Kaplan Publishing are constantly finding new ways to make a difference to y~~ou~~ ~~an~~d our exciting online resources r~~ea~~ ~~som~~ething different to students lookin~~g for succes~~s.

D1387047

This book comes with free EN-gage online resources so that you can study anytime, anywhere.

Having purchased this book, you have access to the following online study materials:

CONTENT	ACCA (including FFA,FAB,FMA)		AAT		FIA (excluding FFA,FAB,FMA)	
	Text	Kit	Text	Kit	Text	Kit
iPaper version of the book	✓	✓	✓	✓	✓	✓
Interactive electronic version of the book	✓					
Fixed tests / progress tests with instant answers	✓		✓			
Mock assessments online			✓	✓		
Material updates	✓	✓	✓	✓	✓	✓
Latest official ACCA exam questions		✓				
Extra question assistance using the signpost icon*		✓				
Timed questions with an online tutor debrief using the clock icon*		✓				
Interim assessment including questions and answers		✓			✓	
Technical articles	✓	✓			✓	✓

* Excludes F1, F2, F3, FFA, FAB, FMA

How to access your online resources

WITHDRAWN

Kaplan Financial students will already have a Kaplan EN-gage account and these extra resources will be available to you online. You do not need to register again, as this process was completed when you enrolled. If you are having problems accessing online materials, please ask your course administrator.

If you are already a registered Kaplan EN-gage user go to www.EN-gage.co.uk and log in. Select the 'add a book' feature and enter the ISBN number of this book and the unique pass key at the bottom of this card. Then click 'finished' or 'add another book'. You may add as many books as you have purchased from this screen.

If you purchased through Kaplan Flexible Learning or via the Kaplan Publishing website you will automatically receive an e-mail invitation to Kaplan EN·gage online. Please register your details using this email to gain access to your content. If you do not receive the e-mail or book content, please contact Kaplan Flexible Learning.

If you are a new Kaplan EN-gage user register at www.EN-gage.co.uk and click on the link contained in the email we sent you to activate your account. Then select the 'add a book' feature, enter the ISBN number of this book and the unique pass key at the bottom of this card. Then click 'finished' or 'add another book'.

Your Code and Information

This code can only be used once for the registration of one book online. This registration and your online content will expire when the final sittings for the examinations covered by this book have taken place. Please allow one hour from the time you submit your book details for us to process your request.

Please scratch the film to access your EN-gage code.

Please be aware that this code is case-sensitive and you will need to include the dashes within the passcode, but not when entering the ISBN. For further technical support, please visit www.EN-gage.co.uk

FINANCIAL STATEMENTS

Qualifications and Credit Framework

Level 4 Diploma in Accounting

British Library Cataloguing-in-Publication Data

A catalogue record for this book is available from the British Library.

Published by
Kaplan Publishing UK
Unit 2, The Business Centre
Molly Millars Lane
Wokingham
Berkshire
RG41 2QZ

ISBN 978-0-85732-603-4

Printed and bound in Great Britain.

We are grateful to the Association of Accounting Technicians for permission to reproduce past assessment materials and example tasks based on the new syllabus. The solutions to past answers and similar activities in the style of the new syllabus have been prepared by Kaplan Publishing.

CONTENTS

STUDY TEXT AND WORKBOOK

KAPLAN PUBLISHING

INTRODUCTION

HOW TO USE THESE MATERIALS

These Kaplan Publishing learning materials have been carefully designed to make your learning experience as easy as possible and to give you the best chance of success in your AAT assessments.

They contain a number of features to help you in the study process.

The sections on the Unit Guide, the Assessment and Study Skills should be read before you commence your studies.

They are designed to familiarise you with the nature and content of the assessment and to give you tips on how best to approach your studies.

STUDY TEXT

This study text has been specially prepared for the revised AAT qualification introduced in July 2010.

It is written in a practical and interactive style:

- key terms and concepts are clearly defined

- all topics are illustrated with practical examples with clearly worked solutions based on sample tasks provided by the AAT in the new examining style

- frequent practice activities throughout the chapters ensure that what you have learnt is regularly reinforced

- 'pitfalls' and 'examination tips' help you avoid commonly made mistakes and help you focus on what is required to perform well in your examination.

- clear advice as to which practice activities can be completed is given at the end of each chapter.

WORKBOOK

The workbook comprises:

A question bank of practice activities with solutions, to reinforce the work covered in each chapter.

The questions are divided into their relevant chapters and students may either attempt these questions as they work through the textbook, or leave some or all of these until they have completed the textbook as a final revision of what they have studied

ICONS

The study chapters include the following icons throughout.

They are designed to assist you in your studies by identifying key definitions and the points at which you can test yourself on the knowledge gained.

 Definition

These sections explain important areas of Knowledge which must be understood and reproduced in an assessment

 Example

The illustrative examples can be used to help develop an understanding of topics before attempting the activity exercises

 Activity

These are exercises which give the opportunity to assess your understanding of all the assessment areas.

KAPLAN PUBLISHING

UNIT GUIDE

Financial Statements is divided into two units but for the purposes of assessment these units will be combined.

Principles of Drafting Financial Statements (Knowledge)

4 credits

Drafting Financial Statement (Skills)

6 credits

Purpose of the units

The AAT has stated that the general purpose of these units is to enable learners to demonstrate that they possess the requisite knowledge and skills to be able to accurately draft singular and consolidated financial statements of limited companies, and analyse and interpret the financial statements of limited companies using ratio analysis

Learning objectives

On completion of these units the learner will be able to:

- understand the regulatory framework that underpins financial reporting
- understand the key features of a published set of accounts
- understand basic principles of consolidation
- appreciate the analysis and interpretation of financial statements
- draft statutory financial statements for a limited company
- draft simple consolidated financial statements
- interpret financial statements using ratio analysis.

Learning Outcomes and Assessment criteria

The unit consists of seven learning outcomes, four for Knowledge and three for Skills, which are further broken down into Assessment criteria. These are set out in the following table with Learning Outcomes in bold type and Assessment criteria listed underneath each Learning Outcome. Reference is also made to the relevant chapter within the text.

Knowledge

To perform this unit effectively you will need to know and understand the following:

		Chapter
1	**Understand the regulatory framework that underpins financial reporting**	
1.1	Explain the scope, elements and purpose, for different users, of preparing users, of preparing financial statements for external reporting	1, 2
1.2	Describe legislation and regulation which must be complied with in the preparation of the financial statements	1, 2, 3
1.3	Explain the reason for governance by legislation and regulation	1
1.4	Explain the relevance of accounting standards	1
1.5	Explain the duties and responsibilities of the directors or other responsible parties, of a corporate organisation	1, 2, 3
2	**Understand the key features of a published set of accounts**	
2.1	Describe the key components and the purpose of a statement of financial position	3
2.2	Describe the key components and the purpose of a statement of comprehensive income	3

Skills

To perform this unit effectively you will need to be able to do the following.

		Chapter
1	**Draft statutory financial statements for a limited company**	
1.1	Apply accounting standards and relevant legislation to correctly identify, and accurately adjust, accounting information	12
1.2	Use appropriate information to accurately draft a statement of comprehensive income	12
1.3	Use appropriate information to accurately draft a statement of financial position	12
1.4	Prepare notes to the accounts which satisfy statutory current disclosure requirements, in respect of accounting policies, fixed assets, current and long term liabilities, equity	3 - 12
1.5	Draft an accurate statement of cash flows	13
2	**Draft simple consolidated financial statements**	
2.1	Draft a consolidated income statement for a parent company with one partly owned subsidiary	16
2.2	Draft a consolidated statement of financial position for a parent company with one partly owned subsidiary	15
2.3	Apply current standards to accurately calculate and appropriately deal with the accounting treatment of goodwill, non- controlling interest and post acquisition profits, in the group financial statements	15, 16, 17
3	**Interpret financial statements using ratio analysis**	
3.1	Calculate and interpret the relationship between the elements of the financial statements with regard to profitability, liquidity, efficient use of resources and financial position	14
3.2	Draw valid conclusions from the information contained within the financial statements	14
3.3	Present clearly and concisely issues, analysis and conclusions to the appropriate people	14

KAPLAN PUBLISHING

Delivery guidance

The AAT have provided a comprehensive content guide for the unit in respect of the international financial reporting standards (both IFRS and IAS) which are assessable and lists appropriate formulas for the ratios. The content that is assessable is described under each of the headings.

IFRS 1 – *First-time adoption of IFRS*

- not assessable.

IFRS 2 – *Share based payment*

- not assessable.

IFRS 3 – *Business combinations*

- definitions of acquiree, acquirer, business, business combination, control, fair value, goodwill, identifiable, non-controlling interest (Appendix A)
- identifying a business combination (3 and Appendix B5)
- the acquisition method (4 and 5), identifying the acquirer (6 and 7), determining the acquisition date (8 and 9), recognition and measurement of assets, liabilities and non-controlling interest (10-12)
- measurement principle (18 and 19)
- recognition and measurement of goodwill (32, 34, and 35).

IFRS 4 – *Insurance contracts*

- not assessable

IFRS 5 – *Non-current assets held for sale and discontinued operations*

- requirement to classify a non current asset as held for sale if its carrying amount will be recovered principally through a sale transaction rather than through continuing use (6)
- measurement of non-current assets held for sale at lower or carrying amount and fair value less costs to sell (15)
- definitions (31–32) and requirement to disclose post tax profit or loss of discontinued operations in the statement of comprehensive income (33a).
- disclosure of non-current assets held for sale separately from other assets in the statement of financial position (38).

IFRS 6 – *Exploration for and evaluation of mineral resources*

- not assessable

IFRS 7 – *Financial Instruments: Disclosures*

- not assessable

IFRS 8 – *Operating segments*

- core principle (1)
- application of standard to entities whose debt or equity instruments are publicly traded (2) or to those who voluntarily choose to disclose segment information
- definition of an operating segment (5 and 6)
- requirement to report separately information in respect of each operating segment (11)
- aggregation criteria in respect of reportable segments (12)
- quantitative thresholds in respect of reportable segments (13 and 15).

IAS 1 – *Presentation of financial statements*

- objective of financial statements (9)
- components of financial statements (10)
- reports and statements that are presented outside of financial statements and therefore outside of the scope of IFRS (13 and 14)
- requirement for financial statements to present fairly the financial position, financial performance and cash flows of an entity (15)
- requirement to make a statement in respect of compliance with IFRS (16)
- circumstances in which departure from IFRS allowed and disclosure of departure (19 and 20)
- requirement to assess going concern (25)
- requirement for accrual accounting (27)
- requirement to present each material class of similar items separately (29)
- prohibition of offsetting elements (32)
- requirement to present a complete set of financial statements at least annually (36)
- requirement for comparative information (38)

KAPLAN PUBLISHING

- requirement for consistency of presentation and classification (45)

- requirement to identify clearly the financial statements (49) and each component of the financial statements (51)

- requirement to display other information prominently (51)

- information to be presented on the face of the statement of financial position (54 and 55)

- requirement to separate current and non-current assets and liabilities (60)

- criteria for current assets (66) and current liabilities (69)

- sub-classifications on the face of the statement of financial position or in notes (77 and 78) and disclosure of other items on the face of the statement of financial position or the statement of changes in equity or in notes (79)

[Assessment of the notes in paragraph 79 is restricted to notes (a) (i), (ii) and (iii)]

- requirement to disclose all items of income and expense recognised in the period either in a single statement of comprehensive income or in two separate statements, comprising:

    (i)   an income statement which shows the components of the company's profit or loss, and

    (ii) a statement of comprehensive income which begins with the profit or loss for the period and shows components of the entity's other comprehensive income (81)

[Only the single statement of comprehensive income will be assessed in this unit]

- information to be presented on the face of the statement of comprehensive income (82 – 85)

- prohibition of extraordinary items (87)

- separate disclosure of material items of income and expense (97)

- requirement to analyse expenses based on nature of expenses or their function (99) and criteria of choice (99, 105) with examples of analysis in 102–103). [Only the form of analysis based upon functionality will be assessed]

- requirement to present a statement of changes in equity (106)

- information to be shown in the statement of changes of equity (106) and the treatment of dividends (107)

- general requirements for notes (112), cross referencing (113), disclosure of accounting policies (117) and disclosure of dividends proposed (137).

IAS 2 – *Inventories*

- definition of inventories (6)
- measurement of inventories (9) and definition of net realisable value (6)
- what is included in cost of inventories (10 and 15) and what is excluded (16)
- cost of inventories of items that are not ordinarily interchangeable (23)
- formulas for determining the cost of inventories for interchangeable items i.e. FIFO and weighted average (25)
- recognition as an expense when inventories sold (34).

IAS 7 – *Statement of cash flows*

- requirement for an entity to prepare a statement of cash flows in accordance with this standard (1)
- definitions of terms used in standard (6)
- requirement to report cash flows during the period classified by operating, investing and financing activities (10)
- examples of cash flows from operating activities (14)
- examples of investing activities (16)
- examples of financing activities (17)
- requirement to report cash flows from operating activities using either the direct method or the indirect method (18). Examples of both types of statement can be found in Appendix A of the standard
- requirement to report separately major classes of gross cash receipts and gross cash payments arising from investing and financing activities (21)
- requirement to disclose separately cash flows from interest and dividends received and paid in a consistent manner from period to period as either operating, investing or financing activities (31)
- requirement to disclose separately cash flows from taxes on income as cash flows from operating activities unless they can be specifically identified with financing and investing activities (35)

- requirement to present separately aggregate cash flows from acquisitions and disposals of subsidiaries or other business units as investing activities (39)

- disclosure of components of cash and cash equivalents and the reconciliation of the amounts in the statement of cash flows with the equivalent items reported in the statement of financial position (45).

IAS 8 – *Accounting policies, changes in accounting estimates and errors*

- requirement to apply IRFS (standards and interpretations defined in 5) to transactions, other events or conditions to which they apply (7)

- criteria to be used where judgment is required because there is no standard or interpretation (10,11 and 12)

- requirement for consistency in applying accounting policies (13) as defined (in 5)

- conditions that require a change in accounting policy (14)

- requirement to follow transitional arrangements arising from the initial application of a standard or interpretation where they are included in the standard, otherwise retrospectively (23)

- requirements of retrospective application of a change in accounting policy (22)

- requirement to correct material prior period errors retrospectively (42) as defined (5).

IAS 10 – *Events after the reporting period*

- definitions of events after the reporting period and adjusting and non-adjusting events (3)

- requirement to adjust for adjusting events after the reporting period (8) with examples (9)

- prohibition of adjustment in respect of non-adjusting events after the reporting period (10) with examples (11)

- prohibition on recognition of dividends declared after the reporting period as a liability (12)

- prohibition on preparing financial statements on a going concern basis if there is an intention to liquidate or cease trading (14)

- requirement to disclose date when financial statements were authorised for issue (17)

- requirement to disclose material non-adjusting events (21) with examples (22).

IAS 11 – *Construction contracts*
- not assessable

IAS 12 – *Income taxes*
- requirement for recognition of unpaid current tax (12)
- requirement to recognise a deferred tax liability for all taxable temporary differences (15) including definitions of deferred tax liabilities and taxable temporary differences (5)
- measurement rule for current tax liabilities (46)
- disclosure of tax expense related to profit or loss from ordinary activities in the statement of comprehensive income (77) and of current and deferred tax (81a). [There will be no assessment of the computation of current tax or of deferred tax].

IAS 16 – *Property, plant and equipment*
- definition of property, plant and equipment (6)
- recognition rule for items of property, plant and equipment (7)
- recognition rules for subsequent expenditure (12, 13 and 14)
- measurement rule at recognition (15) and of elements of cost (16, 17 and 19)
- measurement rules after recognition (29) including explanation of cost model (30) and revaluation model (31)
- definitions of fair value (6) and how it is computed (32 and 33)
- rules on frequency of revaluations (34)
- rule that all assets belonging to a class must be revalued if one item in that class is revalued (36) and examples of different classes (37)
- treatment of revaluation surpluses or decreases (39 and 40)
- requirement to depreciate each part of an item of property, plant and equipment separately (43)
- depreciation charge for each period to be recognised in profit or loss (48)
- depreciable amount to be allocated on a systematic basis over the asset's useful life (50)
- requirement to review the residual value at least at the year end and any change to be accounted for as a change in accounting estimate

- rule that depreciation is required even if fair value exceeds carrying amount as long as the residual value does not exceed its carrying amount, in which case depreciation is zero, and not negated by repair and maintenance (52)
- depreciable amount determined after deducting residual value (53)
- factors determining useful life of an asset (56)
- land not depreciated (58)
- rule for determining depreciation method (60) with examples of methods (62) and need for review at least at the year end (61)
- derecognition rule (67)
- treatment of gain and loss (68) and how computed (71)
- disclosure relating to each class of property, plant and equipment (73), depreciation method and useful life or depreciation rates, depreciation and accumulated depreciation (75).

IAS 17 – *Leases*

- classification of leases as finance and operating leases (8) and examples of situations in which a lease would be classified as a finance lease (10 and 11)
- application of distinction between operating and finance leases to leasing of land and buildings (14 and 15)
- initial recognition of finance leases of lessees (20) including related definitions of fair value, minimum lease payments, interest rate implicit in lease and incremental borrowing rate (4)
- subsequent measurement of finance leases of lessees (25 and 26)
- requirement to depreciate assets held under finance leases of lessees (27) including definition of useful life (4)
- accounting requirements for operating leases of lessees (33)

[Computational questions may be set in relation to the accounting of leases for lessees. Accounting for leases in respect of lessors is not assessable].

IAS 18 – *Revenue*

- scope of standard (1)
- definitions of revenue and fair value (7)
- measurement of revenue (9)
- conditions for recognising revenue from the sale of goods (14), rendering of services (20) and dividends (29 and 30).

IAS 19 – *Employee benefits*

- not assessable

IAS 20 – *Accounting for government grants and disclosure of government assistance*

- definitions of government grants, grants related to assets and grants related to income (3)
- recognition of government grants in the financial statements (7)
- recognition of government grants in profit or loss (12)
- presentation of grants related to assets (24 – 27)
- presentation of grants related to income (29)

[Computational questions may be set in relation to the treatment of grants received in respect of assets].

IAS 21 – *The effects of changes in foreign exchange rates*

- not assessable

IAS 23 – *Borrowing costs*

- definitions of borrowing costs and qualifying assets (5)
- recognition of borrowing costs (8) and rules for determining the amount of borrowing costs (12 and 14)
- commencement and cessation of capitalisation of borrowing costs (17 and 22).

IAS 24 – *Related party disclosures*

- not assessable

IAS 26 – *Accounting and reporting by retirement benefit plans*

- not assessable

IAS 27 – *Consolidated and separate financial statements*

- scope of standard (1 and 3)
- definitions of terms used in standard (4)
- requirement to prepare consolidated financial statements (9)

- requirement to include all subsidiaries of the parent (12) and explanation of when control is presumed (13)

- consolidation procedures (18)

- requirement to eliminate intra-group balances, transactions, income and expenses (20 and 21)

- need to use uniform accounting policies in consolidation (24)

- presentation of non-controlling interests (27)

- requirement to include investment in subsidiaries and associates at cost or fair value in accordance with IAS 39 when preparing separate financial statements (38).

IAS 28 – *Investments in associates*

- definitions of terms used in standard (2)

- criteria for significant influence (6 and 7)

- requirement to account for associates using the equity method (13) and description of that method (11)

- need to used uniform accounting policies in applying the equity method (26 and 27).

IAS 29 – *Financial reporting in hyperinflationary economies*

- not assessable

IAS 31 – *Interests in joint ventures*

- not assessable

IAS 32 – *Financial instruments: presentation*

- not assessable

IAS 33 – *Earnings per share*

- scope of standard (2 and 3)

- definition of ordinary share (5)

- measurement of basic earnings per share (9 and 10)

- explanation of amounts attributable to ordinary equity holders of the parent entity (12 and 13)

- need to use weighted average number of ordinary shares in calculating basic earnings per share (19 and 20)
- presentation of basic earnings per share (66).

IAS 34 – *Interim financial reporting*

- not assessable

IAS 36 – *Impairment of assets*

- scope of standard (2 and 4)
- requirement to assess whether there are indications that assets may be impaired and requirement to estimate recoverable amount where there are such indications (9) and definitions of carrying amount and recoverable amount (6)
- an asset becomes impaired when its carrying amount exceeds its recoverable amount (8)
- requirement to assess intangible assets meeting certain criteria and goodwill annually (10)
- indications of impairment (12, 13 and 14)
- explanations of how to determine fair value less costs to sell (25, 26, 27 and 28)
- explanations of how to determine value in use (30 and 31)
- explanations of the discount rate to be used in determining value in use (55)
- recognising and measuring an impairment loss for in individual assets other than goodwill (59 and 60) including definition (6) and revision of depreciation charge (63) including definition of depreciation, depreciable amount and useful life (6)
- requirement to determine recoverable amount for individual assets if possible or for the cash-generating unit to which an asset belongs if not possible (66) along with definition of cash generating unit (6)
- requirement to test goodwill allocated to a cash generating unit for impairment annually by comparing the carrying amount of the unit, including the goodwill, with the recoverable amount of the unit (90)
- requirement to allocate impairment loss first against goodwill and then against other assets of the unit (104)
- disclosure of impairment loss recognised in profit or loss (126a).

KAPLAN PUBLISHING

IAS 37 – *Provisions, contingent liabilities and contingent assets* definitions (10)

- distinction of provisions from other liabilities (11), idea of being contingent in the standard (12) and distinction of provisions from contingent liabilities (13)

- requirement to recognise provisions and criteria (14)

- prohibition on recognising contingent liabilities (27) and contingent assets (31)

- measurement of provision (36)

- determination of amount of provision where effect of the time value of money is material (45)

- requirement to review provisions at the end of each reporting period to reflect current best estimate (59)

- use of provisions (61)

- examples of events that amount to restructuring (70) and determination of constructive obligation to restructure (72) along with amounts to be included in restructuring provision (80)

- disclosure of provisions (84–85)

- disclosure of contingent liabilities (86) and contingent assets (89).

IAS 38 – *Intangible assets*

- definition of an intangible asset (8)

- identifiability criterion in definition of an intangible asset (12)

- recognition criteria for intangible assets (21) including explanation of future economic benefits (17)

- measurement rule for intangible assets (24)

- prohibition on recognition of internally generated goodwill (48)

- rules of recognition of internally generated intangible assets including the need to classify the generation of the asset into a research phase and a development phase (52) and the rules that prohibit the recognition of intangible assets from the research stage (54) and the rules governing the recognition of intangible assets arising from the development stage (57)

- prohibition of the recognition of internally generated brands and similar items (63)

- examples of directly attributable costs for internally generated intangible assets (66) and prohibited costs (67)

- rule on measurement after recognition (72) and explanation of cost model (74) and revaluation model (75) with related definitions (8)

- treatment of revaluation gains (85) and losses (86)

- need to determine whether useful life of an intangible asset is finite or indefinite (88)

- rules for depreciation of intangible assets with finite useful lives (97), residual value (100) and review of amortisation period (104)

- prohibition of amortisation for intangible assets with indefinite useful life (107) and requirement for impairment review in accord with IAS 36 (108) and review of useful life assessment (109).

IAS 39 – *Financial instruments: recognition and measurement*

- not assessable

IAS 40 – *Investment property*

- definitions (5)
- examples of investment property (8)
- recognition rule (16)
- measurement rule at recognition (20)
- requirement to choose as its accounting policy either the fair value model or the cost model after recognition (30)
- explanation of requirements of fair value model (33) and treatment of gains and losses in fair value (35)
- explanation of requirements of cost model in accordance with IAS 16 (56)
- rule for derecognition of investment property (66) and treatment of gains or losses from retirement or disposal (69)
- disclosure of whether the fair value or cost model is used (75a).

IAS 41 – *Agriculture*

- not assessable

Recommended additional reading

'A student's guide to International Financial Reporting Standards' by Clare Finch.

ISBN 978-1-84710-476-2

THE ASSESSMENT

The format of the assessment

The assessment will be divided into two sections.

Section 1:

This section will be focussing on the drafting of financial statements for singular and consolidated financial statements of limited companies.

Section 2:

This section will be focussing on analysis and interpretation.

Learners will normally be assessed by computer based assessment (CBA), which will include extended writing tasks, and will be required to demonstrate competence in both sections of the assessment.

Time allowed

The time allowed for this assessment is **two and half hours.**

STUDY SKILLS

Preparing to study

Devise a study plan

Determine which times of the week you will study.

Split these times into sessions of at least one hour for study of new material. Any shorter periods could be used for revision or practice.

Put the times you plan to study onto a study plan for the weeks from now until the assessment and set yourself targets for each period of study – in your sessions make sure you cover the whole course, activities and the associated questions in the workbook at the back of the manual.

If you are studying more than one unit at a time, try to vary your subjects as this can help to keep you interested and see subjects as part of wider knowledge.

When working through your course, compare your progress with your plan and, if necessary, re-plan your work (perhaps including extra sessions) or, if you are ahead, do some extra revision / practice questions.

Effective studying

Active reading

You are not expected to learn the text by rote, rather, you must understand what you are reading and be able to use it to pass the assessment and develop good practice.

A good technique is to use SQ3Rs – Survey, Question, Read, Recall, Review:

1   **Survey the chapter**

     Look at the headings and read the introduction, knowledge, skills and content, so as to get an overview of what the chapter deals with.

2   **Question**

     Whilst undertaking the survey ask yourself the questions you hope the chapter will answer for you.

3 Read

Read through the chapter thoroughly working through the activities and, at the end, making sure that you can meet the learning objectives highlighted on the first page.

4 Recall

At the end of each section and at the end of the chapter, try to recall the main ideas of the section / chapter without referring to the text. This is best done after short break of a couple of minutes after the reading stage.

5 Review

Check that your recall notes are correct.

You may also find it helpful to re-read the chapter to try and see the topic(s) it deals with as a whole.

Note taking

Taking notes is a useful way of learning, but do not simply copy out the text.

The notes must:

- be in your own words
- be concise
- cover the key points
- well organised
- be modified as you study further chapters in this text or in related ones.

Trying to summarise a chapter without referring to the text can be a useful way of determining which areas you know and which you don't.

Three ways of taking notes

1 Summarise the key points of a chapter

2 Make linear notes

A list of headings, subdivided with sub-headings listing the key points.

If you use linear notes, you can use different colours to highlight key points and keep topic areas together.

Use plenty of space to make your notes easy to use.

3   **Try a diagrammatic form**

The most common of which is a mind map.

To make a mind map, put the main heading in the centre of the paper and put a circle around it.]

Draw lines radiating from this to the main sub-headings which again have circles around them.

Continue the process from the sub-headings to sub-sub-headings.

Highlighting and underlining

You may find it useful to underline or highlight key points in your study text – but do be selective.

You may also wish to make notes in the margins.

Revision phase

Kaplan has produced material specifically designed for your final examination preparation for this unit.

These include pocket revision notes and a bank of revision questions specifically in the style of the new syllabus.

Further guidance on how to approach the final stage of your studies is given in these materials.

Further reading

In addition to this text, you should also read the 'Student section' of the 'Accounting Technician' magazine every month to keep abreast of any guidance from the examiners.

'A student's guide to IFRS' by Clare Finch.

Assessable ratios

PROFITABILITY

Return on capital employed

$$\frac{\text{Profit from operations}}{\text{Total equity} + \text{Non - current liabilities}} \times 100\%$$

Return on total assets

$$\frac{\text{Profit from operations}}{\text{Total assets}} \times 100\%$$

Return on equity

$$\frac{\text{Profit after tax}}{\text{Total equity}} \times 100\%$$

Earnings per share

$$\frac{\text{Profit after tax}}{\text{Number of issued ordinary shares}}$$

Gross profit percentage

$$\frac{\text{Gross profit}}{\text{Revenue}} \times 100\%$$

Expense/revenue percentage

$$\frac{\text{Specified expense}}{\text{Revenue}} \times 100\%$$

Operating profit percentage

$$\frac{\text{Profit from operations}}{\text{Revenue}} \times 100\%$$

LIQUIDITY

Current ratio

$$\frac{\text{Current assets}}{\text{Current liabilities}} \times : 1$$

The quick ratio or "acid test" ratio

$$\frac{\text{Current assets} - \text{inventories}}{\text{Current liabilities}} \times : 1$$

USE OF RESOURCES

Inventory turnover

$$\frac{\text{Cost of sales}}{\text{Inventories}} = \times \text{ times}$$

Inventory holding period

$$\frac{\text{Inventories}}{\text{Cost of sales}} \times 365 \text{ days}$$

Trade receivables collection period

$$\frac{\text{Trade receivables}}{\text{Revenue}} \times 365 \text{ days}$$

Trade payables payment period

$$\frac{\text{Trade payables}}{\text{Cost of sales}} \times 365 \text{ days}$$

Working capital cycle

Inventory days + Receivable days – Payable days

Asset turnover (total assets)

$$\frac{\text{Revenue}}{\text{Total assets}} = \times \text{ times}$$

Asset turnover (net assets)

$$\frac{\text{Revenue}}{\text{Total assets} - \text{current liabilities}} = \times \text{ times}$$

FINANCIAL POSITION

Interest cover

$$\frac{\text{Profit from operations}}{\text{Finance costs}} = \times \text{ times}$$

Gearing

$$\frac{\text{Non - current liabilities}}{\text{Total equity} + \text{non - current liabilities}} \times 100$$

KAPLAN PUBLISHING

The regulatory framework

1

Introduction

In this initial chapter we will be covering background information that is essential for your understanding of the preparation of financial statements for many types of organisation, in particular for limited companies.

KNOWLEDGE
The elements and purposes of financial statements of limited companies as set out in the conceptual framework for financial reporting (1.1)
The general legal framework of limited companies and the obligations of Directors in respect of the financial statements (1.2)
Explain the reasons for governance by legislation and regulation (1.3)
Explain the relevance of accounting standards (1.4)

CONTENTS
1   Introduction
2   The purpose of financial statements
3   The legal framework
4   Accounting standards

1 Introduction

1.1 Background knowledge

In the units accounting preparation I and II your accounting studies took you from ledger accounts to a trial balance to an extended trial balance. On the extended trial balance you will have put through a number of adjustments for inventories, accruals, prepayments, depreciation and irrecoverable and doubtful debts. Each account on the extended trial balance was then balanced and extended into either the income statement columns or the statement of financial position columns depending upon whether the balance was income, expenditure, an asset or a liability.

For this unit your accounting knowledge must be taken further.

1.2 Drafting financial statements

This unit involves the drafting of the relevant financial statements for limited companies. You must be able to prepare a statement of financial position, income statement, statement of other comprehensive income, statement of changes in equity and statement of cash flow in accordance with all the applicable regulations (the Companies Act 2006, accounting standards, etc).

1.3 Interpretation of financial statements

The unit also involves interpretation of limited company financial statements. It is concerned with being able to analyse and understand the structure and purpose of financial statements of limited companies. It requires a sound understanding of the knowledge and skills required to prepare financial statements and an ability to interpret the relationships between these elements of financial statements by using ratio analysis.

In order to understand and interpret limited company financial statements you must be able to understand how they have been prepared. Therefore your knowledge of accounts preparation I and accounts preparation II is extremely important as the knowledge and skills from these units will assist in the understanding of how the financial statements of limited companies are prepared.

In this chapter and the next, however, we will consider the background to the preparation of financial statements for limited companies by considering the regulatory framework and then the conceptual framework within which these financial statements must be prepared.

2 The purpose of financial statements

2.1 Introduction

The main purpose of financial statements is to provide information to a wide range of users.

The **statement of financial position** provides information on the financial position of a business (its assets and liabilities at a point in time).

The **statement of comprehensive income** provides information on the performance of a business (the profit or loss which results from trading over a period of time).

The **statement of other comprehensive income** shows income and expenses that are not recognised in profit or loss.

The **statement of changes in equity** provides information about how the equity of the company has changed over the period.

The **statement of cash flow** provides information on the financial adaptability of a business (the movement of cash into and out of the business over a period of time).

2.2 Stewardship

Financial statements also show the results of the stewardship of an organisation. Stewardship is the accountability of management for the resources entrusted to it by the owners or the Government. This applies to the financial statements of limited companies as well as to central and local government and the National Health Service.

2.3 Needs of users

All users of financial statements need information on financial position, performance and financial adaptability. However, many different groups of people may use financial statements and each group will need particular information.

Users of financial statements may include investors, management, employees, customers, suppliers, lenders, the government and the public.

- Investors need to be able to assess the ability of a business to pay dividends and manage resources.

- Management need information with which to assess performance, take decisions, plan, and control the business.

- Lenders, such as banks, are interested in the ability of the business to pay interest and repay loans. HM Revenue and Customs uses financial statements as the basis for tax assessments.

2.4 Legal requirements

The law requires limited companies to prepare financial statements annually. These financial statements must be filed with the Registrar of Companies and are then available to all interested parties. Most businesses, whether incorporated or not, are required to produce financial statements for submission to HM Revenue and Customs.

In the UK, the form and content of limited company accounts is laid down within the Companies Acts. The preparation of limited company accounts is also subject to regulations issued by the Accounting Standards Board if the company is still following UK standards or the International Accounting Standards Board if the company has adopted international standards.

3 The legal framework

3.1 Introduction

The financial statements of limited companies must usually be prepared within the legal framework relevant to that company. In the case of UK companies, the Companies Act 2006 contains guidance and rules on:

- Formats for the financial statements
- Fundamental accounting principles
- Valuation rules.

The Companies Act 2006 allows companies to use the format of accounts set out in IAS 1(revised) *Presentation of Financial Statements* if they have adopted IFRS or continue to use the format in the Act if they have not.

4 Accounting standards

4.1 IFRSs and IASs

Accounting standards give guidance in specific areas of accounting. The Financial Statements syllabus follows International standards which consist of the following:

- *International Financial Reporting Standards (IFRSs)*

  These are issued by the International Accounting Standards Board. Many countries have used IFRSs for some years. Back in 2002, the Council of Ministers of the European Union (EU) decided that any company which is listed on a European Stock Exchange must prepare their consolidated accounts in line with IFRSs with effect from 1 January 2005.

- *International Accounting Standards (IASs)*

  IASs were created by a body known as the International Accounting Standards Committee (IASC) the predecessor of the IASB. When the IASB was formed it adopted the standards of the IASC which were called IASs. In recent times, the IASB has introduced many new standards so several IASs have now been superseded.

4.2 The structure of the IASC

The structure of the International Financial Reporting Standards Foundation and its subsidiary bodies is shown below:

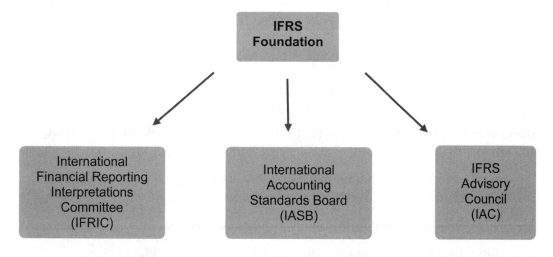

4.3 The IFRS Foundation ('the Foundation')

The IFRS Foundation is an independent not-for profit foundation based in the US. The Trustees of the Foundation appoint the members of the International Accounting Standards Board, the IFRS Advisory Council and the IFRS Interpretations Committee. They are also responsible for setting and approving the budgets of the various bodies, determining strategic direction and promoting IFRS.

4.4 The International Accounting Standards Board ('the IASB')

The IASB has sole responsibility for the setting of international accounting standards. The IASB's objectives are:

(a) to develop a single set of high quality, global accounting standards that require transparent and comparable information in general purpose financial statements;

(b) to promote the use and rigorous application of those standards; and

(c) to work actively with national standard setters to bring about convergence of national accounting standards and IFRSs.

IFRSs set out the recognition, measurement, presentation and disclosure requirements of transactions and events that are important in accounting. They apply to all general purpose financial statements and any limitation in scope of the standard is stated within the standard.

The IASB cooperates with other accounting standard setters with the aim of achieving harmony of accounting practice throughout the world. This has been the case in the UK as the Accounting Standards Board (ASB) has adopted recent IFRSs. There will be minimal difference in accounting practice for companies who have adopted IFRS and those who haven't.

4.5 International Financial Reporting Interpretations Committee ('IFRIC')

The aim of the IFRIC is to assist the IASB in establishing and improving standards of financial accounting and reporting. It promotes the rigorous and uniform application of IFRS. They provide timely guidance on:

1   newly identified financial reporting issues not specifically covered by an accounting standard

2   unsatisfactory interpretations that have developed or may develop.

The guidelines IFRIC publishes are called IFRIC Interpretations. If a company complies with IFRSs, then it is automatically presumed that this includes the IFRIC Interpretations as well as the relevant standards.

4.6   IFRS Advisory Council ('the Council')

The Council provides a forum for organisations and individuals to input into the standard setting process. Their overall objectives are:

(i)   to give advice to the IASB on agenda decisions and priorities

(ii)   to inform the IASB of the views of organisations and individuals, and

(iii)   to give other advice to the IASB or the Trustees.

4.7   The standard setting process

There are a number of steps in the process of developing and issuing a new accounting standard by the IASB. These are detailed below:

(a)   Staff are asked to identify and review all issues associated with a topic and to consider the application of the Conceptual Framework to the issues;

(b)   Study of national accounting requirements and practice and an exchange of views about the issues with national standard-setters;

(c)   Consulting the Council about the advisability of adding the topic to the IASB agenda;

(d)   Formation of an advisory group to give advice to the IASB on the project;

(e)   Publishing for public comment a discussion document;

(f)   Publishing for public comment an exposure draft approved by at least eight members of the IASB, including any dissenting opinions held by IASB members;

(g)   Publishing within an exposure draft a basis for conclusions;

(h)   Consideration of all comments received within the comment period on the discussion documents and exposure drafts;

(i)   Consideration of whether to hold a public hearing and to conduct field tests and, if necessary, holding such hearings and conducting such tests;

(j)   Approval of a standard by at least eight members of the IASB and inclusion in the published standard of any dissenting opinions; and

(k)   Publishing within a standard a basis for conclusions, explaining, among other things the steps in the IASB due process and how the IASB dealt with public comments on the exposure draft.

Activity 1

1   What are the four statements that would be seen in a set of financial statements?

2   What is meant by the term 'stewardship'?

3   What does IFRS stand for?

4   What is the role of the IASB?

5   What is the role of IFRIC?

5   Summary

The regulatory framework for a UK company preparing financial statements under international standards consists of:

- The Companies Act which applies to all UK companies regardless of whether they follow UK or International accounting rules

- The International Accounting Standards Board and its associated bodies who are responsible for the setting of IFRSs.

Answers to chapter activities

Activity 1

1 Statement of financial position, statement of comprehensive income, statement of changes in equity and statement of cash flow.

2 Stewardship is the accountability of management for the resources entrusted to it by the owners or the Government.

3 International Financial Reporting Standard.

4 The role of the IASB is to set accounting standards. They are called International Financial Reporting Standards.

5 IFRIC assists the IASB by producing IFRIC Interpretations which guide on new accounting issues that are not covered by an accounting standard or guide on the correct interpretation of a standard if it is being applied incorrectly.

The conceptual framework

2

Introduction

This chapter provides some essential background knowledge of the principles and concepts that underlie the preparation of financial statements for limited companies. The IASB have produced a framework for the preparation and presentation of financial statements.

KNOWLEDGE
The elements of financial statements of limited companies as set out in the conceptual framework for financial reporting (1.1)
Generally accepted accounting principles and concepts and relevance of accounting standards (1.4)

CONTENTS

1 User groups
2 A conceptual framework
3 Framework for the preparation and presentation of financial statements
4 The objective of financial statements
5 Underlying assumptions
6 The qualitative characteristics of financial statements
7 The elements of financial statements
8 The accounting equation
9 Recognition of the elements of financial statements
10 Measurement of the elements of financial statements
11 The potential benefits and drawbacks of an agreed conceptual framework
12 IAS 8 *Accounting Policies*
13 Other key concepts

1 User groups

1.1 The purpose of accounting

The purpose of accounting is to provide information to users of financial statements. Legally, company financial statements are drawn up for the benefit of the shareholders, so that they can assess the performance of their Board of Directors. However, in practice many other groups will use these financial statements, and these groups will all have different needs. These groups, and their needs, are described below.

1.2 Management

Management will be interested in an analysis of revenues and expenses that will provide information that is useful when plans are formulated and decisions made. Once the budget for a business is complete, the accountant can produce figures for what actually happens as the budget period unfolds, so that they can be compared with the budget. Management will also need to know the cost consequences of a particular course of action to aid their decision making.

1.3 Shareholders and potential shareholders

This group includes the investing public at large and the stockbrokers and commentators who advise them. The shareholders should be informed of the manner in which management has used their funds that have been invested in the business. This is a matter of reporting on past events. However, both shareholders and potential shareholders are also interested in the future performance of the business and use past figures as a guide to the future if they have to vote on proposals or decide whether to sell their shares.

Financial analysts advising investors such as insurance companies, pension funds, unit trusts and investment trusts are among the most sophisticated users of accounting information, and the company contemplating a takeover bid is yet another type of potential shareholder.

1.4 Employees and their trade union representatives

These use accounting information to assess the potential performance of the business. This information is relevant to the employee, who wishes to discover whether the company can offer him safe employment and promotion through growth over a period of years, and also to the trade unionist, who uses past profits and potential profits in his calculations and claims for higher wages or better conditions. The viability of different divisions of a company is of interest to this group.

1.5 Lenders

This group includes some who have financed the business over a long period by lending money which is to be repaid at the end of a number of years, as well as short-term payables such as a bank which allows a company to overdraw its bank account for a number of months, and suppliers of raw materials, which permit a company to buy goods from them and pay in, say, four to twelve weeks' time.

Lenders are interested in the security of their loan, so they will look at an accounting statement to ensure that the company will be able to repay on the due date and meet the interest requirements before that date. The amount of cash available and the value of assets, which form a security for the debt, are of importance to this group. Credit rating agencies are interested in accounts for similar reasons.

1.6 Government agencies

These use accounting information, either when collecting statistical information to reveal trends within the economy as a whole or, in the case of the Inland Revenue, to assess the profit on which the company's tax liability is to be computed.

1.7 The business contact group

Customers of a business may use accounting data to assess the viability of a company if a long-term contract is soon to be placed. Competitors will also use the accounts for purposes of comparison.

1.8 The public

From time to time other groups not included above may have an interest in the company e.g. members of a local community where the company operates, environmental pressure groups, and so on.

Conclusion

Financial statements serve a wide variety of user groups, who have different interests and also different levels of financial sophistication. This makes it particularly difficult to produce accounts that are intelligible to the layman but comprehensive for the expert.

The next section looks at how standards have been developed to try to meet these diverse needs.

2 A conceptual framework

A conceptual framework is a coherent system of inter-related objectives and fundamentals that can lead to consistent standards and that prescribes the nature, function and limits of financial accounting and financial statements. The IASB's conceptual framework is known as the Conceptual Framework for Financial Reporting 2010 ('the Framework').

The basic objective of the conceptual framework is to provide a logical and sensible guide for preparing accounting standards and applying them. In effect it will be the constitution within which accountant's work, while the standards themselves will be the detailed laws enacted to apply these constitutional principles.

3 Framework for the preparation and presentation of financial statements

The Framework is not an accounting standard. Nothing in the Framework overrides a specific international financial reporting standard.

3.1 The matters dealt with in the Framework

The following topics are covered in the Framework:
- The objective of financial statements.
- Underlying assumptions.
- Qualitative characteristics of financial statements.
- Definition of elements of financial statements.
- Recognition of the elements of financial statements.
- Measurement of the elements of financial statements.
- Concepts of capital and capital maintenance.

4 The objective of financial statements

4.1 Usefulness for particular purposes

The objective of financial statements is to provide information about the financial position, performance and changes in financial position of an entity that is useful to a wide range of users in making economic decisions. Financial statements may not provide all the information that users need to make economic decisions as they portray the effect of past events and do not always provide non-financial information.

The two most common 'economic decisions' made by users are:

- to buy or sell shares, and
- to re-elect or replace the Board of Directors.

Users need to be able to evaluate the ability of the entity to generate cash. They also need to be able to predict the timing and certainty of the cash being generated. To be able to do this users need historic information about:

- financial position
- performance
- cash flow of an entity.

(a) The financial position of an entity is affected by:

- the economic resources it controls
- its financial structure
- its liquidity and solvency
- its capacity to adapt to changes in the environment in which it operates.

This information is normally found in the statement of financial position.

(b) Information about the performance of an entity comprises the return obtained by the entity on the resources it controls. This can be found in the income statement and the statement of changes in equity.

(c) Information on cash flows of an entity is useful in providing the user with an additional perspective on the performance of an entity by indicating the amounts and principal sources of its cash inflows and outflows.

This is provided by the statement of cash flow.

Each statement reflects different aspects of the same transactions and events. A user should study all of the statements before making any decisions.

4.2 User groups

Traditionally financial statements were prepared for the benefit of the shareholders (the owners) and the creditors. The Framework recognises that other user groups may have a reasonable right to information, and that financial statements should take their needs into account.

The Framework identifies the following users:

- equity investors (existing and potential)
- employees (existing, potential and past)
- lenders, existing and potential, including providers of short-term loans
- suppliers and other trade creditors
- customers
- government, including tax authorities
- the public.

5 Underlying assumptions

The underlying assumptions governing financial statements are:

- *The accrual basis*

  The accrual basis of accounting means that the effects of transactions and other events are recognised as they occur and not as cash or its equivalent is received or paid.

- *Going concern*

  The going concern basis assumes that the entity will continue in operation for the foreseeable future and has neither the need nor the intention to liquidate or curtail materially the scale of its operations.

KAPLAN PUBLISHING

6 The qualitative characteristics of financial statements

6.1 Overview

The Framework identifies two fundamental qualitative characteristics of useful financial information:

- relevance, and
- faithful representation.

These are supported by four enhancing qualitative characteristics:

- comparability
- verifiability
- timeliness, and
- understandability.

🔍 Definitions

Relevance

Financial information is regarded as relevant if it is capable of influencing the decisions of users.

Faithful representation

This means that financial information must be complete, neutral and free from error.

Comparability

It should be possible to compare an entity over time and with similar information about other entities.

Verifiability

If information can be verified (e.g. through an audit) this provides assurance to the users that it is both credible and reliable.

Timeliness

Information should be provided to users within a timescale suitable for their decision making purposes.

Understandability

Information should be understandable to those that might want to review and use it. This can be facilitated through appropriate classification, characterisation and presentation of information.

6.2 True and fair view/fair presentation

Financial statements are frequently described as giving a true and fair view, or presenting fairly the position, performance and changes in financial position of an entity. The Framework does not define the concept of a true and fair view, but by following accounting standards as well as the qualitative characteristics above financial statements should present a true and fair view.

One of the concepts embodied in the concept of truth and fairness is that of reasonable accuracy, rather than absolute accuracy. For example, consider a large multinational corporation with revenues of hundreds of billions of dollars per year; would the users' decisions be affected by an error that overstated profits in the financial statements by one thousand dollars? Of course it would not; the financial statements would be rounded to the nearest billion dollars so the error is totally irrelevant. Would an error that understated liabilities by two billion dollars affect their decisions? The answer to this is that it might; this is a significant amount of debt missing from the statement of financial position and the debt position of a business is crucial to decision makers, particularly lenders.

This leads to the concept of materiality; to be true and fair financial statements should be free from material misstatement.

 Definition

Information is material if its omission or misstatement, either individually or in aggregate with other omissions or misstatements, could influence the economic decisions of the users of the financial statements.

7 The elements of financial statements

The Framework identifies five elements of financial statements:

- assets
- liabilities
- equity interest
- income
- expenses.

7.1   Assets

The Framework defines an asset as:

'A resource controlled by the entity as a result of past events and from which future economic benefits are expected to flow to the entity.'

'Controlled by the entity'

Control is the ability to obtain economic benefits from an

asset through use or sale. It also includes the ability to restrict other people's access to an asset. Control does not require ownership of the asset.

'Past events'

Assets arise from past events. For example land arises from a purchase and trade receivables from a sale.

'Future economic benefits'

Ultimately, an asset generates cash. A trade receivable should realise cash directly. A machine will make goods that will be sold, creating trade receivables that will realise cash.

7.2   Liabilities

The Framework defines a liability as:

'A present obligation of the entity arising from past events, the settlement of which is expected to result in an outflow from the entity of resources embodying economic benefits.'

'Obligations'

These may be legal or not. A trade payable is a legal obligation. A warranty provision arises from sales during the year, but won't become a legal liability until a customer makes a claim.

'Outflow of economic benefits'

This could be the transfer of cash or another asset, or the provision of a service. It also includes refraining from profitable activities.

'Past transactions or events'

For example, a tax liability arises from past profits.

Complementary nature of assets and liabilities

Assets and liabilities should normally be recognised separately. Sometimes they may be offset, e.g. issuing a credit note reduces the value of the trade receivable.

7.3 Equity interest

The Framework defines equity as:

'The residual interest in the assets of the entity after deducting all its liabilities.'

In other words, equity is what is left when all liabilities have been settled. This is essentially the net assets of a business.

Equity interest is usually analysed to distinguish between that arising from owners' contributions and that arising from profits, revaluations or other events.

Share capital and revaluation reserves are normally non-distributable.

7.4 Income

Income consists of both revenue and gains. Revenue arises from a business's ordinary activities such as the sale of goods. Gains represent increases in economic benefits such as a gain on disposal of a non-current asset. Gains are usually shown separately from the revenue generated by the business often because they need to be disclosed separately to give a full understanding of the transaction. Note that contributions from shareholders are not income, they are part of equity.

7.5 Expenses

Expenses are losses as well as expenses that arise in the normal course of business such as cost of sales, wages and depreciation. Losses represent a decrease in economic benefits such as losses on disposal of non-current assets or disasters such as fire or flood. As with gains, losses are often shown separately in the financial statements to give a full understanding of the situation. Note that distributions (dividends) to shareholders are not expenses.

8 The accounting equation

This unit requires that the elements of the financial statements should be identified and that the relationships between these elements are also identified.

Earlier in your studies you will have learned the accounting equation:

Assets – Liabilities = Capital + Profits – Drawings

When preparing company financial statements the equation is rearranged as follows:

Assets = Equity + Liabilities

Activity 1

Sabrina Ltd

Statement of Financial Position as at 31 March 20X8

ASSETS	£
Non-current assets	
Property, plant and equipment	20,500
Current assets	17,500
	———
Total assets	**38,000**
	———
EQUITY AND LIABILITIES	
Share capital	12,000
Share premium	3,000
Retained earnings	5,000
	———
	20,000
Non-current liabilities	5,000
Current liabilities	13,000
	———
Total equity and liabilities	**38,000**
	———

What are the monetary values of the equity, the assets and the liabilities in Sabrina Ltd as at 31 March 20X8 and how are they related in the accounting equation?

9 Recognition of the elements of financial statements

9.1 General recognition criteria

An item should be recognised in the financial statements if:

- it meets one of the definitions of an element (asset, liability, equity, income, expense).

- it is probable that any future economic benefit associated with the item will flow to or from the entity (for example, income is recognised when a sale is made, not when an order is received).

- the item has a cost or value that can be measured with reliability.

Normally the monetary amount will come straight from the sale or purchase invoice. However, reasonable, reliable and prudent estimates can be recognised, for example, a property revaluation or a warranty provision.

The recognition process

Recognition is triggered where a past event indicates that there has been a measurable change in the assets or liabilities of the entity.

The effect of uncertainty

The more evidence there is for an item, the more reliable its recognition and measurement will be.

 Activity 2

The framework for the preparation and presentation of financial statements states 'the objective of financial statements is to provide information about the financial position, performance and changes in financial position of an entity.'

Additionally it states 'financial statements also show the results of the stewardship of management.'

(a) What is meant by saying that financial statements show the results of 'stewardship of management'?

(b) What is meant by 'Equity'? How is it related to other elements in the accounting equation?

---

10 Measurement of the elements of financial statements

The Framework identifies four possible measurement bases:

- historical cost
- current cost
- realisable value
- present value.

10.1 Historical cost

Assets are recorded at the amount of cash paid to acquire them. Sometimes the terms, cash equivalents or fair value at acquisition will be used instead.

Liabilities are recorded at the proceeds received in exchange for the obligation.

10.2 Current cost

Assets are carried at their current purchase price (i.e. their price now, not their price when originally purchased).

Liabilities are carried at the undiscounted amount currently required to settle them.

10.3 Realisable value

Assets are carried at the amount, which could currently be obtained by an orderly disposal. Liabilities are carried at their settlement values – the amount to be paid to satisfy them in the normal course of business.

10.4 Present value

Assets are carried at the present discounted value of the future net cash inflows that the item is expected to generate in the normal course of business.

Liabilities are carried at the present discounted value of the expected cash outflows necessary to settle them.

Although historical cost is the most common basis, the others are often used to modify historical cost. For example, inventories are usually carried at the lower of cost and net realisable value, investments may be carried at market value and pension liabilities are carried at their present value.

11 The potential benefits and drawbacks of an agreed conceptual framework

Potential benefits

The potential benefits of a conceptual framework are:

- A framework for setting future accounting standards.

- A basis for resolving disputes as the elements of financial statements are clearly defined.

- Fundamental principles do not have to be repeated in accounting standards.

- There should be a reduction in pressure from vested interests who wish to pursue a particular policy out of self-interest rather than satisfying the general needs of users.

Potential drawbacks

Drawbacks to a conceptual framework include:

- Due to their general nature the principles may not, in practice, reduce the options available.

- There may be further disagreement as to the contents of the framework in addition to disagreement over the contents of standards.

12 IAS 8 *Accounting Policies*

Accounting policies are the specific principles, bases, conventions, rules and practices applied by an entity in preparing and presenting financial statements.

Management should select and apply appropriate accounting policies so that the financial statements comply with all international standards (IFRSs and IASs) and IFRIC Interpretations.

If there is no specific standard for a particular item then management should choose policies that are relevant and reliable. Management should refer to IFRSs, IASs and Interpretations dealing with similar issues and to the Framework.

All material accounting policies should be disclosed and explained in the notes to the financial statements.

An entity should select and apply accounting policies consistently for similar transactions.

13 Other key concepts

13.1 Substance over form

Under this concept, transactions and other events are accounted for and presented in financial statements in accordance with their economic substance and financial reality and not merely with their legal form.

For example, leasehold buildings are owned by the landlord rather than the occupier, but the occupier is using them for his business in the same way as if they were freehold. Thus it may be appropriate to treat them as a fixed asset in the occupier's statement of financial position, provided that it is made clear that the premises are leasehold.

13.2 The consistency concept

Like items are treated in a similar manner within each accounting period and from one period to the next. This aids comparison of results over time.

 Activity 3

The accounting equation is:

$$\text{Assets} - \text{Liabilities} = \text{Equity or}$$

$$\text{Assets} = \text{Equity} + \text{Liabilities}$$

(a) Define the following elements of financial statements:

    (i) Assets

    (ii) Liabilities

    (iii) Equity

(b) Explain why inventory is an asset of a company.

Activity 4

1   Which group is seen to be the main user of financial statements?

2   What does management require from financial information?

3   What would potential shareholders' interests be in the financial statements?

4   What is a conceptual framework?

5   What is meant by the relevance of information?

6   How does the IASB Framework define:

  • assets

  • liabilities?

7   What is the going concern concept?

8   What is the accruals concept?

14   Summary

The framework for the preparation and presentation of financial statements sets out two fundamental accounting concepts:

• going concern

• accruals.

The objective of financial statements is to provide information about the reporting entity's financial performance and financial position that is useful to a wide range of users for assessing the stewardship of management and for making economic decisions.

The two fundamental qualitative characteristics of financial information are:

• relevance

• faithful representation

The four enhancing qualitative characteristics of financial information are:

- comparability
- verifiability
- timeliness
- understandability.

The elements of financial statements are:

- assets
- liabilities
- equity interest
- income
- expenses.

Answers to chapter activities

 Activity 1

Sabrina Ltd

The monetary values are as follows:

	£
Equity	20,000
Assets	38,000
Liabilities	18,000

The figures are related in the accounting equation as follows

Assets – Liabilities = Equity

38,000 – 18,000   = 20,000 or

Assets = Equity + Liabilities

38,000= 20,000 +18,000

 Activity 2

(a) Management is accountable for the safe-keeping of the entity's resources and for their proper, efficient and profitable use.

In other words, they are the 'stewards' of the resources of the entity and are responsible to shareholders for the management of the resources to ensure that they generate adequate profit and cash flows to give them a return and to ensure that lenders to the business are repaid.

(b) Equity is 'the residual amount found by deducting all of the entity's liabilities from all of the entity's assets'. The equity is related to the other elements in the accounting equation as follows:

Assets – Liabilities = Equity

Activity 3

(a) The elements of financial statements are defined by the framework for the preparation and presentation of financial statements as follows:

(i) 'Assets' are rights or other access to future economic benefits controlled by an entity as a result of past transactions or events.

(ii) 'Liabilities' are obligations of an entity to transfer economic benefits as a result of past transactions or events.

(iii) Equity is 'the residual amount found by deducting all of the entity's liabilities from all of the entity's assets'.

(b) Inventory fits the definition of an asset in that:

- the purchase of inventory for resale gives rise to a right to future economic benefits in that the entity can sell the inventory or use the inventory to manufacture products that are sold to generate future economic benefits

- this is as a result of a past transaction.

 Activity 4

1 Shareholders

2 Management will be interested in an analysis of revenues and expenses that will provide information that is useful when plans are formulated and decisions made. Once the budget for a business is complete, the accountant can produce figures for what actually happens as the budget period unfolds, so that they can be compared with the budget. Management will also need to know the cost consequences of a particular course of action to aid their decision making.

3 The future performance of the business.

4 A conceptual framework is a coherent system of inter-related objectives and fundamentals that can lead to consistent standards and that prescribes the nature, function and limits of financial accounting and financial statements.

5   Information must be relevant to the decision-making needs of users.

6   An asset is a resource controlled by the entity as a result of past events and from which future economic benefits are expected to flow to the enterprise. A liability is a present obligation of the entity arising from past events, the settlement of which is expected to result in an outflow of economic benefits.

7   Going concern

     The going concern basis assumes that the entity will continue in operation for the foreseeable future and has neither the need nor the intention to liquidate or curtail materially the scale of its operations.

8   The accruals concept

     The accrual basis of accounting means that the effects of transactions and other events are recognised as they occur and not as cash or its equivalent is received or paid.

15 Test your knowledge

 Workbook Activity 5

A major objective of published financial statements is 'to provide information about the financial position, performance and financial adaptability of an enterprise that is useful to a wide range of users for assessing the stewardship of management and for making economic decisions'.

What characteristics contribute to making financial information useful in terms of both content and presentation, and how do these characteristics fulfil their objective?

 Workbook Activity 6

The elements of financial statements comprise:

- Assets
- Liabilities
- Equity interest
- Income
- Expenses

Define these terms and state which of these terms comprise the 'accounting equation'.

 Workbook Activity 7

Data

The accounting equation of a business is as follows:

Assets £1,200 – Liabilities £800 = Equity Interest £400

The business subsequently makes two transactions:

(1) it purchases on credit inventories costing £120; and

(2) it sells the inventories purchased in (1) for £180 cash.

Task

(a) Explain what is meant by 'assets', 'liabilities' and 'equity interest'.

(b) Explain the effect of each transaction on the elements in the statement of financial position.

(c) State the accounting equation for the business after the two transactions have taken place.

(d) Draft a simple income statement for the two transactions.

(e) Give an example of a user who might be interested in an income statement.

Explain how the user you have chosen might find the statement useful.

 Workbook Activity 8

Data

The Framework for the Preparation and Presentation of Financial Statements says that:

The elements of the financial statements are:

(a) Assets

(b) Liabilities

(c) Equity interest

(d) Income

(e) Expenses

Task

(a) (i) In which primary financial statement are 'assets', 'liabilities' and 'equity interest' shown?

(ii) How are they related to each other in that statement?

(b) What is meant by 'income' and 'expenses' and in which primary financial statements are they shown?

KAPLAN PUBLISHING

Workbook Activity 9

(a) What sort of information in the financial statements does the Conceptual Framework for Financial Reporting 2010 say that potential investors are interested in and for what purpose?

(b) How do inventories meet the definition of an asset in accordance with the Framework?

Limited company financial statements

3

Introduction

In this chapter we will consider the presentation of financial statements for limited companies and consider the legal and regulatory requirements for the presentation of those financial statements.

KNOWLEDGE

Describe key components and the purpose of a statement of financial position (2.1)

Describe the key components and the purpose of a statement of comprehensive income (2.3)

Explain the content and purpose of disclosure notes to the accounts (2.4)

Identify accounting standards and the effect of these on the preparation of the financial statements (2.5)

SKILLS

Apply accounting standards and relevant legislation to correctly identify and accurately adjust accounting information (1.1)

Use appropriate information to accurately draft a statement of comprehensive income and a statement of financial position (1.2, 1.3)

Prepare notes to the accounts which satisfy statutory current disclosure requirements, in respect of accounting policies, non-current assets, current and long term liabilities, equity (1.4)

CONTENTS

1 Distinctive features of limited companies
2 Key differences between a sole trader's accounts and limited company accounts
3 Introduction to company accounts
4 The statement of financial position for publication
5 The statement of comprehensive income for publication
6 Notes to the accounts
7 Statement of changes in equity

1 Distinctive features of limited companies

1.1 Differences between a sole trader and a limited company

A limited company is a separate legal entity and is distinct from its owners. This is in contrast to a sole trader who in law is not a separate entity from his business, even though he is treated as such for accounting purposes.

The key advantage of this is the limited liability that an investment in shares offers the shareholder. While a sole trader has unlimited liability for the debts of his business, shareholders have limited liability for the debts of the company in which they hold shares.

1.2 Types of limited company

There are two types of limited company, public and private. A public company must include in its name the letters 'plc' standing for public limited company. Private companies must include Limited or Ltd in their name. The main difference is that a private company may not offer its shares to the public and so all companies listed on the Stock Exchange are public companies.

1.3 Advantages and disadvantages of incorporated status

There are certain advantages and disadvantages associated with trading as a company rather than as a sole trader.

The advantages are as follows:

- If a company goes into liquidation the owners of the company (the shareholders) are only liable to pay any amounts that they have not yet paid for the shares that they hold. A sole trader would be personally liable for any outstanding debts of the business.

- The shareholders can share in the profits of the business without necessarily having to work day-to-day for the business.

- Companies are in a better position when borrowing money; for example they can issue debentures.

- The company will continue in existence even if shareholders die. If a sole trader dies the business will only continue if the business is sold. This is known as 'perpetual succession.'

The disadvantages are as follows:

- A large company (i.e. one that meets certain size criteria) must normally have an audit of its accounts and therefore must pay auditors' fees. However an audit also offers benefits to the company.

- A company must prepare its accounts in a format prescribed by legislation.

- A company suffers a greater administrative burden than a sole trader. For example, it must file its accounts each year with the Registrar of Companies and must hold an Annual General Meeting of its shareholders.

1.4 Accounting distinctions between a limited company and a sole trader

There are three main differences between the final accounts of a company and those of a sole trader:

- the way in which profit and tax are dealt with in the income statement

- the composition of capital in the statement of financial position

- the statutory requirements of the Companies Act 2006.

The accounts prepared by a company for its own internal use can be in any format that the managers choose. It is only the accounts filed publicly with the Registrar of Companies each year that have to follow the statutory formats. These formats are reproduced later in the chapter.

 Activity 1

What is the difference between a private and a public company?

2 Key differences between a sole trader's accounts and limited company accounts

There are a few differences between the format and content of a sole trader's accounts and the published financial statements of a limited company. The key differences are explained below.

2.1 Capital and accumulated profits

The capital introduced by the shareholders is classified separately in the statement of financial position. It is split between nominal value and share premium. The nominal value is defined by law. The premium is any extra money received by the company when the shares were first issued.

Accumulated profits consist of the brought forward accumulated retained profits, plus the net profit for the year, less dividends. The movement on accumulated profits is reported in the statement of changes in equity.

2.2 Dividends

Dividends for limited companies are the equivalent of drawings for a sole trader. Dividends are reported in the statement of changes in equity (dealt with later). Dividends are recognised on a cash basis when they are paid. Dividends declared but not paid at the year end are disclosed in the notes to the financial statements.

2.3 Taxation

Tax does not appear in a sole trader's income statement. However, limited companies pay their own income tax, and this will be charged to the income statement. The tax will not be paid until after the year-end, and so the charge for the year will be a liability at the year-end. The closing liability is an estimate, and any over or under estimate is reversed out through the following year's income statement.

2.4 Cost of sales and other expenses

Cost of sales and other expenses can be reported in two ways.

The most common way is the **function of expenditure** method. This groups together expenses under three headings: cost of sales, distribution costs and administrative expenses.

Some manufacturing industries use the **nature of expenditure** method. This itemises out expenditure according to its nature, e.g. depreciation, staff costs.

2.5 Non-current assets

Non-current assets such as buildings, machinery or vehicles are analysed out in a note to the accounts. Only the total carrying value appears in the statement of financial position.

2.6 Notes and workings

Notes are printed and published as part of the financial statements. Their contents are normally specified by an accounting standard.

Workings are confidential. They will not be published.

3 Introduction to company accounts

3.1 The content of company accounts

The financial statements of a company comprise the following elements.

- Statement of financial position and notes
- Statement of comprehensive income and notes
- Statement of changes in equity
- Statement of cash flow and notes
- Accounting policies note
- Comparative figures

3.2 Regulations governing company accounts

The main sources of regulations are the Companies Act 2006 (CA 06) and accounting standards.

IAS 1 (Revised) *(Presentation of Financial Statements)* is the main source for the required formats and disclosures in the published statement of comprehensive income, statement of financial position and statement of changes in equity. IAS 7 provides guidance with regard to the statement of cash flows.

4 The statement of financial position for publication

Company statement of financial position as at 31 December 20XX

	£000
Non-current assets	
Goodwill	X
Other intangible assets	X
Property, plant and equipment	X
Investments in subsidiaries	X
Investments in associates	X
	X
Current assets	
Inventories	X
Trade and other receivables	X
Cash and cash equivalents	X
	X
Total assets	**X**
Equity and Liabilities	
Equity	
Share capital	X
Share premium account	X
Revaluation reserve	X
Retained earnings	X
Total equity	X
Non-current liabilities	
Bank loans	X
Long-term provisions	X
	X

Current liabilities	
Trade and other payables	X
Tax liabilities	X
Bank overdrafts and loans	X
	———
	X
	———
Total liabilities	**X**
	———
Total equity and liabilities	**X**
	———

As well as the statement of financial position figures for this year, comparative figures as at the previous year-end must also be shown in a statutory statement of financial position.

Any line item with a nil value this year and the previous year need not be shown in the statement of financial position.

5 The statement of comprehensive income for publication

Company statement of comprehensive income for the year ended 31 December 20XX

	£000
Continuing operations	
Revenue	X
Cost of sales	(X)
	___
Gross profit	X
	___
Distribution costs	(X)
	___
Administrative expense	(X)
	___
Profit from operations	X
	___
Finance costs	(X)
	___
Profit before tax	X
	___
Tax	(X)
	___
Profit for the period from continuing operations	X
Discontinued operations	
Loss for the period from discounted operations	(X)
	___
Profit for the period attributable to equity holders	X
	___
Other comprehensive income	
Gain/loss on property revaluation	X
	___
Total comprehensive income for the year	X
	___

6 Notes to the accounts

6.1 Accounting policies

The notes to the accounts must state the accounting policies adopted by the company for all material items in the financial statements, for example, depreciation of property, plant and equipment and valuation of inventories.

6.2 Notes to the statement of financial position – non-current assets

Classification of non-current assets

Assets are classified as non-current assets if they are intended for use on a continuing basis in the company's activities.

Non-current assets are subdivided as follows:

- **Intangible non-current assets**   These are assets that have no physical form, such as patents and goodwill.

  The notes to the accounts will detail the total intangible non-current assets in the statement of financial position.

	20XX £000
Development costs	X
Concessions, patents, licences and trade marks	X
Goodwill	X
	———
	X
	———

- **Tangible assets (property, plant and equipment)**   These assets have physical form, such as buildings.

- **Investments**   This relates to long-term investments in other companies. It includes shares and loans made to other companies.

- **Property, plant and equipment**

The property, plant and equipment note analyses the total carrying value shown in the statement of financial position by category, and by cost and cumulative depreciation.

The movements for the year (by category, cost and depreciation) are disclosed as follows:

- Opening balance
- Additions/charges for the year
- Effect of revaluations
- Disposals
- Closing balance

An example of a property, plant and equipment note is shown below.

	Land and buildings	Plant and machinery	Fixtures, fittings, tools and equipment	Payments on account and assets in course of construction	Total
	£000	£000	£000	£000	£000
Cost or valuation:					
At 1 January 20XX	X	X	X	X	X
Additions	X	X	X	X	X
Disposals	–	(X)	(X)	–	(X)
At 31 December 20XX	X	X	X	X	X
Accumulated depreciation:					
At 1 January 20XX	X	X	X	–	X
Charge for year	X	X	X	X	X
Disposals	–	(X)	(X)	–	(X)
At 31 December 20XX	X	X	X	X	X
Carrying amount:					
At 1 January 20XX	X	X	X	X	X
At 31 December 20XX	X	X	X	X	X

- **Non-current asset investments**

These are investments that the company intends to keep for more than 12 months from the statement of financial position date. They will normally be stated at cost.

KAPLAN PUBLISHING

6.3 Notes to the statement of financial position – current assets

Classification of current assets

Current assets are assets that are expected to be converted into cash within 12 months. For example, inventories will be sold and converted into cash or receivables. Receivables in turn will settle their debts in cash. If it becomes apparent that the amount of cash that will be received will be less than the book value of the asset, then the asset should be written down to its recoverable amount. This is the basis for valuing inventories at the lower of cost and net realisable value, and for making allowances for doubtful receivables.

Inventories

Inventories are stated at the lower of cost and net realisable value. They will be analysed as follows:

	20XX £000
Raw materials and consumables	X
Work in progress	X
Finished goods and goods for resale	X
	——
	X
	——

6.4 Notes to the statement of financial position – liabilities

Non-current liabilities do not have to be repaid within the next 12 months. Current liabilities are payable within the next 12 months.

Liabilities include provisions. Provisions are made for liabilities of uncertain timing or amount.

6.5 Notes to the statement of financial position – capital and reserves

Called Up Share Capital

	20XX £000
Allotted and fully paid:	
Ordinary shares of £1 each	X
Ordinary shares of 50p each	X
	——
	X
	——

Any movement in the share capital of the company should be disclosed. This is done in the statement of changes in equity. The authorised share capital should also be disclosed.

Reserves

The movement in reserves is analysed out in the statement of changes in equity.

6.6   Notes to the income statement

Revenue

IFRS 8 *Operating Segments* requires disclosure of the analysis of revenue by business segment.

Operating costs and revenues

Disclose all material items of income and expense for example:

*   Disposals of non-current assets

*   Cost associated with discontinued operations etc.

Auditors' remuneration (all remuneration to the auditor, whether for audit or other services) – per CA06.

Example

Profit from operations

Profit is stated after charging the following

	£000	£000
Loss on sale of property plant and equipment		X
Auditors' remuneration		X
In capacity as auditor	X	
In other capacities	X	
	——	
		X
Exceptional write off of receivable		X

Tax on profit on ordinary activities

There are three elements to the tax charge, all of which are disclosed in the tax note:

Example

	20XX £000
Taxation on the profit for the year	
Income tax – estimate for the year	X
Under (over) provision in previous year	X/(X)
Transfer to/(from)Deferred tax	X/(X)
	X

Activity 2

Florabundi, a limited liability company, shows an overprovision of £3,400 on its tax liability account at the end of the year ended 31 December 20X8 before accounting for that year's tax charge.

It estimates tax on profits for the year to be £67,900.

What amounts should be shown in the financial statements for the year ended 31 December 20X8 in respect of tax?

A   £67,900 tax charge £67,900 tax payable

B   £64,500 tax charge £64,500 tax payable

C   £64,500 tax charge £67,900 tax payable

D   £71,300 tax charge £67,900 tax payable

7 Statement of changes in equity

The statement of changes in equity brings together all the gains and losses for the period, including items which do not pass through the income statement.

The most common example of an item which does not pass through the income statement is a gain on the revaluation of a non-current asset. Revaluation gains cannot be taken to the income statement because they are unrealised, but nevertheless, they may form an important part of a company's overall performance.

The statement of changes in equity highlights the effect of revaluations and other items such as prior period adjustments and helps users of the financial statements to appreciate their impact upon the company's overall financial performance.

Example plc

Statement of changes in equity

	Share capital £000	Share premium £000	Revalua -tion £000	Other reserves £000	Retained earnings £000	Total £000
At January 20X8	X	X	X	X	X	X
Revaluation			X			X
Transfer between reserves				X	(X)	
Profit for the year					X	X
Dividends paid					(X)	(X)
At 31 December 20X8	X	X	X	X	X	X

Activity 3

According to IAS 1 *Presentation of Financial statements* which of the following items should appear in the statement of changes in equity:

1   Total comprehensive income for the year

2   Dividends paid

3   Loss on sale of investments

4   Issue of share capital

A   1, 2 and 4 only

B   1,3 and 4 only

C   1 and 3 only

D   1,2,3 and 4

8   Summary

In order to prepare limited company financial statements you need:

•   a detailed knowledge of the disclosure requirements IAS 1

•   the ability to get the knowledge onto paper quickly and neatly.

•   Apply a methodical approach and show workings

Published accounts' is primarily a practical subject, so take the opportunity to learn from financial statements which you come across in practice.

Answers to chapter activities

 Activity 1

There are two types of Limited company:

Public companies must include 'PLC' in its name.

PLC's are listed on the stock exchange and can sell shares to the public.

Private companies must include 'Ltd' or Limited after in their name and are not listed on the stock exchange therefore cannot offer their shares to the public.

 Activity 2

Answer is C

Over provision b/fwd	(3,400)
Current years estimated tax	67,900
Tax charge	64,500
Tax Liability	67,900

Activity 3

Answer is A

9 Test your knowledge

Workbook Activity 4 (revision of API and APII)

You work as an accounting technician for a firm of chartered accountants. Karl Hayes, a self-employed builder, is one of your clients and the following issues relate to his year end accounts.

(1) The trade receivables balance is £19,100. A debt of £400 is considered to be irrecoverable and is to be written off. The balance on the allowance for doubtful debts account is currently £735 and the allowance is to be revised to 5% of trade receivables.

The amount to be charged to the income statement for the change in the doubtful debt allowance is:

A   £935

B   £735

C   £200

D   £220

(2) During the year a non-current asset had been disposed of. The profit on sale was £750. The cost of the asset had been £3,400 and the proceeds on sale were £2,150.

The accumulated depreciation to date was:

A   £2,150

B   £2,650

C   £2,000

D   £1,250

(3) The balance on the rent and rates account as shown on the trial balance was £2,850 Dr.

At the year end, rates had been prepaid by £720 and the rent was due at the year end of £500.

The amount to be charged to the income statement for the year was:

A   £2,630

B   £3,070

C   £1,630

D   £4,070

(4) The following information relates to items in the purchase ledger control account:

Opening balance	£15,100 Cr
Payments to suppliers	£83,200
Returns to suppliers	£1,100
Discounts received	£4,100
Amounts offset against items in the sales ledger	£1,560
Purchases on credit from suppliers	£96,000

(**NB:** A supplier was also a customer.)

The closing balance on the purchase ledger account would be:

A   £34,660

B   £23,340

C   £21,140

D   None of these

(5) The trial balance included the following information:

Revenue £131,700, returns outward £1,100, returns inward £1,700, purchases £96,000, opening inventory valuation £16,200 and a note to the information showed that the closing inventory valuation was £17,220 and that goods which had cost £1,500 had been used by Karl for his own use.

(a) The cost of goods sold for the period was:

A   £91,780

B   £94,420

C   £95,380

D   £92,380

(b) The gross profit for the period was:

    A   £32,080

    B   £37,620

    C   £38,220

    D   None of these

Property, plant and equipment

Introduction

For this unit you need to be able to draft limited company year-end financial statements and for that purpose you need to be aware of the main requirements of relevant accounting standards.

In this chapter we will consider the detailed requirements of IAS 16 *Property, Plant and Equipment*. For this IFRS all aspects are assessable both discursive and computational tasks. We will also consider IAS 40 Investment Property and IAS 23 Borrowing Costs.

KNOWLEDGE
Describe legislation and regulation which must be complied with in the preparation of the financial statements (1.2)
Explain the relevance of accounting standards (1.4)
Identify accounting standards and the effect of these on the preparation of the financial statements (2.5)

SKILLS
Apply accounting standards and relevant legislation to correctly identify, and accurately adjust, accounting information (1.1)
Prepare notes to the accounts which satisfy statutory current disclosure requirements, in respect of accounting policies, non-current assets, current and long term liabilities, equity (1.4)

CONTENTS

1   IAS 16 *Property, Plant and Equipment*
2   IAS 40 *Investment Property*

1 IAS 16 *Property, Plant and Equipment*

1.1 Introduction

IAS 16 *Property, Plant and Equipment* considers recognition of assets, determination of carrying amount and the depreciation charges and impairment losses to be recognised in relation to them.

1.2 Initial measurement

Initial measurement of property, plant and equipment (whether acquired or self-constructed) should be at its cost.

Cost should include all costs directly attributable to bringing the asset into working condition for its intended use. Cost can include finance costs – see 1.3.

If the carrying amount of the property, plant or equipment exceeds its recoverable amount (defined as the higher of net realisable value and value in use) then the asset is impaired and it should be written down to its recoverable amount – see IAS 36 in the next chapter.

1.3 IAS 23 *Borrowing Costs*

Finance costs (such as interest payable) directly attributable to the construction of a tangible non-current asset may be capitalised as part of the cost of the asset.

Conditions:

- Finance costs capitalised in a period must not exceed finance costs incurred in the period.

- Capitalisation should begin when:
    - finance costs are being incurred; and
    - expenditure for the asset is being incurred; and
    - work has begun on the asset or on getting it ready for use

- Capitalisation should cease when:
    - substantially all the activities necessary to get the asset ready for use are complete

---

🔆 Example

AB plc incurs the following costs in constructing a new non-current asset which takes three months.

	£
Site clearance	2,000
Cost of materials used in asset	30,000
Legal fees to secure a license	1,000
Interest at 10% pa on £40,000 loan raised to finance the asset's construction: 3-month construction period (10% × £40,000 × $^3/_{12}$)	1,000
Cost of materials wasted in a flood	500
Cost of labour used in asset	8,000
Cost of industrial dispute	1,500

Which of the above costs can be capitalised into the initial cost of the non-current asset?

Solution

The directly attributable costs are:

	£
Site clearance	2,000
Cost of materials in asset	30,000
Necessary legal fee	1,000
Interest during construction period	1,000
Cost of labour in asset	8,000
	_____
	42,000
	_____

The cost of the wasted materials and the industrial dispute are not direct costs and must be written off to the income statement as incurred.

1.4 Subsequent expenditure

Subsequent expenditure should be capitalised if it enhances the economic benefits of the asset in excess of its previously assessed standard of performance. Otherwise, subsequent expenditure that helps to maintain the asset's standard of performance (e.g. routine repairs and maintenance) should be charged to the income statement as it is incurred.

1.5   Valuation

Revaluation of property, plant and equipment is allowed if a policy of revaluation is adopted. Any gains or losses on revaluation must be disclosed in both the statement of other comprehensive income and the statement of changes in equity.

Conditions:

- All assets of the same class must be revalued. For example, if certain land and buildings were to be revalued, this would not require the revaluation of plant and machinery, but would require the revaluation of all land and buildings held.

- Once revalued, the carrying amount in each statement of financial position must be current value. This is fair value at date of valuation less any subsequent accumulated depreciation and subsequent accumulated impairment losses.

- Revaluations should be made regularly to ensure carrying value does not differ materially from fair value at statement of financial position date. (Some items may require annual revaluation others only every three to five years.)

1.6   Reporting valuation gains and losses

- Gains

  - These are recorded in equity as a revaluation reserve. They can be seen in the statement of other comprehensive income and the statement of changes in equity (SOCIE). If the increase reverses a previous loss which was recognised in the income statement, then it can be taken to the income statement to the extent that it reverses a previous revaluation loss on the same asset.

- Losses

  - These are recognised in the income statement unless there is already a balance in the revaluation reserve for that asset. In this case, the loss is taken to the revaluation reserve to the extent of any previous surplus and is also seen in the statement of changes in equity and the statement of other comprehensive income.

Example

A building costing £200,000 was purchased on 1 January 20X8. It is being depreciated over its useful life of 20 years on a straight line basis down to a nil residual value. At 31 December 20X8 the building was revalued at £247,000 and at 31 December 20X9 it was revalued at £150,000.

Show how these revaluations should be dealt with in the financial statements as at 31 December 20X8 and 20X9.

Solution

(a)   In the year ended 31 December 20X8, depreciation of $\dfrac{£200,000}{20} =$

£10,000 would originally be charged so the carrying value at the date of revaluation is £190,000.

The revaluation gain is £57,000 (from a carrying value of £190,000 up to £247,000). This gain would be reported in the SOCE and statement of other comprehensive income and would be shown in the statement of financial position as a revaluation reserve.

The double entry for the revaluation is:

	£	£
DR Building (247 – 200)	47,000	
DR Accumulated depreciation	10,000	
CR Revaluation reserve		57,000

As the asset is being used, it is possible to transfer some of the revaluation reserve to retained earnings. The amount that is transferred (as the revaluation reserve is non-distributable) is the amount of the revaluation reserve for the asset divided by the remaining life or alternatively the difference between the original depreciation based on cost and the depreciation based on the revaluated amount.

In our example the journal would be:

	£	£
DR Revaluation reserve (57,000 ÷ 19)	3,000	
CR Retained earnings (13,000 – 10,000)		3,000
(**Note:** £247,000 ÷ 19 = £13,000)		

The journal above shows both methods of calculating this transfer. This realises a proportion of the revaluation reserve each year the asset is being depreciated and is disclosed in the SOCE.

(b) In the year ended 31 December 20X9, depreciation of $\dfrac{£247,000}{19} =$

£13,000 would originally be charged, so the carrying value at the date of the second revaluation is £234,000.

Once the asset has been revalued it is depreciated over its remaining useful life, hence the depreciation was over a period of 19 years and not 20.

The revaluation loss is £84,000 (from a carrying value of £234,000 down to £150,000).

This loss can be offset against the previous revaluation gain, to the extent that there is enough gain available.

The previous revaluation surplus is now £54,000 (£57,000 – £3,000 transfer) so this part of the loss can be offset reducing the revaluation reserve to zero.

The remainder of the loss is £30,000 and this must be charged to the income statement.

The double entry for the revaluation is:

	£	£
DR Accumulated depreciation	13,000	
DR Income statement	30,000	
DR Revaluation reserve	54,000	
CR Building (150 – 247)		97,000

Activity 1

At the end of its financial year, Tanner has the following non-current assets:

Land and buildings at cost	£10.4 million
Land and buildings: accumulated depreciation	£0.12 million

The company has decided to revalue its land and buildings at the year end to £15 million.

What will be the amount of the adjustment on revaluation?

A   £4.48m

B   £4.6m

C   £4.72m

D   £15.12m

1.7   Gains and losses on disposal

Gains and losses on disposal of tangible non-current assets are shown in the income statement and are calculated as the difference between proceeds and carrying amount at the date of sale.

1.8   Depreciation

The depreciable amount (cost or valuation, less residual value) of a tangible non-current asset should be allocated on a systematic basis over its useful life. The following factors need to be considered when determining the useful life, residual value and depreciation method of an asset:

- Expected usage

- Expected physical wear and tear

- Economic or technological obsolescence

- Legal or similar limits on use, such as the expiry dates of related leases

Note that land is not depreciated. This is because it is not expected to have a finite life, whereas other assets such as buildings or machinery will have a finite life.

IAS 16 does not stipulate a particular method of depreciation. It is up to the directors to choose the most appropriate method possible.

1.9 Useful economic lives and residual values

The length of a non-current asset's life is clearly a very important number in a depreciation calculation. However, it is an estimate, as it is necessary to make predictions about the future.

Both the useful economic life and the residual value (if material) of a tangible non-current asset should be reviewed at the end of each reporting period. They should be revised 'if expectations are significantly different from previous estimates'.

 Activity 2

Ford plc

The following property, plant and equipment balances have been extracted from the books of Ford plc as at 31 December 20X7.

	£000	£000
Freehold factory cost at 1 January 20X7	1,440	
Freehold factory revaluation	760	
Freehold factory additions	500	
Freehold factory depreciation at 1 January 20X7		144
Freehold factory revaluation adjustment	144	
Freehold factory depreciation charge		60
Plant and machinery cost at 1 January 20X7	1,968	
Plant and machinery additions	75	
Plant and machinery depreciation at 1 January 20X7		257
Plant and machinery depreciation charge		233
Motor vehicles cost at 1 January 20X7	449	
Motor vehicles additions	35	
Motor vehicles depreciation at 1 January 20X7		194
Motor vehicles depreciation charge		87
Office equipment and fixtures cost at 1 January 20X7	888	
Office equipment and fixtures additions	22	
Office equipment and fixtures depreciation at 1 January 20X7		583
Office equipment and fixtures depreciation charge		182

You are given the following information for the year ended 31 December 20X7:

(1) The factory was acquired in March 20X2 and is being depreciated over 50 years.

(2) At 1 January 20X7, depreciation was provided on cost on a straight-line basis. The rates used were 20% for office equipment and fixtures, 25% for motor vehicles and 10% for plant and machinery.

(3)   Early in the year the factory was revalued to an open market value of £2.2 million and an extension was built costing £500,000.

(4)   It is the company's policy to charge a full year's depreciation in the year of acquisition.

Required:

Prepare the accounting policy and property, plant and equipment notes for the year ended 31 December 20X7 as required by IAS 16 and IAS 1 in so far as the information permits.

2   IAS 40 *Investment Property*

2.1   Definition

An investment property is property held to earn rentals or for capital appreciation or both. Investment property is not:

(a)   Property intended for sale in the ordinary course of business

(b)   Property being constructed on behalf of third parties

(c)   Owner occupied property or property occupied by the parent or subsidiary company

(d)   Property that is leased to another entity under a finance lease.

Example

Which of the following are investment properties?

(a)   Land which is leased out at an arm's length rental to a third party for use as a car park.

(b)   A building used by the owning company as the company head office.

(c)   A building leased to a subsidiary at an arm's length rental.

Solution

(a)   This is an investment property.

(b)   This is not an investment property, since it is occupied by the owning company for its own purposes.

(c)   In the parents statement of financial position the building is an investment property, it is only owner occupied in the consolidated financial position and thus recorded in property, plant and equipment under IAS 16.

2.2   Accounting treatment

Investment properties should be measured initially at cost, after initial recognition an entity must choose either the fair value model or the cost model to value its investment property.

Fair value model – After initial recognition, all investment property is recognised at fair value. Fair value is the price the property could be exchanged between willing knowledgeable parties in an arm's length transaction.

Any gains or losses arising from a change in fair value shall be recognised in the income statement for period in which it arises. Under this model, investment properties are not depreciated.

Cost model – The asset is measured at cost and depreciated as per IAS 16 *Property, Plant and Equipment*.

The method used, whether the fair value or cost model, must be disclosed.

 Activity 3

X Ltd (part of Question 1 June 2004)

X Ltd owns the freehold of a building which they constructed for investment purposes. The building is currently rented to another company on commercial terms. The property is not recorded at its historical cost and has not been depreciated.

What is the correct accounting treatment for this property?

Activity 4

1   Is the capitalisation of finance costs into the cost of tangible non-current assets mandatory or optional?

2   How should directors choose the depreciation method to be used?

3   At what value should investment properties be shown in the statement of financial position?

3 Summary

IAS 16 covers the accounting for property, plant and equipment. Property, plant and equipment should initially be shown at cost. Interest is be capitalised into the cost of non-current asset in accordance with IAS 23 Borrowing costs.

Subsequently they may either be shown at cost less depreciation, or revalued to fair value. Where revalued, all similar items should be revalued and the revaluation must be kept up to date.

IAS 40 requires that investment properties should be valued using either the fair value model or cost model.

Answers to chapter activities

Activity 1

Answer is C

	£m
Non-current assets at cost	10.40
Accumulated depreciation	(0.12)
Carrying value	10.28
Revaluation amount	15.00
Gain to revaluation reserve	4.72

The accounting entry is:

Dr	accumulated depreciation	0.12	
Dr	land	4.6	
	Cr revaluation reserve		4.72

Activity 2

Ford plc   Accounting policy note

(1) Property, plant and equipment

Interests in buildings are stated at a valuation.

Other property, plant and equipment are stated at cost, together with any incidental expenses of acquisition.

Depreciation is calculated so as to write off the net cost or valuation of property, plant and equipment over their expected useful economic lives. A full year's charge is provided in the year of acquisition. The rates and bases used are as follows:

Buildings – on the straight-line basis	2% pa
Plant and machinery – on the straight-line basis	10% pa
Office equipment and fixtures – on the straight-line basis	20% pa
Motor vehicles – on the straight-line basis	25% pa

KAPLAN PUBLISHING

(2)   Property, plant and equipment

	Freehold land and buildings	Plant and machinery	Motor vehicles	Fixtures, fittings, tools and equipment	Total
	£000	£000	£000	£000	£000
Cost or valuation					
At 1 January 20X7	1,440	1,968	449	888	4,745
Additions	500	75	35	22	632
Revaluations	760	–	–	–	760
At 31 December 20X7	2,700	2,043	484	910	6,137
Depreciation					
At 1 January 20X7	144	257	194	583	1,178
Revaluation adjustment	(144)				(144)
Charge for year	60	233	87	182	562
At 31 December 20X7	60	490	281	765	1,596
Carrying value					
At 1 January 20X7	1,296	1,711	255	305	3,567
At 31 December 20X7	2,640	1,553	203	145	4,541

 Activity 3

X Ltd

Assuming that the other company is not a member of the same group as X Ltd then this property is an investment property as defined by IAS 40. It is rented out on commercial terms and should therefore be classified in the statement of financial position as a non-current asset under the heading Investment property.

The property shall be valued using either the fair value model or the cost model.

The fair value model is the price that could be achieved if the asset was sold to a knowledgeable willing party at an arm's length transaction.

The cost model is initial construction cost less accumulated depreciation. The valuation model chosen must be disclosed.

Activity 4

1   Mandatory.

2   The depreciation method should reflect the pattern in which the asset's economic benefits are consumed.

3   Fair value or cost less depreciation.

4 Test your knowledge

 ## Workbook Activity 5

The objective of IAS 16 is to prescribe the accounting treatment for property, plant and equipment.

(a) Identify the principal issues in the accounting treatment of property, plant and equipment.

(b) When should items of property, plant and equipment be recognised as assets?

(c) Which costs should be included on initial recognition of property, plant and equipment.

 ## Workbook Activity 6

Bill Ltd has provided the following information:

	£
List price of machinery	600,000
Transportation costs	3,500
Site preparation costs	1,500
Installation costs	3,800
Pre production testing	5,300
Two year maintenance contract cost	15,000
Warranty cost	7,600
Annual insurance	3,200

The company received a 5% trade discount on the list price.

What is the initial measurement value (capitalised cost) of the machinery?

A £614,100

B £584,100

C £591,700

D £609,900

Workbook Activity 7

The following is provided by Ivan Ltd:

	£
Land at cost	500,000
Buildings at cost	450,000
Buildings – accumulated depreciation	(180,000)
Carrying value	770,000

Land was revalued to £600,000 and buildings to £600,000.

What is the correct double entry to record the revaluation of land and buildings?

		£
A	Dr Land	100,000
	Dr Buildings	150,000
	Cr Revaluation reserve	350,000
B	Dr Revaluation reserve	430,000
	Cr Land	100,000
	Cr Buildings	150,000
	Cr Building depreciation	180,000
C	Dr Buildings	270,000
	Dr Land	100,000
	Cr Revaluation reserve	370,000
D	Dr Land	100,000
	Dr Buildings	150,000
	Dr Buildings accumulated depreciation	180,000
	Cr Revaluation reserve	430,000

Intangible assets and impairment of assets

5

Introduction

For this unit you need knowledge of aspects of IAS 38 *Intangible assets* and of IAS 36 *Impairment of assets.*

KNOWLEDGE
Describe legislation and regulation which must be complied with in the preparation of the financial statements (1.2)
Explain the relevance of accounting standards (1.4)
Identify accounting standards and the effect of these on the preparation of the financial statements (2.5)

SKILLS
Apply accounting standards and relevant legislation to correctly identify, and accurately adjust, accounting information (1.1)
Prepare notes to the accounts which satisfy statutory current disclosure requirements, in respect of accounting policies, non-current assets, current and long term liabilities, equity (1.4)

CONTENTS

1 IAS 38 *Intangible Assets*
2 IAS 36 *Impairment of Assets*

1 IAS 38 *Intangible Assets*

1.1 Introduction

In the previous chapter you studied the accounting for property, plant and equipment such as buildings, cars and computers. Property, plant and equipment have physical form, so you can see what the company has paid for. Sometimes a company will pay money to acquire an intangible asset which has no physical form.

1.2 Criteria of an Intangible asset

An intangible asset is an identifiable, non-monetary asset without physical substance.

To be identified as an intangible asset, an asset must either:

- be capable of being separated or divided from the entity and sold, transferred, licensed, rented or exchanged either individually or together with a related contract, asset or liability or

- arise from contractual or other legal rights.

The definition requires an intangible asset to be identifiable to distinguish it from goodwill. In an acquisition, goodwill represents the payment made by the acquirer in anticipation of future benefits from the assets purchased. These benefits may result from cost savings when the businesses are combined, but cannot be separately identified as an asset.

Internally generated goodwill should not be recognised as an asset as it is not a separable asset or arise from contractual rights as seen above and it cannot be measured reliably.

1.3 Recognition and measurement

An intangible asset shall only be recognised if:

- it is probable that the expected future economic benefits that are attributable to the asset will flow to the entity; and

- the cost of the asset can be measured reliably.

Future economic benefits includes revenue from sale of products or services, cost savings, or other benefits resulting from use of the asset by the entity.

An intangible asset shall initially be measured at cost.

1.4 Internally generated intangible assets

To assess whether an internally generated intangible asset meets the criteria for recognition, an entity classifies the generation of the asset into:

- research phase
- development phase.

No intangible asset arising from research or from the research phase shall be recognised. Expenditure on the research phase is recognised as an expense in the income statement when it is incurred.

An intangible asset arising from the development or the development phase shall be recognised if an entity can demonstrate all of the following:

(a) technical feasibility of completing the intangible asset so it is available for use or sale

(b) intention to complete the intangible asset and use or sell it

(c) ability to use or sell the intangible asset

(d) how the intangible asset will generate probable future economic benefits. E.g. how the entity can demonstrate the existence of a market for the output of the intangible asset or the intangible asset itself

(e) availability of adequate technical, financial and other resources to complete the development and to use or sell the intangible asset

(f) ability to measure reliably the expenditure attributable to the intangible asset during its development

Internally generated brands, publishing titles, customer lists and similar items shall not be recognised as intangible assets.

1.5 Cost of an internally generated intangible asset

Cost comprises all directly attributable cost necessary to create, produce and prepare the asset for use. This will include the following:

- Costs of materials and services used or consumed in generating the intangible asset
- Costs of employee benefits arising from the generation of the intangible asset
- Fees to register a legal right
- Amortisation of patents and licences that are used to generate the intangible asset.

The following are not components of cost:

- Selling, administrative, and other general overhead expenses
- Identified inefficiencies and initial operating losses incurred before the asset achieves planned performance
- The cost of training staff to operate the asset.

1.6 Measurement after recognition

An entity shall choose either the cost model or revaluation model as its accounting policy.

Cost model: The asset is carried at cost less any accumulated depreciation and any accumulated impairment losses.

Revaluation model: The asset is carried at its revalued amount. This is its fair value at the date of revaluation less any subsequent accumulated amortisation and any subsequent impairment losses. The valuation must be reviewed regularly.

Intangible assets are usually not revalued as they are unique and it is unlikely that there is an active market, meaning: a number of willing buyers and sellers; similar items traded are homogenous: and that sale prices are readily available to the public.

1.7 Revaluation gains or losses

A revaluation gain should be credited to the revaluation reserve. It will be recognised in the statement of changes in equity and shown in the statement of comprehensive income.

A revaluation loss will be debited to the income statement (unless reversing a previous gain in which case the loss will be debited to the relevant revaluation reserve).

1.8 Useful life

An entity needs to determine whether the useful life of an intangible asset is finite or indefinite.

Finite life

If finite then the entity must determine the length of the life. Amortisation shall begin when the asset is available for use and cease when the asset is either classified as held for sale or the date the asset is derecognised.

The amortisation method chosen should reflect the pattern in which the assets' benefits are expected to be consumed. If this cannot be reliably measured then the straight-line method shall be used. The amortisation charge for each period shall be recognised in the income statement.

The residual value of an intangible asset shall be deemed to be zero unless:

- there is a commitment by a third party to purchase the asset at the end of its useful life or

- there is an active market for the asset and a residual value can be determined and the active market will still exist at the end of the assets useful life.

The amortisation period and method shall be reviewed at each financial year end.

Indefinite life

If an asset has an indefinite life it shall not be amortised.

The asset must be tested for impairment in accordance with IAS 36 *Impairment of Assets.*

An entity must compare the recoverable amount with the carrying amount of the asset. This must be done annually and whenever there is an indication that the asset may be impaired.

The useful life must be reviewed each period to ensure events and circumstances still support an indefinite useful life assessment for that asset.

 Activity 1

(a) Describe the difference between purchased and non-purchased good will, stating how each is created and how it should be accounted for.

(b) Explain the criteria in IAS 38 for capitalising research and development expenditure.

2 IAS 36 *Impairment of Assets*

2.1 Introduction

We have already met impairment in this text:

IAS 16 requires property, plant and equipment to be written down to their recoverable amounts when it is known that the carrying amount exceeds the recoverable amount.

IAS 38 requires annual impairment reviews to be carried out whenever an intangible asset is deemed to have an indefinite useful life.

Definition

Impairment is the reduction in the recoverable amount of a non-current asset or goodwill below its carrying amount.

Recoverable amount is the higher of net selling price and value in use.

Net realisable value is the amount at which an asset could be disposed of, less any direct selling costs (fair value less selling costs).

Value in use is the present value of the future cash flows arising from an asset's continued use, including those resulting from its ultimate disposal.

 Example

A machine has a carrying value of £5,000 in the draft statement of financial position as at 31 December 20X9. It could be sold now for £4,000, or retained in the business where it's value in use is £4,476. Assess whether the machine is impaired at 31 December 20X9.

Solution

Current carrying value (= carrying amount) = £5,000

Compare this with the recoverable amount:

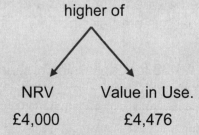

higher of

NRV   Value in Use.

£4,000   £4,476

Therefore recoverable amount = £4,476

The machine has a book value of £5,000 but a recoverable amount of only £4,476. It is impaired and should be written down to £4,476 in the statement of financial position. An impairment loss of £5,000 – £4,476 = £524 must be recognised.

2.2 Identifying an asset that may be impaired

An entity shall assess at each reporting date whether there is any indication that an asset may be impaired.

Regardless of any indication an entity shall also:

- test an intangible asset with an indefinite useful economic life for impairment (this may be performed at any time during the year, provided it is performed at the same time each year)

- test goodwill acquired in a business combination for impairment annually.

2.3 Indicators of impairment

Examples of indications that impairment may have occurred are as follows.

External sources of information:

- a significant decline in a non-current asset's market value during the period

- a significant adverse change in the market in which the business operates

- changes in the economic environment, such as interest rates or inflation

- changes in the legal system.

Internal sources of information:

- evidence of physical damage to, or obsolescence of, the asset

- a current period operating loss

- net cash outflow from operating activities

- a management commitment to undertake a significant reorganisation

- a major loss of key employees.

2.4 Determining fair value

The best evidence of an asset's fair value is a price in a binding sale agreement in an arm's length transaction.

If no binding sale agreement exists but the asset is traded on the active market then this value (less sales cost) could be used.

If neither of these exist then fair value less costs to sell is based on the best available information e.g. look at recent transactions for similar assets within the industry etc.

2.5 Determining value in use

The following shall be reflected in determining value in use:

(a) estimate of the future cash flows the entity expects to derive from the asset

(b) expectations about possible changes of those future cash flows

(c) time value of money

(d) price for bearing the uncertainty inherent in the asset

(e) other factors (such as illiquidity) that market participants would reflect in pricing the future cash flows the entity expects to derive from the asset.

Estimating value in use involves:

(a) estimating future cash flows to be derived from the continuing use of the asset

(b) applying the appropriate discount rate to these cash flows. (The discount rate shall be pre-tax and reflect the time value of money and the specific risks to that asset.)

2.6 Accounting for impairment losses

Impairment losses must be recognised in the income statement, unless they arise on a previously revalued asset. Impairment losses on revalued assets are recognised in the revaluations reserve which is part of the statement of changes in equity.

After recognition of the impairment loss the depreciation (amortisation) charge for the asset shall be adjusted to allocate the asset's revised carrying amount over its useful economic life.

2.7 Cash generating units

If there is an indication that an asset has been impaired, then the recoverable amount shall be estimated for that individual asset.

If this is not possible to do for an individual asset, then an entity shall determine the recoverable amount of the cash generating unit to which the asset belongs.

 Definition

A cash generating unit is the smallest identifiable group of assets which generate income independently of other assets.

For example; in a restaurant chain one individual restaurant may be classed as a CGU. In a college a classroom and its associated furniture and technology might be classed as a CGU.

2.8 Timing of impairment tests for goodwill

The annual impairment test for a cash generating unit to which goodwill has been allocated may be performed at any time during an annual period, provided the test is performed at the same time each year.

If an impairment loss is found for a cash generating unit then the loss shall be allocated firstly to any assets that are specifically impaired and then as follows:

(a)   to reduce the carrying amount of goodwill

(b)   to reduce the carrying amount of the other assets in the unit on a pro rata basis.

2.9 Disclosure requirements

An entity shall disclose the amount of the impairment losses recognised during the period and the line item(s) of the income statement in which those impairment losses are included.

 Activity 2

The directors of Smokey Ltd are carrying out a review of four assets which they consider may have become impaired.

	Carrying amount	Fair value less costs to sell	Value in use
	£	£	£
A	20,000	24,000	28,000
B	16,000	18,000	11,600
C	14,000	15,200	14,400
D	18,000	8,600	10,400

In accordance with IAS 36 Impairment of assets, which of the above assets will be impaired?

Activity 3

1   What is purchased goodwill?

2   What is the required accounting treatment for costs during the research phase?

3   What is the accounting treatment of goodwill?

4   Explain how the recoverable amount of an asset is estimated.

3   Summary

This chapter has covered two important accounting standards:

*   IAS 38 *Intangible Assets*

   This requires intangibles to be capitalised and amortised over their useful economic lives.

   It discusses the treatment of costs in the research and development phases of a product.

*   IAS 36 *Impairment of Assets*

   IAS 36 requires impaired assets (those for which the carrying value exceeds the recoverable amount) to be written down to their recoverable amount. The impairment loss is normally recognised in the income statement.

Answers to chapter activities

 Activity 1

Purchased goodwill is goodwill which is established as a result of a purchase of a business. Under these circumstances goodwill is measured as the difference between the value of the business as a whole and the aggregate value of the separable tangible and intangible assets. This represents a valuation of goodwill at the time of acquisition.

All other forms of goodwill are considered to be non-purchased goodwill. Whilst it is possible to speculate about how such goodwill has come into existence, (e.g. from the reputation of the business as a supplier of quality goods, good customer and/or staff relations, advantageous location etc) any list such as the foregoing cannot be considered either complete or definitive. Any expenditure incurred in creating circumstances where goodwill may arise cannot be directly related to the value of the resulting goodwill, and indeed may be completely unrelated to any goodwill in the business.

Purchased positive goodwill should be capitalised. Goodwill is regarded as having an indefinite useful economic life and therefore, it should not be amortised.

An annual impairment review must be performed in order to identify any fall in value. The value of the goodwill should then be written down if necessary. Purchased goodwill should be capitalised for the following reasons.

- Including goodwill in the statement of financial position means that users of the financial statements recognise that it is part of the cost of an investment, a cost for which management remains accountable.

- There is consistency between the treatment of goodwill and other assets.

Non-purchased goodwill should not be capitalised.

It can be argued that goodwill meets the definition of an asset in the IASB's Framework for the preparation and presentation of financial statements. However, only where the historical costs of creating or acquiring an asset are known is it capable of being measured with sufficient reliability to be recognised in the financial statements.

Where goodwill has been purchased, the cost of the goodwill has been established by an actual transaction, and is a matter of fact. Where goodwill has been generated internally any valuation can only be subjective. For this reason non-purchased goodwill cannot be included in the statement of financial position.

(b) Expenditure on the research phase must be recognised as an expense in the income statement when it is incurred and can never be capitalised.

An intangible arising from the development or development phase shall be recognised if an entity can demonstrate all of the following:

(a) technical feasibility of completing the intangible asset so it is available for use or sale

(b) intention to complete the intangible asset and use or sell it

(c) ability to use or sell the intangible asset

(d) how the intangible asset will generate probable future economic benefits e.g. how the entity can demonstrate the existence of a market for the output of the intangible asset or the intangible asset itself

(e) availability of adequate technical, financial and other resources to complete the development and to use or sell the intangible asset

(f) ability to measure reliably the expenditure attributable to the intangible asset during its development.

 Activity 2

Answer is D

According to IAS 36 an asset is impaired when its carrying amount exceeds its recoverable amount, where the recoverable amount of an asset is the higher of its fair value less costs to sell and its value in use.

Carrying amount = 18,000

The higher of recoverable amount is value in use = 10,400

Therefore only asset D is impaired by (18,000 – 10,400) = 7,600

Activity 3

1   Purchased goodwill arises when the cost of purchasing a company is greater than the aggregate of the fair values of the net assets it acquires.

2   Costs during the research phase must be written off as incurred.

3   Purchased goodwill is capitalised. Annual impairment reviews must be carried out. Internally generated goodwill can never be capitalised.

4   Recoverable amount is the higher of net realisable value and value in use.

4   Test your knowledge

 Workbook Activity 4

Prepare brief notes for the directors to answer the following questions:

(a)   What is meant by an intangible asset according to IAS 38?

(b)   What would Harris plc have to demonstrate about development costs before these costs can be recognised as an intangible assets in the financial statements according to IAS 38?

 Workbook Activity 5

Which of the following statements are true according to IAS 38?

(i)   All development expenditure must be written off immediately to the income statement as soon as the expenditure is incurred.

(ii)   Amortisation of development costs can be based on the future sales revenue of the product.

(iii)   All research expenditure should be capitalised as an intangible asset.

(iv)   Development expenditure that is capitalised should be treated as a tangible non-current asset.

(v)   One of the criteria to be met in considering whether or not development expenditure can be capitalised is whether the project is technically feasible.

     A   Only (ii) and (v).

     B   Only (i), (iii) and (v)

     C   Only (ii) and (iv)

     D   Only (iii) and (iv)

Workbook Activity 6

Which of the following statements are true according to IAS 36?

(i)   Impairment arises when the recoverable amount exceeds the carrying amount.

(ii)   The recoverable amount is the higher of the net selling price and the value in use.

(iii)   The value in use is the net present value of future cash flows.

(iv)   An impairment charge is recorded by debiting the asset account and crediting the income statement.

(v)   The value in use of an asset can be affected by both internal and external factors.

    A   Only (i), (ii) and (v).

    B   Only (ii), (iii) and (v)

    C   Only (ii), (iii) and (iv)

    D   Only (i), (iv) and (iv)

Inventory

Introduction

In order to prepare a set of limited company accounts you need to know how to deal with the valuation of inventories. This is covered by IAS 2 *Inventories*.

KNOWLEDGE
Describe legislation and regulation which must be complied with in the preparation of the financial statements (1.2)
Explain the relevance of accounting standards (1.4)
Identify accounting standards and the effect of these on the preparation of the financial statements (2.5)

SKILLS
Apply accounting standards and relevant legislation to correctly identify, and accurately adjust, accounting information (1.1)

CONTENTS

1 Valuation of inventories
2 Methods of costing inventories

1 Valuation of inventories

1.1 The basic rule

Inventories should be stated at the **lower of cost and net realisable value,** on an item by item basis.

1.2 Cost

IAS 2 *Inventories* defines cost as comprising: 'all costs of purchase, costs of conversion and other costs incurred in bringing the inventories to their present location and condition'.

Specifically excluded are:

(a)   abnormal amounts of wasted materials, labour and other production costs

(b)   storage costs, unless necessary in the production process before a further production stage

(c)   administrative overheads that do not contribute to bringing inventories to their present location and condition

(d)   selling costs.

This means that two identical items may have different costs if they are in different locations. For example, the cost of an item which has been shipped to a distribution centre in France will include the normal transport costs to France and hence will have a higher cost than a similar item held in the factory in England.

Note that only costs incurred In the normal course of business should be included. If the lorry taking items to France broke down, the costs of the breakdown would not be included as part of the transport costs since they are considered abnormal.

Example

The Standard Company plc has inventories at 31 December 20X7 and has gathered the following information together in order to determine its cost.

	£
Cost of original materials	16,000
Cost of work on material: Labour 1,000 hours @ £2.50	2,500
Variable overhead	700
Fixed production overhead during the period 1 October to 31 December 20X7	40,000
Number of hours worked in the period 1 October to 31 December 20X7	18,000 hours

You also discovered that an additional 2,000 hours of work were lost during December due to an industrial dispute over the holiday work programme.

Selling and distribution costs during the quarter were £10,000.

What is the cost of the inventories held at 31 December 20X7?

Solution

	£
Material cost	16,000
Labour cost	2,500
Variable overhead	700
Fixed overhead $\dfrac{40,000}{20,000\ \text{hrs}} \times 1,000$ hrs	2,000
	21,200

Fixed overheads are absorbed on the basis of the labour hours worked, 1,000 hours, as a proportion of normal working hours for the period, 20,000 hours (18,000 + 2,000).

The industrial dispute will not increase the value of the inventories even though it reduced the number of hours actually worked in the quarter.

Selling and distribution overheads have been ignored as the inventories have not been sold or distributed.

1.3 Net realisable value

The expected selling price in the ordinary course of business less any costs to complete and sell.

2 Methods of costing inventories

2.1 Acceptable inventory accounting methods

When a number of identical items of inventories have been purchased or made at different times, the actual cost of the items in inventories at the yearend may not be known, so assumptions have to be made of the way in which the inventory items flowed through the business. Only methods that give the fairest practicable approximation to actual cost are acceptable.

2.2 Acceptable methods

IAS 2 accepts the use of any one of the following methods, consistently applied:

(i)   **Unit cost** – The actual cost of purchasing or manufacturing identifiable units of inventory.

(ii) **Weighted average cost** – The calculation of the cost of inventories and work in progress on the basis of the application to the units of inventories on hand of an average price computed by dividing the total cost of units by the total number of such units (this average price may be arrived at by means of a continuous calculation, a periodic calculation or a moving periodic calculation).

(iii) **FIFO (first in, first out)** – The calculation of the cost of inventories and work in progress on the basis that the quantities in hand represent the latest purchases or production.

Example

RJ plc made the following purchases and sales of grommets in May 20X1:

1 May	Opening stock	Nil
8 May	Bought 200 units	@ £5 each
13 May	Bought 400 units	@ £5.60 each
20 May	Sold 300 units	@ £8 each

Determine the closing inventories valuation at 31 May and the gross profit for the month using:

(a)   FIFO

(b)   Weighted average cost.

Solution

(a) There are 300 units in inventory and the FIFO method assumes that these consist of the purchases on 13 May as the earlier purchase has all been sold.

Closing inventories = 300 units @ £5.60 = £1,680

Gross profit:	£
Sales (300 × £8)	2,400
Less cost of sales ((200 × £5) +(100 × £5.60))	(1,560)
Gross profit	840

(b) The WAC method calculates an average price for the inventory purchases.

$$\text{Average price} = \frac{(200 \times £5) + (400 \times £5.60)}{600 \text{ units}} = £5.40$$

Closing inventories = 300 × £5.40 = £1,620

	£
Sales (300 × £8)	2,400
Less cost of sales (300 × £5.40)	(1,620)
Gross profit	780

 Activity 1

S Ltd is a manufacturing company. It held its annual inventory count on 31 March 20X2, the company's year-end. The accounts department is currently working its way through the inventory sheets placing a value on the physical inventories. The company has had a difficult year and profits are likely to be lower than in the previous year.

Raw materials

Inventories of raw materials are valued at cost. The finance director has suggested that the cost has been understated in previous years because the company has not taken the costs of delivery or insurance into account. These can be substantial in the case of imported goods. It has been proposed that these costs be taken into account in the valuation of closing inventories of raw materials.

Finished goods

Finished goods have already been valued at £400,000. This figure includes some obsolete goods which cost £70,000 to produce, but which are likely to be sold at a scrap value of £500. There are also several batches of a new product which will be launched early in the new financial year. These cost £90,000 to manufacture. Independent market research suggests that it is very likely that the new product will be sold for considerably more than this. If, however, the launch is unsuccessful, the new product will have to be sold as scrap for £1,000. The finance director has said that the aggregate net realisable value of all closing inventories of finished goods is at least £500,000 and so there is no need to worry about the obsolete and new inventory products.

Required:

(a) Explain whether the costs of delivery and insurance should be included in the valuation of raw materials.

(b) (i) Explain whether the valuation of closing inventories at the lower of cost and net realisable value should be done on an item–by–item basis or on the basis of the aggregate cost of all items as compared with their aggregate net realisable value.

  (ii) State how you would value the obsolete items and the new product line, giving reasons for your valuation in each case.

 Activity 2

(a) Why Is an adjustment made for closing inventories in the financial statements?

(b) How should inventories be valued in the financial statements?

 Activity 3

1 A company has closing inventories of 100 items of Unit X. Each unit cost £4 but can only be sold for £3.50. What is the total closing inventories valuation?

2 State two circumstances when NRV is likely to be lower than cost.

3 What methods of valuation can be used per IAS 2?

4 Give two examples of items excluded from the cost of inventories.

---

3 Summary

IAS 2 requires that inventories should be stated in the statement of financial position at the lower of cost and net realisable value.

Cost comprises all expenditure which has been incurred in the normal course of business in bringing the product or service to its present location and condition.

NRV is the expected selling price less further costs to completion and costs to be incurred in selling the item.

If the actual costs of the items in closing inventories are not known (since the items are interchangeable), an assumption has to be made of how the items physically flow through the business. The usual assumption is FIFO (First In First Out).

Answers to chapter activities

 Activity 1

S Ltd

(a) Raw materials should be valued at the lower of cost and net realisable value where cost includes all costs in bringing the items to their statement of financial position location and conditions.

Both delivery and insurance costs could be included in this definition and so legitimately be added to the valuation, as long as they have been incurred in bringing the inventory items to their present location and condition.

(b) (i) Valuation at cost or net realisable value should be carried out on a product line-by-line basis. The value of assets and liabilities should be determined for individual items not in aggregate. The finance director's statement is therefore incorrect.

(ii) Obsolete items must be valued at £500, their net realisable value since this is lower than cost.

New product line. It seems likely from the initial market research that net realisable value will be considerably greater than the cost of £90,000. These items should thus be included at £90,000. If in a later period the launch proves unsuccessful the inventories will need to be written down to £1,000 and, if material, may be shown as an exceptional item.

 Activity 2

(a) We must match costs with related revenues. The cost of unsold inventories is therefore carried forward to be matched with revenue when it arises. So the cost of inventories is not shown in the year in which the cost is incurred but rather in the year the sale is made.

(b) Inventories should be valued at the lower of cost and net realisable value.

Activity 3

1   100 × £3.50 = £350.

2   Physical deterioration, obsolescence.

3   Cost, FIFO, Weighted average.

4   Select from:

- abnormal amounts of wasted materials, labour and other production costs

- storage costs, unless necessary in the production process before a further production stage

- administrative overheads that do not contribute to bringing inventories to their present location and condition

- selling costs.

4 Test your knowledge

 Workbook Activity 4

Tim's business sells two products A and B. The following information is available at the year end:

Product	A per unit	B per unit
Purchase price	£10	£12
Carriage inwards costs	£2	£3
Estimated selling price	£15	£14
Estimated sales commission	£1	£6
Units of inventory	20	25

At what value should total inventory be stated in Tim's financial statements according to IAS 2 Inventories?

A   £500

B   £440

C   £615

D   £480

Workbook Activity 5

Which of the following statements is correct?

(i)   Inventory is valued at the lower of replacement cost or net selling price.

(ii)   When valuing the cost of inventory all overheads should be absorbed at the actual level of activity.

(iii) LIFO method of valuation of inventory is an acceptable method under IAS 2.

(iv)   The FIFO method of valuation of inventory values inventories still held at the year-end at the most recent prices.

(v)   Normally there are three categories of inventory namely: raw materials, work in progress and finished goods

    A   Only (ii), (iii) and (iv).

    B   Only (i), (ii) and (v).

    C   Only (i), (iii) and (iv).

    D   Only (iv) and (v).

KAPLAN PUBLISHING

Taxation

7

Introduction

In order to prepare a set of limited company accounts you need to know how to deal with tax in the statement of comprehensive income and the statement of financial position.

This is covered by IAS 12 *Income Taxes*. You also need to know the definition of deferred tax and the circumstances in which it should be accounted for and where disclosed.

KNOWLEDGE
Describe legislation and regulation which must be complied with in the preparation of the financial statements (1.2)
Explain the relevance of accounting standards (1.4)
Identify accounting standards and the effect of these on the preparation of the financial statements (2.5)

SKILLS
Apply accounting standards and relevant legislation to correctly identify, and accurately adjust, accounting information (1.1)

CONTENTS

1 IAS 12 *Income Taxes*
2 Deferred tax
3 Disclosure

1 IAS 12 *Income Taxes*

1.1 Introduction

The current tax for a company is the amount of corporation tax estimated to be payable in respect of the taxable profit for the year, along with adjustments to estimates in respect of previous periods.

1.2 Corporation tax

Companies pay corporation tax on their profits. In principle, the amount of current corporation tax should be calculated using the tax rates that the legislation has laid down for the company's financial year. In the exam you will normally be told the rate, and often the amount, of corporation tax.

It is obvious that corporation tax cannot be calculated until after the profit figure for the year is known. When preparing a statement of financial position, current tax for current and prior periods is recognised as a liability. If the amount already paid in respect of current and prior periods exceeds the amount due for those periods, the excess shall be recognised as an asset.

1.3 Adjustments relating to prior years

When the provision for corporation tax is made in the accounts, it is only an estimate of the actual liability which will eventually be agreed with the HM Revenue and Customs (HMRC). Any difference between the original estimate and the actual figure will be adjusted in the next year's provision. If material this figure will be shown separately.

 Example

A company makes an operating profit before taxation of £300,000. Corporation tax is estimated at £105,000. (The corporation tax charge is not 30% of the accounting profits before tax, since accounting profits are adjusted to calculate the taxable profit before tax.)

Solution

Statement of comprehensive income (extract) for the year end 31 December 20X7

	£
Profit before taxation	300,000
Tax on profit	(105,000)
Profit after taxation	195,000

Corporation tax liability account

	£		£
31 Dec X7 Balance c/d	105,000	Income statement charge	105,000
	105,000		105,000
		1 Jan X8 Balance b/d	105,000

The balance on the corporation tax account is carried forward and will appear on the statement of financial position under the 'current liabilities' heading.

 Example

Continuing with the previous example, suppose that in 20X8 the company pays £99,000 corporation tax on the 20X7 profit, not the £105,000 as estimated.

The profit for the year 20X8 is £400,000 and corporation tax is estimated at £132,000.

Statement of comprehensive income (extract) 20X8

	£	£
Profit before taxation		400,000
Tax		
Corporation tax based on the profit of the year @ 30%	132,000	
Adjustment for over provision in previous year	(6,000)	(126,000)
Profit after taxation		274,000

Corporation tax account

	£		£
01 Oct X8 Bank	99,000	01 Jan X8 Balance b/d	105,000
31 Dec X8 Over provision	6,000	31 Dec X8 Income statement	132,000
31 Dec X8 Balance c/d	132,000		
	237,000		237,000
		01 Jan X9 Balance b/d	132,000

The double entry for the over provision is:

Debit Tax liability £6,000

Credit Tax charge in the statement of comprehensive income £6,000

This reduces both the liability and the charge.

 Activity 1

Rubislaw plc

Rubislaw was formed in 20X0. It has a 31 December year-end.

The balance on its tax liability account at 1 January 20X3 was £74,000. During 20X3 this liability was settled for £69,000. The taxable profits for 20X3 are estimated to be £150,000, and the tax rate is 30%.

Required:

Disclose how the above should be presented in the statement of comprehensive income for the year ended 31 December 20X3 and in the statement of financial position as at that date

2 Deferred tax

Deferred tax arises due to the differences in the way financial statements and tax computations are prepared. For example, a piece of IT equipment may be depreciated over four years in the financial statements. However, that same piece of equipment might be written down (the same as depreciation) by 100% in its first year of ownership in the tax computation, depending on the fiscal laws in place.

The result is a different depreciation charge in the financial statements to the one in the tax computation and a different reported profit in each document. In the example above the 100% depreciation of the asset in the tax computation would lead to a lower reported profit than the financial statements and a reduced tax charge. However, in consequent years, the profits reported in the tax computation would be higher than the financial statements as there would be no further depreciation in the tax computation.

Therefore due to differences in financial reporting standards and tax laws the company in the example would suffer lower taxable profits in year one and higher taxable profits in years 2, 3 and 4. Financial accounting requires that we recognise this future liability for increased tax as a provision in the financial statements. This is referred to as deferred tax.

Note: Deferred tax is purely an accounting concept reflected in the financial statements. It is not a tax that is paid to the government or something reflected in fiscal law.

 Definition

A deferred tax liability shall be recognised for all **taxable temporary differences**.

A temporary difference is the difference between the carrying amount of an asset (or liability) in the statement of financial position and its tax base (i.e. its carrying value in the tax computation).

2.1 Example of a tax charge calculation

 Example

XY Ltd expects the tax liability for the current year to be £46,000. There was an under provision of £3,000 in the previous year. The deferred tax balance at the beginning of the year was £20,000 and this is to increase to £26,000 at the year end.

Calculate the tax charge for the current year.

Solution

The tax charge in the statement of comprehensive income consists of three things:

Tax on profits	X
Under /(Over) provision from prior year	X
Movement on deferred tax provision	X
	___
Tax charge	X
	___

To calculate the movement on the deferred tax provision, we just take the difference between the opening and closing provision. This will be a £6,000 increase (£26,000 – £20,000). This is an increase in the liability so the double entry will be:

DR Tax expense	£6,000
CR Deferred tax liability	£6,000

The tax charge will be as follows:

Tax on profits	46,000
Under /(Over) provision from prior year	3,000
Movement on deferred tax provision	6,000
Tax charge	55,000

Activity 2

1   A company has a profit for the period of £100,000. The tax rate is 30%. Last year there was an over provision of £2,000. How much should be charged in this period's statement of comprehensive income?

2   Give an example of a taxable temporary difference.

3 Disclosure

The tax charge related to profit or loss for the period shall be presented on the face of the statement of comprehensive income.

The aggregate current and deferred tax relating to items that are charged or credited to equity must be disclosed separately.

4 Summary

This chapter has summarised all the information regarding tax that you need for the preparation of a set of limited company financial statements.

The current corporation tax provision appears as an expense in the statement of comprehensive income and as a current liability in the statement of financial position.

If there is a balance on the corporation tax account already this will represent an under or over provision from the previous year. This is also included as part of the current year tax charge.

Deferred tax is a tax adjustment to reflect taxable temporary differences.

Answers to chapter activities

Activity 1

Rubislaw plc

Statement of comprehensive income (extract) for the year ended 31 December 20X3

	£
Tax on profit (W1)	40,000

Statement of financial position (extract) at 31 December 20X4

	£
Current liabilities	
Tax liabilities	45,000

Workings

		£
1	*Tax for account period ended 31.12.X3*	
	Profits	150,000
	Tax at 30%	45,000

	£
Tax charge for the year	
Tax for year ended 31.12.X3	45,000
Overprovision for 31.12.X2 (£74,000 – £69,000)	(5,000)
	40,000

Activity 2

1 £28,000 (£30,000 – £2,000).

2 Capital allowances versus depreciation.

Leases

Introduction

Leases are covered by IAS 17 *Leases*. For this unit you need an appreciation of the difference between finance and operating leases and an overview of the differences in accounting treatment. Both written and computational questions can be examined.

KNOWLEDGE

Describe legislation and regulation which must be complied with in the preparation of the financial statements (1.2)

Explain the relevance of accounting standards (1.4)

Identify accounting standards and the effect of these on the preparation of the financial statements (2.5)

SKILLS

Apply accounting standards and relevant legislation to correctly identify, and accurately adjust, accounting information (1.1)

CONTENTS

1 Types of extended credit agreement
2 Accounting for finance leases
3 Operating leases

1 Types of extended credit agreement

1.1 Introduction

A business may acquire the use of a non-current asset by outright purchase (cash or credit) or by some form of 'extended credit' agreement – credit sale, hire purchase, a finance lease or operating lease.

If these 'extended credit' transactions were to be recorded according to their strict legal form, the picture presented by the statement of financial position and statement of comprehensive income of the business using the asset could be quite misleading. This is because neither the asset used nor the liabiiity for future payments would be recognised in the statement of financial position.

IAS 17 *Leases* ensures that transactions that are in substance loans to acquire an asset, even if not in legal form, are treated as any other loan agreement or asset purchase.

1.2 Leases

Lease – involves a contract to hire out an asset between the lessor (who owns the asset and will continue to own the asset) and the lessee (who gains the right to use the asset for an agreed period of time).

IAS 17 distinguishes between two types of lease, finance and operating:

A finance lease is a lease that effectively is the sale of the asset to the lessee. The terms of the lease transfers substantially all the risks and rewards of ownership of an asset to the lessee.

If a leased asset meets any of the following criteria it would be considered a finance lease:

(a) lease transfers ownership of the asset to the lessee by the end of the lease term

(b) lessee has the option to purchase the asset at a price that is expected to be sufficiently lower than the fair value at the date the option becomes exercisable so that it is reasonably certain, at the inception of the lease, that the option will be exercised

(c) the lease term is for the major part of the economic life of the asset

(d) at inception the present value of the minimum lease payments amounts to at least substantially all of the fair value of the leased asset

(e)   the leased assets are of such a specialised nature that only the lessee can use them without major modifications.

(f)   the lessee can cancel the lease and the lessors loss associated with the cancellation is borne by the lessee

(g)   gains or losses from the fluctuation in the fair value of the residual accrue to the lessee

(h)   lessee has the ability to continue the lease for a secondary period at a rent that is substantially lower than market rent.

For a lease to be considered as a finance lease, the term of the lease would be close to the life of the asset and the present value of total rentals paid would be close to the value of the asset. Finance leases are capitalised in the lessee's accounts.

An operating lease is a lease other than a finance lease. Operating leases are not capitalised.

1.3   Land and buildings

Land

A characteristic of land is that it normally has an indefinite economic life and if title is not expected to pass to the lessee by the end of the lease term, the lessee normally does not receive substantially all the risks and rewards of ownership. Therefore leases of land are classified as operating leases.

Buildings

Buildings can be treated separately to land even if the contract entered into is a joint one to lease land and buildings. Therefore if the lease covers the life of the building, then it can be classified as a finance lease even if the land element is classified as an operating lease.

2   Accounting for finance leases

2.1   Capitalisation of finance leases in the lessee accounts

The two critical questions to be answered are:

(a)   At what value should the asset be capitalised?

(b)   What finance charge should be made in the statement of comprehensive income?

2.2 The capitalised value in the statement of financial position

At the start of the lease, the sum to be recorded both as an asset and as a liability should be the fair value of the leased asset or, if lower, the present value of the minimum lease payments, derived by discounting them at the interest rate implicit in the lease.

Minimum lease payments – the payments over the lease term that the lessee is required to make.

Interest rate implicit in the lease – this will approximate to the rate of interest on a loan to purchase the asset.

Implicit means the rate of interest is not specifically quoted. For example: a business pays £18 per month for 12 months to lease some equipment, rather than paying the current market price of £200. The company pays a total of £216 (£18 × 12 months) which suggests total finance charges (or interest) of £16.

The asset that is capitalised must also be depreciated in accordance with similar types of assets held by the entity. The depreciation should be calculated in accordance with IAS 16 *Property, plant and equipment* or IAS 38 *Intangible Assets*.

2.3 The finance charge

The excess of the minimum lease payments over the initial capitalised value represents the finance charge. The total finance charge should be allocated to accounting periods during the lease term so as to produce a constant periodic rate of charge on the remaining balance of the obligation for each accounting period (i.e. the actuarial method), or a reasonable approximation.

 Example

A lessee enters into a lease on 1 January 20X8 for an item of plant with a life of five years. The following details are relevant:

Fair value of asset   £10,000

Residual value   Nil after five years

Lease terms   £2,500 pa in advance for five years, the first rental payable on 1.1.X8

The interest rate implicit in the lease is 12.6%.

Required:

Show how this transaction would be recorded in the ledger accounts of the lessee for the first two years, and show also how the transaction would be reflected in the statement of comprehensive income and statement of financial position over the five years.

Solution

The total amount payable for the lease is £12,500 (5 × £2,500). Included in these payments will be the interest element. When the lease starts, the fair value of the asset (£10,000) is capitalised into non-current assets and shown as the lease payable. As the payments are made at the beginning of the year, the first payment of £2,500 is all capital and will reduce the payable to the £7,500 shown below.

The finance charge will be calculated as follows for each year:

End of year	Amount outstanding	Interest @ 12.6%	Total	Repayment on 1 January following
	£	£	£	£
1	7,500	945	8,445	2,500
2	5,945	749	6,694	2,500
3	4,194	528	4,722	2,500
4	2,222	278	2,500	2,500
5	–	–		–
		2,500		

The annual depreciation charge will be:

$$\frac{£10,000}{5} = £2,000 \text{ pa}$$

The ledger entry at the beginning of the lease will be:

	£	£
Dr Leased assets	10,000	
Cr Obligation under finance leases		10,000

Being the recording of the 'purchase' of an asset under a finance lease at its fair value and the assumption of a liability.

Thereafter the entries in the leased asset account and the depreciation account will be exactly the same as for a purchased asset.

The entries in the leasing obligation account will be as follows:

Obligation under finance leases account

	£		£
1.1.X1 Cash	2,500	1.1.X1 Leased asset	10,000
31.12.X1 Balance c/d	8,445	31.12.X1 Interest expense	945
	10,945		10,945
1.1.X2 Cash	2,500	1.1.X2 Balance b/d	8,445
31.12.X2 Balance c/d	6,694	31.12.X2 Interest expense	749
		(8,445 – 2,500) × 12.6%	
	9,194		9,194
		1.1.X3 Balance b/d	6,694

The charges to the statement of comprehensive income over the period of the lease are:

Year	1	2	3	4	5	Total
	£	£	£	£	£	£
Depreciation	2,000	2,000	2,000	2,000	2,000	10,000
Interest	945	749	528	278	–	2,500
	2,945	2,749	2,528	2,278	2,000	12,500

The statement of financial position would reflect the carrying value of the asset and the outstanding principal of the loan together with the accrued interest for the year which will be paid on the first day of the next period.

Statement of financial position

Year	1	2	3	4	5
	£	£	£	£	£
Fixed assets					
Leased plant					
Cost	10,000	10,000	10,000	10,000	10,000
Accumulated dep'n	(2,000)	(4,000)	(6,000)	(8,000)	(10,000)
Carrying value	8,000	6,000	4,000	2,000	–

KAPLAN PUBLISHING

Year	1	2	3	4	5
	£	£	£	£	£
Current liabilities					
Obligations under finance leases:					
Principal	1,555	1,751	1,972	2,222	–
Accrued interest	945	749	528	278	–
	2,500	2,500	2,500	2,500	–
Non-current liabilities					
Obligations under finance leases (principal only)	5,945	4,194	2,222	–	–
	8,445	6,694	4,722	2,500	–

Obligations under finance leases have been split between the current portion (payable within 12 months of the statement of financial position date) and the long-term liability for the remaining lease term.

 Activity 1

Finch

Finch Ltd entered into a leasing agreement with Tyrrell plc on 1 October 20X5. This involves a specialised piece of manufacturing machinery which was purchased by Tyrrell plc to Finch Ltd's specifications.

The contract involves an annual payment in arrears of £1,200,000 for five years.

At the start of the lease with Tyrrell plc the present value of the minimum lease payments was calculated in accordance with the rules contained in IAS 17 and found to be £4,100,000. The fair value of the machinery at the commencement of the contract was £4,680,000.

Finch Ltd is responsible for the maintenance of the machinery and is required to insure it against accidental damage.

The machinery would normally be expected to have a useful life of approximately seven years. Finch Ltd depreciates its property, plant and equipment on the straight line basis.

The implied rate of interest is 14.2% per annum.

Required:

(a) Discuss how you would classify this lease with reference to the rules in IAS 17.

(b) Describe the impact in the accounts of Finch Ltd on the assumption you decide to classify the lease as a finance lease.

3 Operating leases

An operating lease is a lease other than a finance lease, under which there is no suggestion that the risks and rewards of ownership are transferred from the lessor to the lessee.

A business may lease a photocopier or fax machine under this type of shorter-term lease.

Thus the asset is treated as a fixed asset in the books of the lessor and the rental is treated as income for the lessor and as expense for the lessee.

The treatment of operating leases in the lessee's books is that the rental should be charged on a straight-line basis over the lease term.

 Activity 2

1   A lessor hires out an asset with a five-year life to a lessee for a period of five years. Is this a finance lease or an operating lease?

2   Are assets which are the subject of operating leases shown on the lessee's statement of financial position?

3   Explain briefly how IAS 17 requires finance leases to be shown on the statement of financial position.

4 Summary

The important matters which you must appreciate are:

(a) the distinction between a finance lease and an operating lease

(b) looking at the substance of the transaction rather than the form of the contract

(c) the capitalisation of finance leases in the lessee's books and the recognition of the obligation

(d) the treatment of operating lease rentals in the lessee's books.

Answers to chapter activities

 Activity 1

Finch

(a) IAS 17 explains that a finance lease is a lease that transfers substantially all the risks and rewards of ownership to the lessee. It should be presumed that such a transfer of risks and rewards occurs if, at the inception of a lease, the present value of the minimum lease payments, including any initial payment, amounts to substantially all of the fair value of the leased asset.

In this case the present value of the minimum lease payments is £4,100,000 and the fair value of the machinery was £4,680,000. This amounts to:

$$\frac{4,100,000}{4,680,000} \times 100 = 88\% \text{ of the fair value of the machinery}$$

Additionally, the machinery was purchased by Tyrrell plc to Finch Ltd's specifications and it is therefore unlikely that Tyrrell plc would be able to lease it to any other organisation. Secondly, the lease period covers five years of the seven-year useful life of the machinery, which provides further evidence that it would be difficult to lease the asset to another organisation as it will effectively be obsolete at the end of the current lease. Thirdly, Finch Ltd is responsible for the maintenance and insurance of the machinery.

The lease should therefore be classified as a finance lease.

(b) If we treat the lease as a finance lease we capitalise it at fair value or at the present value of the minimum lease payments if this is lower. This means we will include it in the statement of financial position as an asset and as an obligation to pay future rentals, i.e. a liability. The asset will then be depreciated over the shorter of the lease term and its useful life.

The income statement will be charged with a finance charge.

The accounting treatment required for the statement of financial position is to debit non-current assets and credit payables with £4,100,000.

KAPLAN PUBLISHING

Activity 2

1   Finance lease. The term of the lease is for the entire useful life of the leased asset.

2   No.

3   IAS 17 requires lessees to show assets acquired under finance leases, and the related obligation, on the statement of financial position.

5 Test your knowledge

 Workbook Activity 3

MP Ltd entered in a four year finance lease agreement on 1 January 20X1 for a machine with a fair value of £69,740. The lease rentals of £20,000 are payable in advance. The implicit interest rate is 10%.

What is the depreciation charge, finance charge, the carrying value of the machine and total lease obligation (split between non-current and current obligation) for the year ended 31 December 20X1?

	Depreciation charge £	Finance charge £	Carrying value £	Non-current obligation £	Current obligation £
A	17,435	4,974	52,305	34,714	20,000
B	17,435	6,974	52,305	42,385	14,329
C	20,000	4,974	39,740	54,714	20,000
D	17,435	6,974	52,305	56,714	14,329

Events after the reporting period, provisions and contingencies

Introduction

For this unit you need to know all aspects of IAS 10 *Events After the Reporting period* and almost all aspects of IAS 37 *Provisions, Contingent Liabilities and Contingent Assets*.

KNOWLEDGE

Describe legislation and regulation which must be complied with in the preparation of the financial statements (1.2)

Explain the relevance of accounting standards (1.4)

Identify accounting standards and the effect of these on the preparation of the financial statements (2.5)

SKILLS

Apply accounting standards and relevant legislation to correctly identify, and accurately adjust, accounting information (1.1)

CONTENTS

1   IAS 10 *Events after the Reporting Period*
2   IAS 37 *Provisions, Contingent Liabilities and Contingent Assets*

1   IAS 10 *Events after the Reporting Period*

1.1   Introduction

Events after the statement of financial position date are those events, both favourable and unfavourable, which occur between the statement of financial position date and the date on which the financial statements are authorised for issue. There are two types of event:

(a)   adjusting events, which require the accounts to be adjusted to reflect their impact; and

(b)   non-adjusting events, which are merely noted in the accounts if material.

1.2   Adjusting events

These are events which provide additional evidence of conditions existing at the statement of financial position date. Such events are relevant because they relate to items appearing in the accounts or transactions reported in them. Examples of adjusting events are:

(a)   The settlement post year end of a court case that confirms that the entity had a present obligation at the statement of financial position date. The entity must adjust any previously recognised provisions related to the court case in accordance with IAS 37 Provisions, Contingent Liabilities and Contingent Assets or recognise a new provision.

(b)   The receipt of information post year end indicating an asset was impaired at the statement of financial position date, or the amount of a previously recognised impairment loss for that asset needs to be adjusted. For example:

  (i)   bankruptcy of a customer usually confirms that a loss existed at the statement of financial position date on a trade receivable and the entity needs to adjust the carrying amount of the trade receivable;

  (ii)   sale of inventories after the statement of financial position date may give evidence about their net realisable value at the statement of financial position date.

(c)   The subsequent determination of the purchase price or of the proceeds of sale of assets purchased or sold before the year-end.

(d)   The determination after the statement of financial position date of the amount of profit-sharing or bonus payments, if the entity had a present legal or constructive obligation at the statement of financial position date to make such payments as a result of events before that date.

(e)   The discovery of errors or frauds which show that the financial statements were incorrect.

1.3   Non-adjusting events

These events concern conditions which did not exist at the statement of financial position date. These events therefore shall not be adjusted for in the financial statements. Some examples of non-adjusting events are:

(a)   mergers and acquisitions;

(b)   reconstructions;

(c)   issues of shares and debentures;

(d)   purchases and sales of non-current assets and investments;

(e)   losses of non-current assets or inventories as a result of a catastrophe, such as a fire or flood;

(f)   decline in the value of property and investments held as non-current assets, if it can be demonstrated that the decline occurred after the year end

1.4   Dividends

If an entity declares dividends after the statement of financial position date, the entity shall not recognise those dividends as a liability at the statement of financial position date.

1.5   Going concern

The financial statements should not be prepared on a going concern basis if management determines after the statement of financial position date that it intends to liquidate or cease trading.

1.6   Disclosure

The date the financial statements were authorised for issue and who gave that authorisation.

Material non-adjusting events

(i)   the nature of the event; and

(ii)   an estimate of the financial effect, or a statement that it is not practicable to make such an estimate.

(**Note:** You do not 'disclose' adjusting events; when accounts are actually adjusted.)

Example

How would the following events be accounted for in the financial statements for the year to 31 December 20X9?

Assume that each event is material in size in the context of the accounts as a whole.

(a) On 5 January 20X10 a large receivable went into liquidation owing £100,000 as at the statement of financial position date. It is likely that this receivable balance will realise nothing.

(b) On 10 January 20X10 all the inventories in the Dudley warehouse were destroyed by fire. They had a cost at that date of £50,000 and a net realisable value of £70,000. Although this loss is serious, it is not so serious that the company is no longer able to continue as a going concern.

Solution

(a) This is an adjusting event giving additional information on the receivables figure at the year end. The £100,000 irrecoverable debt must be written off in the 20X9 accounts.

(b) This is a non-adjusting event as the fire occurred after the statement of financial position date. The damage to the inventory occurred post year end so the year end position is not affected. This should be described in a note to the accounts.

 Activity 1

Ribblesdale prepares its accounts to a 30 September year end. Its accounts for the year ended 30 September 20X8 are approved on 12 January 20X9 and issued on 20 February 20X9.

Which of the following is an adjusting event after the reporting period?

A   A flood destroys inventory which cost £1,700 on 3 December 20X8.

B   A credit customer with an outstanding balance at the year end was declared bankrupt on 20 January 20X9.

C   Inventory valued at a cost of £800 in the year end accounts was sold for £650 on 11 January 20X9.

D   An ordinary dividend of 4p per share was declared on 1 December 20X8.

2 IAS 37 *Provision, Contingent Liabilities and Contingent Assets*

2.1 Introduction

The objective of the IAS 37 is to ensure that:

- provisions and contingencies are recognised and measured consistently
- sufficient information is disclosed to enable a user of the accounts to understand the nature, timing and amount of any provisions and contingencies included in the accounts.

Definition

Provision – liability of uncertain timing or amount.

Liability – present obligation of the entity arising from past events, the settlement of which is expected to result in an outflow from the entity of resources embodying economic benefits.

Obligating event – an event that creates a legal or constructive obligation that results in the entity having no realistic alternative to settling the obligation.

Constructive obligation – A constructive obligation arises from the entity's past actions, where there is a pattern of past practice that indicates that an entity will behave in a certain way, for example:

- A retail store that habitually refunds purchases for dissatisfied customers and could not change its policy without damaging its reputation.

- An entity that has caused environmental damage and is obliged to rectify this because of its published policies and previous actions, even though there may be no legal obligation for it to do so.

Contingent liability – a possible obligation from a past event whose existence will be confirmed only by the occurrence or non-occurrence of one or more uncertain future events not wholly within the control of the entity; or a present obligation that arises from past events that is not recognised because the outflow required to settle the obligation is not probable or the amount of the obligation cannot be measured with sufficient reliability.

Contingent asset – a possible asset that arises from past events and whose existence will be confirmed only by the occurrence or non-occurrence of one or more uncertain future events not wholly within the control.

2.2 Provisions versus other liabilities versus contingent liabilities

A provision is a liability of uncertain timing or amount. This means that a provision can only be recognised if it meets the definition and recognition criteria of a liability. These are as follows:

(1) A present obligation must exist at the statement of financial position date as a result of a past transaction or event, and

(2) It is probable that an outflow of economic resources will be required to settle the obligation; and

(3) A reliable estimate can be made of the amount of the obligation.

Other liabilities such as trade payables, are liabilities to pay for goods that have been received and invoiced, therefore there is no uncertainty over their timing or amount. This makes them different.

Contingent liabilities are never recognised in the financial statements because their existence will be confirmed only by the occurrence or non-occurrence of one or more uncertain future events not wholly within the control of the entity.

2.3 Recognition

The amount recognised as a provision shall be the best estimate of the expenditure required to settle the present obligation at the statement of financial position date.

Where the time value of money is material, the amount of the provision shall be the present value of the expenditures expected to be required to settle the obligation.

The provisions must be reviewed at each statement of financial position date and adjusted to reflect the current best estimate. If it is no longer probable an outflow of resources will be required to settle the obligation then the provision shall be reversed.

The provision must only be used for expenditures for which the provision was originally recognised.

*   Contingent assets are never recognised

*   Contingent liabilities are never recognised

2.4 Restructuring provisions

A restructuring is a programme that is planned and controlled by management and materially changes either:

(a)   the scope of a business undertaken by an entity: or

(b)   the manner in which the business is conducted.

The following are examples of events that may fall under the definition of restructuring:

- Sale or termination of a line of business
- Closure of business locations in a country or region or relocation from one country/region to another
- Changes in management structure
- Fundamental reorganisations

A constructive obligation to restructure arises when an entity:

(a)   has a detailed formal plan for the restructuring and

(b)   has raised a valid expectation to those affected that it will carry out the restructuring by starting to implement the plan or announcing its main features to those affected.

In the above case therefore a restructuring provision may be recognised as there is:

(i)   an obligation (detailed plan and people know about it)

(ii)   probable outflow of resources (cost of relocation or redundancy etc.)

(iii)   reliable estimate of the expenditure can be made

The restructuring provision shall include only the direct expenditures arising from the restructuring, which are those that are both: (a) necessarily entailed by the restructuring: and (b) not associated with the ongoing activities of the entity.

2.5 Disclosure of contingent liabilities and contingent assets

The accounts should give the following disclosures for each material class of contingent liability and asset that are not recognised in the statement of financial position, unless the possibility of transfer of economic benefits is remote:

- The nature of the contingency
- The uncertainties expected to affect the ultimate outcome
- An estimate of the potential financial effect.

Activity 2

Hill plc

The year end of Hill plc is 31 March 20X0. Hill plc is a very diverse group. One of its consistent features is that it has a reputation as an ethical organisation. Much is made of the company's policies with regard to recycling, controls over emission of noxious substances and making use only of renewable resources.

Many of its goods in its beauty and cosmetic range (Sophie Beauty Products) use ingredients that are sourced overseas and the company publishes full details of its environmental policies as part of its annual report.

You are the chief accountant of the group and your assistant has prepared draft accounts for the year ended 31 March 20X0. Your assistant, however, is uncertain as to the application of IAS 37 *Provisions, Contingent Liabilities and Contingent Assets* to three material items described below and has requested your advice.

Required:

(a) Explain the circumstances under which a provision should be recognised in the financial statements according to IAS 37.

(b) Explain how each of the following issues should be treated in the consolidated financial statements for the year ended 31 March 20X0.

(i) On 12 February 20X0 the board of Hill plc decided to close down a large factory in Aylesbury. The board expects that production will be transferred to other factories. No formal plan has yet been drawn up but it is expected the closure will occur on 31 August 20X0. As at the statement of financial position date this decision has not been announced to the employees or to any other interested parties. The overall costs of this closure are foreseen as £79 million.

(ii) During the year to 31 March 20X0, a customer started legal proceedings claiming one of the products from the 'Sophie Beauty' range had caused a skin complaint. The group's lawyers have advised that the chances of this action succeeding are remote.

(iii) The group has an overseas subsidiary 'Melinat' that is involved in mining certain minerals. These activities cause significant damage to the environment, including deforestation. The company expects to abandon the mine in eight years time. The country where the subsidiary is based has no environmental legislation obligating companies to rectify environmental damage and it is unlikely that such legislation will be enacted within the next eight years. It has been estimated that the cost of putting right the site will be £10 million if the tree re-planting were successful at the first attempt, but it will probably be necessary to have a further attempt costing an additional £5 million.

 Activity 3

1   A receivable goes into liquidation on 12 January 20X8, owing £300,000 to the company on its statement of financial position date of 31 December 20X7. Is this an adjusting or a non-adjusting event? *adj*

2   A company issues new shares soon after its statement of financial position date. Is this an adjusting or a non-adjusting event? *Non*

3   Should contingent assets be shown on the statement of financial position? *No*

3 Summary

You need to be able to recognise both adjusting and non-adjusting events. You should also ensure that you understand what is meant by a provision and when provisions should be shown as a liability in the statement of financial position. You should be able to distinguish a provision from a contingent liability and understand the different treatment of contingent liabilities and contingent assets. The key in deciding whether a provision should be recognised is to ask whether:

1   A present **obligation** must exist at the statement of financial position date as a result of a past transaction or event, and

2   It is **probable** that an outflow of economic resources will be required to settle the obligation; and

3   A **reliable estimate** can be made of the amount of the obligation.

If these factors can be satisfied then a provision should be made in the financial statements otherwise it is a contingent liability which should just be disclosed.

Answers to chapter activities

 ### Activity 1

Answer is C

- A flood does not provide additional information to conditions existing at the year end and therefore is non adjusting.

- The credit customer's bankruptcy occurs after the accounts are approved.

- The declaration of an ordinary dividend is a non adjusting event

 ### Activity 2

Hill plc

(a) A provision should be recognised when, and only when:

  (1) A present **obligation** must exist at the statement of financial position date as a result of a past transaction or event, and

  (2) It is **probable** that an outflow of economic resources will be required to settle the obligation; and

  (3) A **reliable estimate** can be made of the amount of the obligation.

  An obligation exists when the entity has no realistic alternative to making a transfer of economic benefits. This is the case only where the obligation can be enforced by law or in the case of constructive obligation (see below).

(b) (i) *Factory closure*

  The key issue is whether or not a provision should be made for the £79 million cost of restructuring. This will depend on whether the group has an obligation to incur this expenditure.

  There is clearly no legal obligation to close this factory but there may be a constructive obligation. A constructive obligation only exists if the group has created valid expectations in other parties such as customers, employees and suppliers that the restructuring will be carried out.

As no formal plan exists and no announcements have been made to any of the affected parties, no constructive obligation exists. A board decision alone is not sufficient – no provision should be made.

(ii) *Legal proceedings*

It is unlikely the group has a present obligation to compensate the customer and therefore no provision should be recognised.

There may be a contingent liability but as the possibility of a transfer of economic benefit is remote we can ignore this in the accounts.

(iii) *Environmental damage*

The company has no legal obligation to rectify this damage, but through its published policies it has created expectation on the part of those affected that it will take action to do so. There is therefore a constructive obligation to rectify the damage. It is probable that a transfer of economic benefits will take place and an estimate of the amount involved can be made.

A provision should be made of the best estimate of the cost involved, i.e. the full amount of £15 million should be provided for.

Activity 3

1   Adjusting event.

2   Non-adjusting event.

3   No. Contingent assets should be disclosed in a note to the accounts.

4 Test your knowledge

 Workbook Activity 4

Caroline Ltd has a year end of 30 September 20X9. The accounts are anticipated to be approved in a couple of month's time.

How would the following events be accounted for in the Financial Statements?

(Assume all amounts are material to the organisation.)

(i)   On 2 October 20X9 a fire completely destroyed the entire inventory in its warehouse. The total cost of the inventory was £10million. The company unfortunately did not update its insurance cover for fire and consequential damages.

The maximum the company can recover from the insurance company is £4 million. The company's trading operations have been extensively disrupted due to the fire and therefore it is going to incur huge losses in the foreseeable future.

(ii)   On 20 October 20X9 the directors proposed a dividend amounting to £120,000.

Workbook Activity 5

John Ltd is currently being sued by an ex-employee for £45,000. The company's solicitors have the stated that the claim may possibly succeed. The company's solicitor's fees will amount to £3,000. This fee will have to be paid whether the ex-employee's claim is successful or not.

What should be the treatment of the above in the John Ltd's financial statements?

A   Provide a liability for £48,000 comprising the £45,000 claim by the ex-employee and the solicitor's fees.

B   Provide for £45,000.

C   Disclose a total of £48,000 comprising the £45,000 claim by the ex-employee and the solicitor's fees.

D   Provide a liability for £3,000 for the solicitor's fees and disclose £45,000 for the claim by the ex-employee.

Other accounting standards

Introduction

In this chapter we will briefly consider the few remaining accounting standards that have not been covered earlier in this text. In each case the knowledge that will be assessed for each of these standards is very limited and we will only cover what is required for the exam.

KNOWLEDGE
Describe legislation and regulation which must be complied with in the preparation of the financial statements (1.2)
Explain the relevance of accounting standards (1.4)
Identify accounting standards and the effect of these on the preparation of the financial statements (2.5)

SKILLS
Apply accounting standards and relevant legislation to correctly identify, and accurately adjust, accounting information (1.1)

CONTENTS

1   IFRS 5 *Non-current Assets Held for Sale and Discontinued Operations*
2   IFRS 8 *Operating Segments*
3   IAS 18 *Revenue*
4   IAS 33 *Earnings per Share*
5   IAS 20 *Accounting for government grants and disclosure of government assistance*
6   IAS 8 *Accounting policies, changes in accounting estimates and errors*

1 IFRS 5 *Non-current Assets Held for Sale and Discontinued Operations*

1.1 Introduction

This IFRS specifies accounting for assets held for sale and the presentation of discontinued operations.

1.2 Non-current assets as held for sale

An entity should classify a non-current asset as held for sale if its carrying amount will be recovered principally through a sale transaction rather than continuing use.

To be classified as held for sale the following conditions must be met:

- the asset must be available for immediate sale in its present condition

- the sale must be highly probable, meaning that:
  - management are committed to a plan to sell the asset
  - there is an active programme to locate a buyer, and
  - the asset is being actively marketed

- the sale is expected to be completed within 12 months of its classification as held for sale

- it is unlikely that the plan will be significantly changed or withdrawn.

The asset held for sale should be valued at the lower of its carrying amount and fair value less costs to sell.

An entity shall present a non-current asset held for sale separately on the statement of financial position. The major classes of assets held for resale should be separately disclosed either on the face of the statement of financial position or in the notes.

1.3 Discontinued operations

A discontinued operation is a component of an entity that either has been disposed of or is classified as held for sale and:

(a) represents a separate major line of business or geographical area of operations

(b) is part of a single co-ordinated plan to dispose of a separate major line of business or geographical area of operations or

(c) is a subsidiary acquired exclusively with a view to resale

The entity must disclose a single amount on the face of the income statement showing the post tax profit or loss of discontinued operations (see chapter 3 for the pro-forma statement of comprehensive income).

 Activity 1

On 1 January 20X3 NJP Ltd bought an item of plant for £80,000. It had an expected useful life of 5 years. On 31 December 20X5 NJP Ltd decides to sell the plant and takes actions to find a buyer. The plant is expected to be sold in the early part of 20X6. The current expected market value is £33,000 and expected costs to sell is anticipated to be £1,100. The plant meets the criteria of a non-current asset held for sale.

At what value should the plant be stated in the statement of financial position at 31 December 20X5?

A   £48,000

B   £31,900

C   £32,000

D   £30,900

 Activity 2

Which of the following statements is correct?

(i)   A non-current asset held for sale should be depreciated at the year end and shown under the heading of non-current assets in the statement of financial position.

(ii)   If the fair value less costs to sell is greater than the carrying value of a non-current asset held for sale then an impairment charge will arise.

(iii)   A subsidiary acquired exclusively for resale can be treated as a discontinued operation.

(iv)   Showing discontinued operations separately satisfies the qualitative information characteristic of relevance.

A   Only (i) and (ii).

B   Only (i) and (iv).

C   Only (ii) and (iii).

D   Only (iii) and (iv).

2 IFRS 8 *Operating Segments*

2.1 Introduction

IFRS 8 requires an entity to disclose information about each of its operating segments. The purpose is to enable users of the financial statements to evaluate the nature and financial effects of the business activities in which it engages and the economic environments in which it operates.

🔍 Definition

IFRS 8 defines an operating segment as a component of an entity:

- that engages in business activities from which it may earn revenues and incur expenses

- whose operating results are regularly reviewed by the entity's chief operating decision maker to make decisions about resources to be allocated to the segment and assess its performance

- for which discrete financial information is available.

2.2 Scope and definitions

Under IFRS 8 segment information reflects the way that the entity is actually managed. An entity's reportable segments are those that are used in its internal management reports. Therefore management identifies the operating segments.

This standard applies only to entities whose equity or debt is publicly traded or those who voluntarily wish to disclose segmental information.

2.3 Thresholds

An entity must separately report information about an operating segment that meets any of the following quantitative thresholds:

- its reported revenue is ten per cent or more of the combined revenue of all operating segments

- its reported profit or loss is ten per cent or more of:

  - the combined reported profit of all operating segments, or

  - the combined reported loss of all operating segments.

- its assets are ten per cent or more of the combined assets of all operating segments.

At least 75% of the entity's external revenue should be included in reportable segments. So if the test results in disclosure of less than this other segments should be identified as until 75% is reached.

Information about other business activities and operating segments that are not reportable are combined into an 'all other segments' category.

2.4 Information disclosed

For each reportable segment an entity should report:

- a measure of profit or loss
- a measure of total assets
- a measure of total liabilities (if such an amount is regularly used in decision making).

 Activity 3

Which of the following statements is correct?

(i) According to IFRS 8 an operating segment can include a component of an entity for which discrete financial information is available.

(ii) An entity must separately report information about a segment that contributes more than 10% of combined profit.

(iii) A reportable segment is an operating segment or aggregations of operating segments that meet specified criteria.

(iv) If after allocating segments according to the 10% rule, the revenue of reportable segments is less than 75% of the external revenue of the entity, additional segments will be classified as reportable segments even though they do not meet the 10% rule.

A   All the above statements are false.

B   All the above statements are true.

3   IAS 18 *Revenue*

3.1   Introduction

Revenue is recognised when it is probable that future economic benefits will flow to the entity and these benefits can be measured reliably. This standard identifies the circumstances in which these criteria will be met and therefore revenue recognised.

3.2   Scope and definitions

This standard applies when accounting for revenue from sales of goods, the rendering of services and the use by others of the entities assets yielding dividends.

Revenue is the gross inflow of economic benefits during the period arising in the course of the ordinary activities of an entity when those inflows result in increases in equity, other than increases relating to contributions from equity participants.

3.3   Recognition and measurement

Revenue shall be measured at the fair value of the consideration received or receivable.

Revenue from the sale of goods shall be recognised when all the following conditions have been satisfied:

(a)   entity has transferred to the buyer the significant risks and rewards of ownership of the goods;

(b)   entity retains neither continuing managerial involvement to the degree usually associated with ownership nor effective control over the goods sold;

(c)   amount of revenue can be measured reliably;

(d)   probable that the economic benefits associated with the transaction will flow to the entity

(e)   costs incurred or to be incurred in respect of the transaction can be measured reliably.

Revenue from the rendering of services should only be recognised when it can be estimated reliably. Revenue associated with the transaction shall be recognised by reference to the stage of completion of the transaction at the statement of financial position date.

The outcome can be estimated reliably when all the following are satisfied:

(a) amount of revenue can be measured reliably;

(b) it is probable that the economic benefits associated with the transaction will flow to the entity;

(c) the stage of completion of the transaction at the statement of financial position can be measured reliably; and

(d) costs incurred for the transaction and the costs to complete the transaction can be measured reliably.

Revenue arising from the use by others of entity assets yielding dividends shall be recognised when the shareholder's rights to receive payment is established and

(a) it is probable that the economic benefits associated with the transaction will flow to the entity;

(b) the amount of the revenue can be measured reliably.

 Activity 4

Which of the following statements is correct?

(i) Revenue from sale of goods should be recognised when risks and rewards of ownership have been transferred to the buyer.

(ii) Revenue from services should be recognised when it is reasonably certain that the stage of completion can be measured reliably.

(iii) Revenue can only be recognised when payment has been received from the buyer.

(iv) The total revenue of a business can include both cash and credit sales.

(v) An allowance (provision) for irrecoverable debts is calculated on both the cash and credit sales of a business.

A   Only (i), (ii) and (iii).

B   Only (i), (ii) and (iv).

C   Only (i), (iii) and (v).

D   Only (ii), (iii) and (iv).

---

4 IAS 33 *Earnings per Share*

4.1 Introduction

This standard prescribes principles for the determination and presentation of earnings per share so at to improve performance comparisons between different entities in the same reporting period and between different reporting periods for the same entity.

4.2 Scope

This standard applies to all entities whose shares are publicly traded.

4.3 Measurement

The basic earnings per share (EPS) calculation is simply:

$$\frac{\text{Earnings for the year}}{\text{Number of shares in issue}}$$

Here 'earnings' means the profit attributable to ordinary equity holders; and 'shares' means the weighted average number of ordinary shares in issue during the period.

Profit attributable to ordinary equity holders is after tax and must be adjusted for preference dividends.

Using the weighted average number of ordinary shares outstanding during the period reflects the possibility that the amount of shareholders' capital varied during the period as a result of issuing or redeeming shares.

Example

Gerard plc

Draft statement of comprehensive income for the year ended 31 December 20X8

	£000	£000
Profit before tax		5,060
Taxation		(2,300)
Profit after tax		2,760
Dividends		
Paid – preference dividend	276	
Paid – ordinary dividend	368	

On 1 January 20X8 the issued share capital of Gerard plc was 9,200,000 3% preference shares of £1 each and 8,280,000 ordinary shares of £1 each.

Required:

Calculate the earnings per share (EPS) in respect of the year ended 31 December 20X8 on the basis that there was no change in the issued share capital of the company during the year.

Solution

The amount of earnings available to the ordinary shares (i.e. excluding the preference dividend) is divided by the number of ordinary shares.

$$\frac{£2,760,000 - £276,000}{8,280,000} = 30p$$

The EPS of 30p would be disclosed at the bottom of the statement of comprehensive income for the year 20X8.

4.4 Issue of shares during the year (to show weighted average number of shares)

In the example of Gerard plc, suppose that the company had issued 3,312,000 new ordinary shares at their full market value on 30 June 20X8. The money raised would have had an impact on the earnings from 30 June. We would need to reflect this in the earnings per share working by recognising the impact on the earnings using a weighted average number of shares.

Date	Actual number of shares	Fraction of year	Total
1 January 20X8	8,280,000	$\frac{6}{12}$	4,140,000
30 June 20X8	11,592,000 (W1)	$\frac{6}{12}$	5,796,000
Number of shares in EPS calculation			9,936,000

(W1) New number of shares

Original number	8,280,000
New issue	3,312,000
New number	11,592,000

The earnings per share for 20X8 would now be calculated as:

$$\frac{£2,760,000 - £276,000}{9,936,000} = 25p$$

5 IAS 20 *Accounting for government grants and disclosure of government assistance*

5.1 Introduction

Governments often provide money or incentives to companies to export or promote local employment.

Government grants could be:

- Revenue grants, e.g. money towards wages

- Capital grants, e.g. money towards purchases of non-current assets.

5.2 General principles

IAS 20 follows two general principles when determining the treatment of grants:

Prudence: grants should not be recognised until the conditions for receipt have been complied with and there is reasonable assurance the grant will be received.

Accruals: grants should be matched with the expenditure towards which they were intended to contribute.

5.3 Revenue grants

The recognition of the grant will depend upon the circumstances.

- If the grant is paid when evidence is produced that certain expenditure has been incurred, the grant should be matched with that expenditure.

- If the grant is paid on a different basis, e.g. achievement of a non-financial objective, such as the creation of a specified number of new jobs, the grant should be matched with the identifiable costs of achieving that objective.

5.4 Presentation of revenue grants

IAS 20 allows such grants to either:

- Be presented as a credit in the income statement, or

- Deducted from the related expense

5.5 Capital grants

IAS 20 permits two treatments:

- Write off the grant against the cost of the non-current asset and depreciate the reduced cost.

- Treat the grant as a deferred credit and transfer a portion to revenue each year, so offsetting the higher depreciation charge on the original cost.

6 IAS 8 *Accounting policies, changes in accounting estimates and errors*

6.1 Introduction

IAS 8 governs the following topics:

- Selection of accounting policies

- Changes in accounting policies

- Changes in accounting estimates

- Correction of prior period adjustments

6.2 Accounting policies

Accounting policies are the principles, bases, conventions, rules and practices applied by an entity which specify how the effects of transactions and other events are reflected in the financial statements.

Accounting policies should be selected so as to comply with the requirements of IASs.

If however, there are no specific policies for a particular transaction, the accounting policy should be developed so as to meet the following objectives:

- Relevant to the decision- making needs of users

- Reliable i.e.
    - Report a faithful representation

    - Report the substance of transactions in preference to legal form

    - Neutral

    - Prudent

    - Complete

- Entities should consider IAS's that deal with similar and related issues. They should also consider the definitions, recognition criteria and measurement concepts contained in the framework.

6.3 Changes in accounting policies

Selected policies should be applied consistently as far as possible. Changes should only be made if:

- a new IFRS requires a change in policy, or

- the changes improve the relevance and faithful presentation of the financial statements. For example, changing to a policy of revaluing tangible non-current assets may improve the reliability of reported carrying values on the statement of financial position as they would better reflect the current market, or fair, value.

A change in accounting policy should be applied retrospectively, i.e. as if the new policy had always been applied. Any resulting adjustment should be reported as an adjustment to the opening balance of retained earnings. Comparative information should be restated.

6.4 Changes in accounting estimates

When preparing financial statements, inherent uncertainties result in estimates having to be made and subsequently, these estimates may need to be revised.

Distinguishing between changes in accounting policies and accounting estimates may be difficult. In these circumstances, the change is to be treated as a change in an accounting estimate.

Changes in accounting estimates should be accounted for prospectively. This means that the revised estimate should be included in the calculation of net profit or loss for the current period and future periods if appropriate.

6.5   Errors

Prior period errors are omissions from, and misstatements in, the entity's financial statements for one or more periods arising from a failure to use, or misuse of, reliable information that:

- was available when financial statements for these periods were authorised for issue; and

- could reasonably be expected to have been obtained and taken into account in the preparation and presentation of those financial statements.

 Activity 5

Which **ONE** of the following would be regarded as a change of an accounting policy according to IAS 8 *Accounting Policies, Changes in estimates and errors*?

A   An entity changed the depreciation method on plant from 10% per annum straight line to 15% per annum reducing balance basis.

B   An entity increased its provision for irrecoverable debts by 3%.

C   An entity started capitalising development costs from this year. In the past all development costs were written off.

D   An entity included some items of damaged inventory at net selling price.

---

7   Summary

IFRS 5 states that assets held for re-sale must be classified separately on the statement of financial position and post tax profit from discontinued operations must be disclosed separately on the face of the statement of comprehensive income.

IFRS 8 states that PLCs must disclose segmental information relating to the business or geographical segments of the entity.

IAS 18 states that revenues should be recognised at fair value and only when they are probable and can be measured reliably.

IAS 33 states that PLCs must disclose their EPS at the bottom of the statement of comprehensive income.

IAS 20 states that government grants should be recognised according to revenue and capital grants received.

IAS 8 states that accounting policies should be selected so as to comply with the requirements of IASs.

 Activity 6

1   How should assets held for sale be valued?

2   What is the definition of revenue?

3   An entity has earnings of £19,200 and share capital of £120,000 comprising 240,000 shares at 50p each. What is the EPS?

Answers to chapter activities

 Activity 1

Answer B

"An asset held for sale" on the statement of financial position should be valued at the **lower** of its:

Carrying value – cost less depreciation for three years (20X3, 20X4 and 20X5).

Cost	£80,000
Less: Accumulated depreciation	
3/5 × £80,000	(£48,000)
	————
	£32,000
	————

Fair value less costs to sell

Expected market value	£33,000
Less: expected costs to sell	(£1,100)
	————
	£31,900
	————

The asset held for sale should be valued at the lower of its carrying amount and fair value less costs to sell.

 Activity 2

Answer D

A non-current asset held for sale should not be depreciated at the year end.

An impairment charge will arise if the carrying value is greater than fair value less costs to sell.

Activity 3

Answer B

 Activity 4

Answer B

Revenue can be recognised before payment has been received from the buyer e.g. on a credit sale transaction.

An allowance (provision) for irrecoverable debts is calculated on the credit sales of a business.

 Activity 5

Answer C

 Activity 6

1   The asset held for sale should be valued at the lower of its carrying amount and fair value less costs to sell.

2   Gross inflow of economic benefits during the period arising in the course of the ordinary activities of an entity when those inflows result in increases in equity, other than increases relating to contributions from equity participants.

3   £0.08 (8 pence) (£19,200/240,000 = £0.08)

8 Test your knowledge

 Workbook Activity 7

The directors of Mattesich Limited are to hold a board meeting next week to consider the performance of the company in the past year. They will also discuss the accounting policy for valuing non-current assets. The company accountant, who would normally prepare the documents for the meeting, is ill. He has completed the extended trial balance for the year ended 30 September 20X0 which is set out below.

Description	Debit £000	Credit £000	Debit £000	Credit £000	Debit £000	Credit £000	Debit £000	Credit £000
Buildings – accumulated depreciation		2,731						2,731
Office equipment – accumulated depreciation		2,456						2,456
Motor vehicles – accumulated depreciation		5,502						5,502
Fixtures and fittings – accumulated depreciation		2,698						2,698
Loss on disposal of discont'd operation	473				473			
Trade payables		2,727						2,727
Trade receivables	6,654						6,654	
Distribution costs	5,695		206	38	5,863			
Admin. expenses	3,337		181	49	3,469			
Land – cost	8,721						8,721	
Buildings – cost	12,873						12,873	
Office equipment – cost	6,182						6,182	
Motor vehicles – cost	11,522						11,522	
Fixtures and fittings – cost	6,913						6,913	
Interest	544				544			
Revenue		40,448				40,448		
Loan		6,800						6,800
Ordinary share capital		14,000						14,000
Inventories	12,973		13,482	13,482	12,973	13,482	13,482	
Retained earnings		12,214						12,214
Accruals				387				387
Share premium		7,200						7,200
Interim dividend	2,100				2,100			
Prepayments			87				87	
Cash at bank and in hand	107						107	
Purchases	18,682				18,682			
Profit						9,826		9,826
	96,776	96,776	13,956	13,956	53,930	53,930	66,541	66,541

You have been given the following further information:

The share capital of the business consists of ordinary shares with a nominal value of £1.

- The company paid an interim dividend of 15 pence per share this year. No final dividend has been proposed

- Depreciation has been calculated on all the non-current assets of the business and has already been entered into the distribution expenses and administrative expenses ledger balances as shown on the extended trial balance.

- The corporation tax charge for the year has been estimated at £3,813,000, all of which relates to continuing activities.

During the year the company discontinued part of its operations. The results for the discontinued operation for the year have already been analysed by the company accountant.

All of these results are included in the figures in the extended trial balance.

The analysed results are set out below:

	Discontinued operations £000
Revenue	1,213
Cost of sales	(788)
	———
Gross profit	425
Distribution costs	(234)
Administration expenses	(178)
	———
Net profit	13
	———

Required:

Using the proforma income statement which follows, draft an income statement for the year ended 30 September 20X0.

Note: You do NOT need to prepare any of the notes to the financial statements. You do NOT need to prepare journal entries for any additional adjustments that may be necessary as a result of the further information given above.

You do NOT need to do an analysis of distribution costs and administrative expenses.

Mattesich Limited Income statement for the year ended 30 September 20X0

	£000
Revenue	
Cost of sales	
	_____
Gross profit	
Distribution costs	
Administrative expenses	
	_____
Profit from operations	
Finance costs	
	_____
Profit before taxation	
Tax	
	_____
Profit for the year from continuing operations	_____
Profit for the year from discontinued operations	_____
Profit for the year	_____

Workbook Activity 8

Which of the following statements is correct?

(i) When there is a change in accounting policy the changes should be applied prospectively.

(ii) When there is a change in an accounting estimate the comparatives must be restated.

(iii) Prior period errors should be accounted for retrospectively.

(iv) A change in accounting policy can be made if it improves the reliability and relevance of the financial statements

A   Only (i) and (ii)

B   Only (ii) and (iii)

C   Only (iii) and (iv)

D   Only (i) and (iv)

 Workbook Activity 9

On 1/9/20X2 a business received a total subscription in advance of £240,000 for 12 monthly publications of a magazine.

At the year ended 31/12/20X2 the business had produced and dispatched four out of the 12 publications.

Using the traditional method of revenue recognition how much revenue should the business recognise in the year ended 31/12/20X2?

A   £240,000

B   £120,000

C   £60,000

D   £80,000

Workbook Activity 10

The following segmental information has been provided by a company:

	Revenue £000
A	186
B	140
C	86
D	24
E	14

What is the **minimum** number of segments that will be classified as reportable segments in accordance with IFRS 8 *Operating Segments*?

Company finance

11

Introduction

This chapter provides additional detail with regards to share issues, debt and different types of reserves.

KNOWLEDGE

The general legal framework of limited companies and the obligations of Directors in respect of the financial statements (1.5)

The statutory form of accounting statements and disclosure requirements (1.2)

SKILLS

Apply accounting standards and relevant legislation to correctly identify, and accurately adjust accounting information (1.1)

Prepare notes to the accounts which satisfy statutory current disclosure requirements, in respect of accounting policies, non-current assets, current and long term liabilities, equity (1.4)

CONTENTS

1 Share capital
2 Types of reserve
3 Finance costs and dividends

1 Share capital

1.1 Introduction

The way in which the assets of a company (non-current assets, inventories, receivables and cash) are financed will vary from one company to another. Part of the finance may be provided by the owners or proprietors of the company (referred to as shareholders), while part may be provided by outsiders including suppliers, banks and other lenders of funds. Companies will also normally be partly financed by their own accumulated profits known as retained earnings.

1.2 The nature and purpose of share capital and reserves

 Definition

Share capital represents the capital invested in the company by its shareholders by the purchase of shares.

 Definition

Reserves represent the balance of net assets belonging to the shareholders. These may include part of past issues of share capital (known as share premium), retained trading profits and revaluation gains on the revaluation of non-current assets.

The total of share capital and reserves represents the book value of the net assets of the company.

1.3 Distinction between nominal value and market value of share capital

 Definition

The nominal value of a share is its face value e.g. £1 ordinary shares or 50p ordinary share.

Each share has a stated nominal (or par) value. This has little practical significance except as a base line price below which further shares may not generally be issued. The nominal value is also used as a means of calculating dividends to shareholders.

 Definition

The market value of a share is the price at which that share could be bought or sold.

The market value of a share is not fixed at any particular date. The market value is related to the market value of the business of the company. For example, if a business is worth £100,000 and there are 1,000 £1 shares in issue in the company, the market value of each share is £100 whereas the nominal value is £1.

If the company is listed on a stock exchange then a price will be quoted for the shares based upon recent transactions between purchasers and sellers of shares.

This is also referred to as the market value of a share, but this may not be the same value that would apply if the entire business was sold and thus all the shares were sold as one transaction.

1.4 Why companies are concerned with the value of their shares

Companies are concerned with the value the stock market places on the shares for two main reasons:

(a) Shareholders will look at a steadily rising price of the shares as evidence of sound management of the company by the directors. It would indicate additional profits being made every year.

(b) If the company wishes to raise further finance through the issue of shares, the current market price will be used as a basis for issuing more shares.

   The higher the price, the fewer shares will need to be issued and the less dilution there will be of the existing shareholders' effective interest in the company.

It is important to appreciate that the market value of a share quoted on the stock exchange has no direct relationship to the nominal value.

1.5 Share capital

The share capital of a company may be divided into various classes. The company's internal regulations (the articles of association) define the respective rights attached to the various shares e.g. as regards dividend entitlement or voting at company meetings. The various classes of share capital are dealt with below. In practice it is usually only larger companies which have different classes of share capital.

1.6 Ordinary shares

 Definition

Ordinary shares are the normal shares issued by a company. The normal rights of ordinary shareholders are to vote at company meetings and to receive dividends from profits.

Ordinary shares are often referred to as equity shares. A special class of ordinary share is the redeemable ordinary share where the terms of issue specify that it is repayable by the company.

There are various accounting terms to describe share capital: authorised, issued, called up and paid up.

(a) When a company is first established it must prepare a Memorandum of Association which will state the maximum amount of shares which the company is allowed to issue to its shareholders. This is the **authorised share capital** of the company.

(b) There is nothing to compel the company to issue to shareholders all of the shares which it is authorised to issue. The number of shares actually issued is known as the **issued share capital**.

(c) Once the company has asked its shareholders to pay for the shares it has issued to them, the shares are said to be **called up**.

(d) Once those shareholders have paid the company for the shares. The shares are said to be **paid up**.

 Activity 1

What are the accounting entries for an issue of shares at their nominal value?

DR

CR

1.7 Share premium account

Each share in the UK has a nominal value, e.g. a company might have in issue 1,000 £1 shares. The share premium is the amount for which a share is issued over and above its nominal value. Thus if a share has a nominal value of £1 and it is issued for £1.50, 50p will be the share premium.

The amounts of share premium received by a company must be credited to a share premium account on the statement of financial position.

 Example

Enterprise Limited makes an issue of 10,000 £1 ordinary shares for £1.60 each. What are the accounting entries?

Solution

Debit	Cash account £16,000 (10,000 × £1.60)
Credit	Share capital account £10,000 (10,000 × £1)
Credit	Share premium account £6,000 (10,000 × £0.60)

The share capital account is only ever credited with the nominal value of the shares issued. Any excess over this nominal value must be credited to the share premium account.

 Activity 2

What are the accounting entries for an issue of 1,000 ordinary £1 shares for £3 each?

DR

CR

1.8 Preference shares

 Definition

Preference shares are shares carrying a fixed rate of dividend, the holders of which have a prior claim to any company profits available for distribution.

The rights and advantages of the shares will be specified in the articles of association.

Special categories of preference shares include:

(i) **Participating preference shares** – where shareholders are entitled to participate together to a specified extent in distributable profits and surpluses on liquidation. Again, the rights of the shareholders are set out in the articles.

(ii) **Redeemable preference shares** – the terms of issue specify that they are repayable by the company.

Redeemable preference shares are more like debt than equity.

1.9 Ordinary and preference shares compared

Aspect	Ordinary shares	Preference shares
Voting power	Carry a vote	Do not carry a vote
Distribution of profits (dividends)	A dividend which may vary from one year to the next after the preference shareholders have received their dividend.	A fixed dividend (fixed percentage of nominal value) in priority to ordinary dividend.
Liquidation of the company	Entitled to surplus assets on liquidation after liabilities and preference shares have been repaid.	Priority of repayment over ordinary shares but not usually entitled to surplus assets on liquidation.

1.10 Debentures or loan stock

A debenture is a written acknowledgement of a loan to a company, given under the company's seal, which carries a fixed rate of interest.

A debenture may relate to a loan from one person. Debenture stock, on the other hand, rather like shares, may be held by a large number of individuals. The conditions and regulations are set out in a debenture trust deed.

Debentures are not part of a company's share capital – they are third party liabilities. Debenture interest is therefore a charge against profit and must be paid whether or not the company makes a profit.

Debentures are shown as liabilities in the statement of financial position, just like any other loan.

1.11 Gearing and risk

Companies with borrowings (such as long-term loans or debentures) or preference shares in their capital structure are said to have 'gearing'. This means that they have raised loans (i.e. borrowed money or raised capital from preference shares) and thereby taken on a degree of financial risk.

The risk comes from the fact that even if the company's financial performance deteriorated badly, the company would still have to pay the annual interest charge and the preference dividend each year. If it was unable to pay these amounts, the company could be wound up.

There is less risk associated with ordinary share capital, since there are no penalties directly associated with not paying an ordinary dividend in one year. If a dividend is not paid on the ordinary shares, this simply means that the owners of the business (the ordinary shareholders) have decided not to pay themselves a dividend – this is their choice.

Gearing is looked at in more detail in the later chapter covering the interpretation of financial statements.

2 Types of reserve

2.1 Introduction

Having looked at share capital we will now consider the different types of reserves a company might have.

2.2 Reserves

The non-current assets and current assets are shown on the top half of a statement of financial position; the non-current liabilities, current liabilities and equity and reserves are shown on the bottom half.

Equity and reserves comprise of:

- Share capital
- Retained earnings
- Capital reserves

2.3 Retained earnings

These comprise the cumulative total of the company's retained profits. In respect of each accounting period the profit attributable to equity holders will be added to retained earnings.

The company may well have more than one revenue reserve depending on the purpose for which the fund is intended, e.g. plant replacement reserve, general reserve etc.

However, they all have one feature in common, namely that they represent the retention of an amount of profit by the company, as opposed to the distribution of that amount by way of dividend to its shareholders.

Appropriation of profits in a limited company

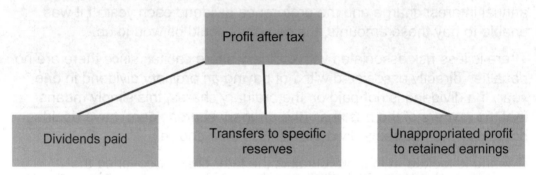

This shows the appropriation of profits firstly to shareholders then to specific named reserves and then finally the retained profits which go to the retained earnings.

The heading 'retained earnings' among the reserves on a statement of financial position refers to the unappropriated profits balance to date.

2.4　Capital reserves

Some reserves are established in certain circumstances by law, for example:

(a)　share premium account

(b)　revaluation reserve.

These may also be referred to as statutory reserves.

The balances on these capital or statutory reserves cannot legally be paid out in dividends, as opposed to retained earnings which could legally be paid out in dividends if the directors wished.

3 Finance costs and dividends

3.1 Finance costs

If a company has debentures in issue then the company usually must pay interest to the debenture holder. Effectively the company is paying interest on the money it has borrowed. Usually the rate is fixed when the debenture is purchased e.g. 10% debentures. This means the company must pay 10% of the issued debentures as interest.

The accounting entries are as follows:

Dr Interest charges (finance costs)

Cr Trade and other payables (current liabilities)

When the interest is paid

Dr Trade and other payables

Cr Cash

3.2 Dividends

When a sole trader withdraws money from their business for personal use it is referred to as drawings and accounted for as follows:

Debit   Drawings account
Credit   Cash

However for a company, where there may be many hundreds of shareholders, it would be far from practical for each one of them to have a drawings account. A system of dividend payments is therefore used. The actual amount of dividend to be paid by a company will be determined by many factors, the main one being the need to retain sufficient profits to provide for the future working capital and fixed assets requirements of the company.

3.3 Interim dividend

Some companies pay an amount on account of the total dividend before the end of the year. This is known as an interim dividend. The bookkeeping entry is as follows:

Debit   Dividend account
Credit   Cash

(The dividend account is a deduction from accumulated profits in the statement of changes in equity.)

3.4   Final dividend

It will only be at the end of the year, when the company's results for the whole accounting period are known, that the directors can declare ('propose') a final dividend. The dividend is usually declared after the year end and therefore is not a liability at the statement of financial position date and so cannot be accounted for until the next period. Any dividends that are proposed but not approved by the year end are disclosed in the financial statements.

 Example

A Ltd pays an interim dividend of £50,000 and proposes to pay a final dividend of £75,000.

The balance on the statement of comprehensive income for the year before any entries for the dividends was £300,000.

Show how these dividends will be presented in the financial statements.

Statement of changes in equity extract

	Accumulated profits
B/f	X
Profit for period	300,000
Dividend paid	(50,000)
C/f	X

Note: A final dividend of £75,000 has been proposed.

4   Summary

You need to understand how to calculate finance costs, debenture interest and dividends in order to make adjustments to company account questions.

You need to have a basic understanding of shares and debentures.

Answers to chapter activities

 Activity 1

DR Bank account

CR Share Capital account

 Activity 2

Debit   Cash account £3,000

Credit   Share capital account £1,000

Credit   Share premium account £2,000

The share capital account is only ever credited with the nominal value of the shares issued. Any excess over this nominal value must be credited to the share premium account.

Preparing financial statements

12

Introduction

In this chapter we will consider the preparation of financial statements for limited companies and consider the legal and regulatory requirements for the presentation of those financial statements.

KNOWLEDGE

Describe key components and the purpose of a statement of financial position (2.1)

Describe the key components and the purpose of a statement of comprehensive income (2.3)

Explain the content and purpose of disclosure notes to the accounts (2.4)

Identify accounting standards and the effect of these on the preparation of the financial statements (2.5)

SKILLS

Apply accounting standards and relevant legislation to correctly identify and accurately adjust accounting information (1.1)

Use appropriate information to accurately draft a statement of comprehensive income and a statement of financial position (1.2, 1.3)

Prepare notes to the accounts which satisfy statutory current disclosure requirements, in respect of accounting policies, non-current assets, current and long term liabilities, equity (1.4)

CONTENTS

1 Drafting financial statements

1 Drafting financial statements

Now that you have studied all the necessary accounting concepts, standards and treatments it is important that you can bring all of this information together to enable you to prepare a complete set of company financial statements. The following example will guide you through this process.

Example

The following trial balance at 30 September 20X9 relates to Pattar Ltd.

	£000	£000
Revenue		103,500
Inventories at 1 October 20X8	5,460	
Purchases	67,206	
Distribution costs	8,000	
Salesmans commissions	2,920	
Administrative salaries	2,280	
Manufacturing wages	2,000	
Interest paid	540	
Administrative expenses	5,000	
3% debenture loans		18,000
Share capital		60,000
Retained earnings at 1 October 20X8		8,495
Cash and cash equivalents	2,685	
Dividends paid	2,820	
Revaluation reserve @ 1 October 20X8		6,000
Trade and other payables		5,861
Land and Buildings – value/cost	92,578	
Accumulated depreciation		25,000
Plant and equipment at cost	35,000	
Accumulated depreciation		15,313
Trade and other receivables	16,395	
Accruals		715
	———	———
	242,884	242,884
	———	———

Further information:

(a) Inventories were valued at £7,850,000 on 30 September 20X9.

(b) Depreciation is to be provided for the year to 30 September 20X9 as follows:

Buildings 10% per annum straight line basis

Plant and equipment 25% per annum reducing balance basis

Depreciation is apportioned as follows:

Cost of sales 60%

Distribution costs 30%

Administrative expenses 10%

Land and Buildings in the trial balance includes a value for Land at £42,578. It is to be revalued at £61,000 and this revaluation is to be included in the financial statements for 30 September 20X9.

(c) An irrecoverable debt of £21,000 which is included in trade receivables is to be written off.

(d) Administrative expenses of £85,000 owing at 30 September 20X9 are to be provided for.

(e) The corporation tax charge for the year has been calculated as £1,500,000.

All operations are continuing operations.

Required:

Prepare the statement of comprehensive income for Pattar Ltd for the year ended 30 September 20X9 and a statement of financial position at that date.

These should be in a form suitable for presentation to the shareholders in accordance with the requirements of IAS 1 and be accompanied by notes to the accounts so far as is possible from the information given above.

You are not required to prepare the note relating to accounting policies.

Solution

Get yourself organised: you will need to prepare a sheet for the statement of comprehensive income and a separate sheet for the statement of financial position

Pattar Ltd Statement of comprehensive income for the year ended 30 September 20X9	Pattar Ltd Statement of financial position as at 30 September 20X9 £ £

You will also need a sheet for notes to the accounts and a sheet for workings.

Pattar Ltd Notes to the accounts	Pattar Ltd Workings

Note: Some of the numbers you require for this answer will come straight out of the question. Some will require a working which is not a note to the accounts. Finally, some will be calculated as part of a note to the accounts. We will go through the answer line by line and indicate how the amount is calculated.

You must let the statutory format dictate the order of working.

Below we show the answer as it will appear in the statutory format, and the workings and notes will follow.

Pattar Ltd – statement of comprehensive income for the year ended 30 September 20X9

	Notes	£000
Revenue (Step 1)		103,500
Cost of sales (W1) (Step 2)		(72,769)
Gross profit		30,731
Distribution costs (W2) (Step 2)		(13,897)
Administrative expenses (W3) (Step 2)		(8,378)
Profit from operations		8,456
Finance costs (Step 3)		(540)
Profit before tax		7,916
Tax (Step 4)	1	(1,500)
Profit for the period from continuing operations		6,416
Other comprehensive income		
Revaluation gain (61,000 – 42,578)		18,422
Total comprehensive income		24,838

Step 1

The revenue figure is taken directly from the question. (**Note:** If there are sales returns listed in the TB this would reduce the value of reported revenue).

Step 2

Cost of sales, distribution costs and administrative expenses

This is found by a working.

(**Note:** Remember that you have to identify cost of sales, distribution costs and administrative costs separately so you need three separate workings.)

In the exam you will need to select the account name and enter the amount in a table as below. (All workings in £000s).

(W1) Expenses – cost of sales

Account name	Cost of sales £000
Opening inventories	5,460
Purchases	67,206
Manufacturing wages	2,000
Closing inventories	(7,850)
Depreciation – buildings(W4)	3,000
Depreciation – plant (W4)	2,953
	72,769

(W2) Expenses – Distribution costs

	Distribution costs £000
Distribution costs	8,000
Salesmans commissions	2,920
Depreciation – buildings (W4)	1,500
Depreciation – plant (W4)	1,477
	13,897

(W3) Expenses – Administrative expenses

	Administrative expenses £000
Administrative salaries	2,280
Administrative expenses	5,000
Depreciation – buildings (W4)	500
Depreciation – plant (W4)	492
Administrative expenses accrued	85
Irrecoverable debt written off	21
	8,378

(W4) Deprecation is calculated as follows:

Buildings £50,000 × 10% = £5,000

The buildings value of £50,000 was calculated by subtracting the land value of £42,578 from the total land and buildings value of £92,578.

Attributable to:

Cost of sales £5,000 × 60% = £3,000

Distribution costs £5,000 × 30% = £1,500

Administrative expenses £5,000 × 10% = £500

Plant and equipment £35,000 – £15,313 = £19,687 × 25% = £4,922

Attributable to:

Cost of sales £4,922 × 60% = £2,953

Distribution costs £4,922 × 30% = £1,477

Administrative expenses £4,922 × 10% = £492

Step 3

Finance costs come straight from the question.

Interest paid = £540

Step 4

When you get as far as taxation, you can then turn your attention to any required notes to the accounts. We shall produce the notes in their correct order even though some cannot be produced because of lack of information. (In the exam only prepare the notes if they are required in the question)

(a) Note 1 usually deals with accounting policies but we are told not to provide this note in the present question.

(b) Note 2 (analysis of revenue) cannot be completed as we are given no information.

(c) Note 3 (operating costs and revenues) There are no material items to disclose however we must always disclose the audit fee.

(d) *Profit from operations*

Profit is stated after charging the following:

	£000
Auditors' remuneration	0

(e) There are detailed disclosure requirements on directors but we do not have the relevant information

(f) The next note is Tax.

Tax on profit (this is the first note we can produce)

	£000
Tax (at 30%) based on profits of the year	1,500
(Over)/under provision for corporation tax in previous year	0
Transfer to/(from) deferred tax	0
	1,500

The tax charge for the year is given in the additional information in the question. This is however only an estimate of the tax for the year – the final figure will be determined by HM Revenue and Customs after the year-end and this figure may be different to this estimated charge of £1,500,000.

The income statement workings and notes are now complete. Record the revaluation gain to complete the income statement.

Step 5

You are now in a position to prepare the statement of financial position using exactly the same approach. Allow the format to take you through the question.

As before we will show the answer below in the correct format and indicate where the numbers come from.

Pattar Ltd Statement of financial position as at 30 September 20X9

Note		£000
	Non-current assets	
2	Property, plant and equipment (W5) (Step 6)	95,765
		95,765
	Current assets	
	Inventories (Step 7)	7,850
	Trade and other receivables (Step 7)	16,374
	Cash and cash equivalents (Step 7)	2,685
		26,909
	Total assets	122,674
	Equity	
	Share capital	60,000
	Retained earnings (Step 10)	12,091
	Revaluation reserve (6,000 + 18,422)	24,422
	Total equity	96,513
	Non-current liabilities (Step 9)	
	Debenture loans	18,000
		18,000
	Current liabilities	
	Trade and other payables (Step 8)	6,661
	Tax liabilities (charge for the year)	1,500
		8,161
	Total liabilities (18,000 + 8,161)	26,161
	Total equity and liabilities	122,674

Step 6

We will continue the statement of financial position notes directly on from the statement of comprehensive income notes. Note 2 will therefore be non-current assets – Property, plant and equipment. This note will also form the working for the figure on the statement of financial position.

(W5) Note 2 Property, plant and equipment

	Land and buildings £000	Plant and machinery £000	Total £000
Cost at 1 October 20X8	92,578	35,000	127,578
Revaluation	18,422		18,422
Cost at 30 September 20X9	111,000	35,000	146,000
Depreciation at 1 October 20X8	25,000	15,313	40,313
Charge for year	5,000	4,922	9,922
Depreciation at 30 September 20X9	30,000	20,235	50,235
CV at 1 October 20X8	67,578	19,687	87,265
CV at 30 September 20X9	81,000	14,765	**95,765**

This can then be taken to the statement of financial position and cross referenced to Note 2.

Step 7

(W6) Investments, inventories, and cash all come directly from the question.

Trade receivables are adjusted for the irrecoverable written off 16,395 – 21 = 16,374.

Step 8

(W7) Current liability workings

(1) You will need a working for trade and other payables

Trade payables	5,861
Accruals	715
Administrative expenses accrued	85
	6,661

(2) Working for tax

Tax estimate for year	1,500

In the exam the tax estimate for the year given in the question will be the current tax liability for the year.

Step 9

Debenture loans come directly from the question.

Step 10

(W8) You are now in a position to complete the statement of financial position with equity.

(a) The called up share capital comes directly from the question.

(b) The retained earnings figure comes from the retained earnings brought forward at 1/10/X8 of 8,495 and profit for the period of 6,416 from the income statement less dividend paid of 2,820.

You should now have completed:

- an income statement
- a statement of financial position
- notes to the accounts
- your working paper.

Required:

Prepare the statement of changes in equity for Pattar Ltd for the year ended 30 September 20X9.

Pattar Ltd

Statement of changes in equity

	Share capital £000	Revaluation £000	Retained earnings £000	Total £000
At 31 October 20X8	60,000	6,000	8,495	74,495
Revaluation		18,422		18,422
Profit for the year			6,416	6,416
Dividends paid			(2,820)	(2,820)
At 30 September 20X9	60,000	24,422	12,091	96,513

Exam focus

- Note that in the computer based assessment you will not be required to show all the workings above and tables will be provided in which you can select the account name from a list and enter the appropriate numerical amount.

- The approach above is given step by step so that you can consolidate your learning and are able to deal with exam type questions.

Activity 1

The following is the trial balance of Transit Ltd at 31 March 20X8.

	£	£
Issued share capital (ordinary shares of £1 each)		42,000
Leasehold properties, at cost	75,000	
Motor vans, at cost (used for distribution)	2,500	
Accumulated depreciation on motor vans to 31 March 20X7		1,000
Administration expenses	7,650	
Distribution costs	10,000	
Inventories at 31 March 20X7	12,000	
Purchases	138,750	
Revenue		206,500
Directors' remuneration (administrative)	25,000	
Rents receivable		3,600
Investments at cost (short-term)	6,750	
Investment income		340
7% Debentures		15,000
Debenture interest	1,050	
Bank interest	162	
Bank overdraft		730
Trade receivables and payables	31,000	23,000
Sales tax control		1,100
Interim dividend paid	1,260	
Retained earnings, 31 March 20X7		17,852
	———	———
	311,122	311,122
	———	———

You are given the following additional information:

• All the motor vans were purchased on 1 April 20X5. Depreciation has been, and is to be, provided at the rate of 20% per annum on cost from the date of purchase.

  Depreciation is to be charged to distribution costs.

• On 31 March 20X8 one van, which had cost £900, was sold for £550, as part settlement of the price of £800 of a new van, but no entries with regard to these transactions were made in the books. The remaining balance due for the new van is payable in 30 days. Depreciation is charged on assets in the year of their disposal, no depreciation is to be charged on the new van.

• The estimated tax liability for the year to 31 March 20X8 is £12,700.

- It is proposed to pay a final dividend of 10% for the year to 31 March 20X8.

- Inventories valued at the lower of cost and net realisable value on 31 March 20X8 are £16,700.

Required:

Using the proformas given prepare:

(a)   a statement of comprehensive income for the year ended 31 March 20X8

(b)   a statement of financial position at that date

(c)   a statement of changes in equity.

Transit limited

Statement of comprehensive income for the year ended 31 March 20X8

£

Revenue

Cost of sales (W1)

Gross profit

Investment income

Rental income

Distribution costs (W2)

Administrative expenses (W3)

Profit from operations

Finance costs

Profit before tax

Tax

Profit for the period from continuing operations

Statement of financial position at 31 March 20X8

£

Non-current assets

Property, Plant and Equipment
(W6)

Current assets

Inventories

Trade and other receivables

Investments held for resale

Total assets

Equity

Share capital

Non-current liabilities

Debentures

Current liabilities

Trade and other payables (W7)

Tax liabilities

Bank overdraft and loans

Total liabilities

Total equity and liabilities

Statement of changes in equity for the year ended 31 March 20X8

	Share capital	Retained earnings	Total
Balance at 31 March 20X7			
Profit for the period			
Dividends			
Balance at 31 March 20X8			

Workings

For (W1), (W2) and (W3) circle the appropriate account name and enter the amount.

(W1) Expenses – cost of sales

Account name	Cost of sales
	£
Opening inventories / Depreciation	
Directors remuneration / Purchases	
Administrative expenses / closing inventories	
	————
Total	
	————

(W2) Expenses – Distribution costs

Account name	Distribution costs
	£
Opening inventories / Distribution costs	
Depreciation / Distribution costs	
Administrative expenses / Profit from disposal of van	
	———
Total	
	———

(W3) Expenses – Administrative expenses

Account name	Administrative expenses
	£
Directors remuneration / Depreciation	
Administrative expenses / closing inventories	
	———
Total	
	———

(W4) Depreciation

(W5) Disposal account (complete the account name and amount)

Account name	£
	———
Profit on disposal	
	———

(W6) Property, plant and equipment

	Leasehold properties	Motor vans	Total
	£	£	£
Cost at 31 March X7			
Additions			
Disposals			
	———	———	———
At 31 March X8			
	———	———	———
Accumulated depreciation at 31 March 20X7			
Charge for year			
Disposals			
	———	———	———
	———	———	———
CV at 31 March 20X7			
CV at 31 March 20X8			

In the exam you will be expected to choose the correct account name and enter the numerical amount. In the table below the narrative has been complete (for guidance), you must enter the amount.

(W7) Trade payables

Account name	£
Trade payables	
Balance due on new motor vehicle	
	———
Total	
	———

2 Summary

In order to prepare limited company financial statements you need:

- a detailed knowledge of the disclosure requirements IAS 1

- the ability to get the knowledge onto paper quickly and neatly.

- Apply a methodical approach and show workings

Published accounts' is primarily a practical subject, so take the opportunity to learn from financial statements which you come across in practice.

Answers to chapter activities

Activity 1

Transit Limited

Statement of comprehensive income for the year ended 31 March 20X8

	£
Revenue	206,500
Cost of sales (W1)	(134,050)
Gross profit	72,450
Investment income	340
Rental income	3,600
Distribution costs (W2)	(10,310)
Administrative expenses (W3)	(32,650)
Profit from operations	33,430
Finance costs (1,050 + 162)	(1,212)
Profit before tax	32,218
Tax	(12,700)
Profit for the period from continuing operations	19,518

Transit Ltd

Statement of financial position at 31 March 20X8

	£
Non-current assets	
Property, plant and equipment (W6)	76,440
	76,440
Current assets	
Inventories	16,700
Trade and other receivables	31,000
Investments held for re-sale	6,750
	54,450
Total assets	130,890
Capital and reserves	
Ordinary shares of £1 each	42,000
Retained earnings (see statement of changes in equity)	36,110
	78,110
Non-current liabilities	
7% Debentures	15,000
	15,000
Current liabilities	
Trade and other payables (W7)	23,250
Tax liabilities (12,700 + 1,100)	13,800
Bank overdraft	730
	37,780
Total Liabilities	52,780
Total Equity and Liabilities	130,890

Statement of changes in equity for the year ended 31 March 20X8

	Share capital	Retained earnings	Total
Balance at 31 March 20X7	42,000	17,852	59,852
Profit for the period	–	19,518	19,518
Dividends	–	(1,260)	(1,260)
Balance at 31 March 20X8	42,000	36,110	78,110

Workings

(W1) Expenses – cost of sales

Account name	Cost of sales
	£
Opening inventories	12,000
Purchases	138,750
Closing inventories	(16,700)
Total	134,050

(W2) Expenses – Distribution costs

Account name	Distribution costs
	£
Distribution costs	10,000
Depreciation (W4)	500
Profit from sale of van (W5)	(190)
Total	10,310

(W3) Expenses – Administrative expenses

Account name	Administrative expenses
	£
Director's remuneration	25,000
Administrative expenses	7,650
Total	32,650

(W4) Depreciation

£2,500 × 20% = £500

(W5) Disposal account

Account name	£
Motor vans cost	900
Accumulated depreciation on disposal (900 × 20% × 3 years)	(540)
Cash proceeds	(550)
	——
Profit on disposal	190
	——

(W6) Property, plant and equipment

	Leasehold properties £	Motor vans £	Total £
Cost at 31 March X7	75,000	2,500	77,500
Additions	–	800	800
Disposals	–	(900)	(900)
At 31 March X8	75,000	2,400	77,400
Accumulated depreciation at 31 March 20X7	–	1,000	1,000
Charge for year (W4)	–	500	500
Disposals	–	(540)	(540)
	–	960	960
CV at 31 March 20X7	75,000	1,500	76,500
CV at 31 March 20X8	75,000	1,440	76,440

(W7) Trade payables

Account name	£
Trade payables	23,000
Balance due on new motor vehicle	250
	———
Total charge for year	23,250
	———

3 Test your knowledge

 Workbook Activity 2

You have been asked to help prepare the financial statements of Laxdale Ltd for the year ended 31 October 20X8. The company's trial balance of the company as at 31 October 20X8 is shown below.

Laxdale Ltd
Trial balance as at 31 October 20X8

	Debit £000	Credit £000
Share capital		16,000
Trade and other payables		2,798
Property, plant and equipment – cost	47,652	
Property, plant and equipment – accumulated depreciation		23,415
Trade and other receivables	5,436	
Accruals		436
8% bank loan repayable 20X2		15,000
Cash at bank	9,774	
Retained earnings		9,786
Interest	600	
Sales		58,975
Purchases	42,398	
Returns inwards	564	
Returns outwards		778
Distribution costs	5,443	
Administration expenses	4,789	
Inventories as at 1 November 20X7	9,032	
Final dividend for year ended 31 October 20X7	850	
Interim dividend for year ended 31 October 20X8	650	
	127,188	127,188

Further information:

- The share capital of the company consists of ordinary shares with a nominal value of £1.

- Inventories at the close of business on 31October 20X8 were valued at £7,878,000.

- The corporation tax charge for the year has been calculated as £2,540,000

- The company began a series of television adverts for the company's range of products on 1 October 20X8 at a cost of £45,000.

  The adverts were run for three months and were to be paid for in full at the end of December 20X8.

- Interest on the bank loan for the last six months of the year has not been included in the accounts in the trial balance.

- All of the operations are continuing operations.

Task 1

Using the proforma provided, and making any adjustments required as a result of the further information given above, draft the income statement for Laxdale Ltd for the year ended 31 October 20X8.

Laxdale Ltd

Income Statement for the year ended 31 October 20X8

	£000
Continuing operations	
Revenue	
Cost of sales	_____
Gross profit	
Distribution costs	
Administrative expenses	_____
	_____
Profit from operations	
Finance costs	_____
Profit before tax	
Tax	_____
Profit for the period from continuing operations	
	_____

Task 2

Using the proforma provided, draft the statement of financial position for Laxdale Ltd as at 31 October 20X8.

Laxdale Ltd

Statement of financial position as at 31 October 20X8

£000

Assets

Non-current assets

_____

_____

Current assets

_____

Total assets _____

Equity and liabilities

Equity

_____

_____

Non-current liabilities

———

———

Current liabilities

———

Total equity and liabilities

———

Workbook Activity 3

Data

You have been asked to help prepare the financial statements of Hightink Ltd for the year ended 31 March 20X2.

The trial balance of the company as at 31 March 20X2 is set out below.

Hightink Ltd
Trial balance as at 31 March 20X2

	£000	£000
Interest	240	
Distribution costs	6,852	
Administrative expenses	3,378	
Trade receivables	5,455	
Trade payables		2,363
Interim dividend	400	
Ordinary share capital		4,000
Revenue		31,710
Long term loan		6,000
Buildings – cost	3,832	
Fixtures and fittings – cost	2,057	
Motor vehicles – cost	3,524	
Office equipment – cost	2,228	
Land – cost	5,000	
Purchases	15,525	
Cash at bank	304	
Retained earnings		6,217
Inventories as at 1 April 20X1	6,531	
Share premium		2,000
Buildings – accumulated depreciation		564
Fixtures and fittings – accumulated depreciation		726
Motor vehicles – accumulated depreciation		1,283
Office equipment – accumulated depreciation		463
	———	———
	55,326	55,326
	———	———

Further information:

- The authorised share capital of the company, all of which has been issued, consists of ordinary shares with a nominal value of £1.

- The company paid an interim dividend of 10p per share during the year. No final dividend has been proposed.

- Inventories at the close of business on 31 March 20X2 were valued at cost at £7,878,000.

- The corporation tax charge for the year has been calculated as £1,920,000.

- Credit sales relating to April 20X2 amounting to £204,000 had been entered incorrectly into the accounts in March 20X2.

- Interest on the long term loan has been paid for six months of the year. No adjustment has been made for the interest due for the final six months of the year. Interest is charged on the loan at a rate of 8% per annum.

- The land has been revalued by professional valuers at £5,500,000. The revaluation is to be included in the financial statements for the year ended 31 March 20X2.

- On 21 April 20X2 there was a fire at the company's premises that destroyed non-current assets and inventory. The losses from the fire amounted to £487,000 and they were not covered by the company's insurance. This amount is considered by the directors to constitute a material loss to the company.

- All of the operations are continuing operations.

Required:

Using the proforma provided, and making any adjustments required as a result of the further information given above, draft a statement of comprehensive income for the year ended 31 March 20X2, a statement of changes in equity and a statement of financial position for Hightink as at that date.

Note: You are NOT required to produce notes to the accounts.

Hightink Ltd

Statement of comprehensive income for the year ended 31 March 20X2

	£000
Revenue	
Cost of sales	_____
Gross profit	
Distribution costs	
Administrative expenses	_____
	_____
Profit from operations	
Finance costs	_____
Profit before tax	
Tax	_____
Profit for the period from continuing operations	_____
Other comprehensive income	
Gain on revaluation	
Total comprehensive income for the year	_____

Statement of changes in equity for the year ended 31 March 20X2

	Share capital	Revaluation reserve	Retained earnings	Total
At 31 March 20X1				
Revaluation				
Profit for year				
Dividends				
At 31 March 20X2				

Hightink Ltd

Statement of financial position as at 31 March 20X2

£000

Non-current assets

Property, plant and equipment

_____

Current assets

Inventories

Trade and other receivables

Cash and cash equivalents

_____

_____

Total assets

_____

Equity

Called-up share capital

Share premium

Revaluation reserve

Retained earnings

_____

_____

Non-current liabilities

Long term loan

_____

Current liabilities

Trade and other payables

Taxation

Bank overdraft and loans

_____

Total equity and liabilities

_____

Workbook Activity 4

An extract from the accounts of Bay Ltd for the year ended 31 March 20X1 showed:

	£000
Revenue	9,320
Cost of sales	(5,120)
Gross profit	4,200
Distribution costs	(1,230)
Admin expenses	(940)
Profit from operations	2,030
Finance costs	(230)
Profit before taxation	1,800
Tax	(480)
Profit for the financial year	1,320

Extract from the statement of financial position

	£000
Equity:	
Share capital	3,500
Share premium	1,400
Revaluation reserve	600
Retained earnings	1,850
	7,350

The revaluation reserve arose in the year ended 31 March 20X1 as a result of land being revalued by a professional valuer. The revaluation is also reflected in the value of the tangible assets.

Dividends paid during the year totalled £420,000.

Task

Prepare a statement of changes in equity for the year ended 31 March 20X1.

Workbook Activity 5

Burysane Ltd

Data

You have been asked to help prepare the financial statements of Burysane Ltd for the year ended 31 March 20X4. The extended trial balance of the company as at 31 March 20X4 is shown as follows.

	Trial balance		Adjustments		Income statement		Statement of financial position	
Burysane Ltd Extended trial balance as at 31 March 20X4								
Description	Debit £000	Credit £000	Debit £000	Credit £000	Debit £000	Credit £000	Debit £000	Credit £000
Trade payables		2,409						2,409
Prepayments			207				207	
Ordinary share capital		18,000						18,000
Inventories	8,912		9,432	9,432	8,912	9,432	9,432	
Share premium		6,000						6,000
Administration expenses	6,143		185	115	6,213			
Distribution costs	9,459		177	92	9,544			
Retained earnings		15,411						15,411
Land – cost	14,000						14,000	
Buildings – cost	12,068						12,068	
Fixtures and fittings – cost	10,217						10,217	
Motor vehicles – cost	18,548						18,548	
Office equipment – cost	3,004						3,004	
Revenue		39,773				39,773		
Trade receivables	1,359						1,359	
Accruals				362				362
Cash at bank	463						463	
Interest	400				400			
Long-term loan		10,000						10,000
Buildings –accumulated depreciation		2,603						2,603
Fixtures and fittings – accumulated depreciation		2,754						2,754
Motor vehicles – accumulated depreciation		5,621						5,621
Office equipment – accumulated depreciation		835						835
Purchases	16,858				16,858			
Interim dividend	2,160						2,160	
Allowance for doubtful receivables		185						185
Profit						7,278		7,278
Total	103,591	103,591	10,001	10,001	49,205	49,205	71,458	71,458

Further information:

- All of the operations are continuing operations

- The authorised share capital of the company, all of which has been issued, consists of ordinary shares with a nominal value of £1.

- The company paid an interim dividend of 12p per share during the year.

- No final dividend has been proposed.

- The corporation tax charge for the year has been calculated as £2,822,000.

- Credit sales relating to March 20X4 amounting to £3,200,000 had not been entered into the accounts at the year end.

- Interest on the long-term loan has been paid for the first six months of the year. No adjustment has been made for the interest due for the last six months of the year. Interest is charged on the loan at a rate of 8% per annum.

- The land has been revalued by professional valuers at £15,000,000. The revaluation is to be included in the financial statements for the year ended 31 March 20X4.

Required:

(a) Draft a statement of comprehensive income for Burysane Ltd for the year ended 31 March 20X4.

(b) Draft a statement of financial position for Burysane Ltd as at 31 March 20X4.

Note: No notes are required.

Statement of cash flows

Introduction

A typical task in the exam might be to draft a statement of cash flows from information provided in the statement of financial position, statement of comprehensive income and additional information.

KNOWLEDGE
Describe the key components and the purpose of a statement of cash flows (2.3)

SKILLS
Draft an accurate statement of cash flows (1.5)

CONTENTS
1 IAS 7 *Statement of cash flows*
2 The elements of a statement of cash flow
3 Preparing a statement of cash flow
4 More complex areas
5 Interpretation of a cash flow

1   IAS 7 *Statement of cash flows*

1.1   The need for a statement of cash flow

IAS 7 requires all financial statements (except those of small companies as defined in the CA 06) to include a statement of cash flow, showing the generation of cash and cash equivalents and the uses of cash and cash equivalents in the period.

One reason why a statement of cash flow is considered necessary is that final profit figures are relatively easy to manipulate. There are many items in an income statement involving judgement, including:

*   Valuation of inventories

*   Depreciation policy

*   Allowance for doubtful debts

This makes it difficult to interpret a company's results with confidence. An IAS 7 statement showing merely inflows and outflows of cash and cash equivalents is easier to understand and more difficult to manipulate.

Cash flows, including net present value calculations, have always been a popular management accounting tool and the requirement to produce a statement of cash flow as part of the financial statements helps to form a basis for any future decision making process.

1.2   The IAS 7 proforma

The standard headings shown in the IAS 7 statement of cash flow are as follows.

*   Cash flows from operating activities

*   Cash flows from investing activities

*   Cash flows from financing activities

*   Net increase in cash and cash equivalents

*   Cash and cash equivalents at beginning of period

*   Cash and cash equivalents at end of the period

The key to producing an accurate statement of cash flow in the examination is to know which cash flows go under which heading. Below is a typical IAS 7 statement showing many of the cash flows one would normally expect to see.

Proforma statement of cash flow for the year ended 31 December 20X9

	£000	£000
Cash flows from operating activities		
Profit from operations	X	
Adjustments for:		
Depreciation/amortisation	X	
	___	
Operating profit before working capital changes	X	
	___	
(Increase)/decrease in inventories	(X)/X	
(Increase)/Decrease in trade and other receivables	(X)/X	
Increase/(Decrease) in trade payables	X/(X)	
	___	
Cash generated from operations	X	
Interest paid	(X)	
Tax paid	(X)	
	___	
Net cash from operating activities		X
Cash flows from investing activities		
Purchase of property plant and equipment	(X)	
Purchase of intangibles	(X)	
Purchase of investments	(X)	
Proceeds from sale of property plant and equipment	X	
Proceeds from sale of intangibles	X	
Proceeds from sale of investments	X	
Interest received	X	
Dividends received	X	
	___	
Net cash used in investing activities		(X)
Cash flows from financing activities		
Proceeds from issue of ordinary shares	X	
Proceeds from issue of preference shares	X	
Proceeds from long-term borrowing	X	
Redemption of long-term borrowings	(X)	
Dividends paid	(X)	
	___	
Net cash used in financing activities		(X)
		___
Net increase in cash and cash equivalents		X
Cash and cash equivalents at beginning of period		X
		___
Cash and cash equivalents at end of period		X
		___

2 The elements of a statement of cash flow

2.1 Net cash flow from operating activities

This is the first heading of the statement of cash flow in the proforma shown above. It can be derived by adjusting the profit before interest and tax figure shown in the income statement.

The profit figure is adjusted for any transactions not involving the movement of cash, e.g. depreciation or profit/loss on disposal of non-current assets.

Note the increase/decrease in inventories, trade receivables and trade payables. An increase in inventories involves an outflow of cash and is, hence, a negative figure. Likewise, if the payables balance has reduced then cash has been spent paying our suppliers and hence this is also a cash outflow which is a negative figure.

The main issue is to understand the impact on cash, i.e. is it a cash outflow or inflow?

Note that any dividends received would be included here whilst dividends paid are disclosed separately; lower down the statement of cash flow (although they could in fact be shown here as well).

Interest paid and tax paid also appear here. This is the amount *paid* during the year, not the amount *charged* in the income statement.

2.2 Direct and indirect methods

In principle, there are two methods of preparing the figure for cash flows from operating activities.

The indirect method and the direct method. You will need to learn both methods.

Proforma statement of cash flow for the year ended 31 December 20X9 – Direct method for calculating cash generated from operations

Cash flows from operating activities	£000
Cash receipts from customers	X
Cash payments to suppliers	(X)
Cash payments to employees	(X)
Cash payments for expenses	(X)
	___
Cash generated from operations	X
	___

Proforma statement of cash flow for the year ended 31 December 20X9 – Indirect method for calculating cash generated from operations

	£000	£000
Cash flows from operating activities		
Profit from operations	X	
Adjustments for:		
Depreciation/amortisation	X	
	―	
Operating before working capital changes	X	
(Increase)/decrease in inventories	(X)/X	
(Increase)/decrease in trade and other receivables	(X)/X	
Increase/(decrease) in trade payables	X/(X)	
	―	
Cash generated from operations	X	

2.3 Cash flows from investing activities

This shows the extent to which the business has spent cash investing in the future of the business. An example is the purchase of non-current assets such as plant and machinery which will be used to generate cash and profits in the future.

2.4 Cash flows from financing

This includes any or all of the following elements.

- Proceeds of share issues
- Proceeds on taking out a new loan or debenture
- Payments to redeem a loan or debenture
- Dividends paid

2.5 Increase/decrease in cash and cash equivalents

This is the net amount of the cash flows from operating, investing and financing activities. It reconciles the opening and closing balances for cash and cash equivalents. The composition of cash and cash equivalents is analysed in a note as below.

Proforma note to the statement of cash flow

Cash and cash equivalents

Cash on hand and balances with banks	X
Short term investments	X
	―
Cash and cash equivalents as previously reported	X

3 Preparing a statement of cash flow

 Example – Indirect method

The following information relates to X plc. The company's accounting year ends on 30 September. Note that 20X9 is on the right.

Statement of financial positions

	30 September 20X8		30 September 20X9	
	£000	£000	£000	£000
ASSETS				
Non-current assets				
Plant property and equipment (Note 1)		945		1,662
Current assets				
Inventories	1,225		1,488	
Trade receivables	700		787	
Short-term liquid investments	175		262	
Cash at bank	184		186	
		2,284		2,723
Total assets		3,229		4,385
EQUITY AND LIABILITIES				
Equity				
Share capital		1,225		1,400
Share premium		–		87
General reserve		525		787
Retained earnings		88		158
		1,838		2,432
Non-current liabilities				
Long-term loan		525		700
Current Liabilities				
Trade and other payables	534		745	
Taxation	280		403	
Bank overdraft	52		105	
		866		1,253
Total Liabilities		1,391		1,953
Total Equity and Liabilities		3,229		4,385

Summary statement of comprehensive income for the year ended 30 September 20X9

	£000
Profit before taxation	735
Tax	(403)
Profit after taxation	332
Transfer to general reserve	(262)
Profit for the period from continuing operations	70

Note 1 Plant, property and equipment

	20X8		20X9	
	Freehold premises	Plant and machinery	Freehold premises	Plant and machinery
	£000	£000	£000	£000
At cost	560	455	560	718
Additions during the year	–	263	280	700
	560	718	840	1,418
Less accumulated depreciation	(35)	(298)	(53)	(543)
Carrying value	525	420	787	875

Prepare a statement of cash flows (using the indirect method) and the related Note for X plc for the year ended 30 September 20X9, conforming to the requirements of IAS 7, in so far as this is possible from the information given.

Solution

Step 1

We start by producing the statement of cash flow and calculating the increase in cash and cash equivalents.

Step 2

Start to work down the proforma statement of cash flow. Only the headings required are used in the answer below.

Remember to tick the numbers you have used in the question as you work through.

Cash flows from operating activities	£000	£000
Profit from operations	735	
Adjustments for:		
Depreciation charges (W1)	263	
	———	
Operating profit before working capital changes	998	
Increase in inventories (1,488 – 1,225) (W2)	(263)	
Increase in trade and other receivables (787 – 700) (W2)	(87)	
Increase in trade payables (745 – 534) (W2)	211	
	———	
Cash generated from operations	859	
Tax paid (W3)	(280)	
Net cash from operating activities		579
Cash flows from investing activities		
Purchase of property plant and equipment (W4)	(980)	
	———	
Net cash used in investing activities		(980)
Cash flows from financing activities		
Proceeds from issue of shares (W5)	262	
Proceeds from long-term borrowing (W6)	175	
Net cash used in financing activities		437
		———
Net increase in cash and cash equivalents (W7)		36
Cash and cash equivalents at beginning of period		307
		———
Cash and cash equivalents at end of period		343
		———

Note 1

Cash and cash equivalents	X8	X9
Cash on hand and balances with banks	132	81
Short-term investments	175	262
	———	———
	307	343
	———	———

(W1) Depreciation

You have to go to the note to the statement of financial position to calculate the depreciation charge as we are not given a detailed income statement. You need to calculate the difference between the accumulated depreciation at the end of the current year and at the end of the previous year. Be careful to find the right line and pick up the right figures.

Freehold premises (53 – 35)	18
Plant and machinery (543 – 298)	245

(W2) Changes in working capital

The other figures are calculated by simply comparing the two statement of financial positions and calculating the increase or decrease in the relevant items.

Inventories have increased in the second year compared to the first year, this means that extra cash has been spent, i.e. a decrease in cash.

Trade receivables have increased, this means that more credit has been offered to customers and therefore cash has not been received.

Trade payables have increased, this means that cash has been conserved so that cash has increased.

(W3) Taxation

The 20X9 tax £403,000 in the summary statement of comprehensive income has not been paid and is a payable in the statement of financial position.

The 20X8 tax £280,000 has been paid and that is the cash that is entered in the statement of cash flow.

(W4) Payments to acquire plant property and equipment

You have to go to Note 1 in the statement of financial position to find the information for this. In the line 'additions during the year' the amounts are given (280 + 700) = 980.

(W5) Issue of ordinary share capital

The ordinary share capital has increased, as has the share premium account. Clearly shares have been issued at a premium. The total amount issued = £(1,400,000 + 87,000 – 1,225,000) = £262,000.

(W6) Loans

Long-term loans have increased. New loans raised = £(700,000 – 525,000) = £175,000.

(W7) Increase in cash and cash equivalents

We can use the note required to produce this. Short-term investments plus cash less overdrafts.
(262 + 186 –105) – (175 + 184 –52) = (343 – 307) = 36

☀ Example – Direct method

The following information relates to Y plc.

Statement of comprehensive income for the year ended 30 September 20X9

	£000
Revenue	444
Cost of sales	(269)
	―――
Gross profit	175
Distribution costs	(35)
Administrative expenses	(8)
	―――
Profit from operations	132
	―――
Finance costs	(18)
	―――
Profit before tax	114
Income tax expense	(42)
	―――
Profit after tax	72
	―――

The expenses can be analysed as follows:

	£000
Wages	72
Auditors remuneration	12
Depreciation	84
Cost of materials used	222
Profit on disposal of non-current assets	(60)
Rental income	(18)
	―――
	312
	―――

The following information is also available:

	30/09/09	30/09/08
	£000	£000
Inventories	42	24
Receivables	48	42
Payables	(30)	(18)

Required:

Prepare the cash generated from operations using the direct method for the year ended 30 September 20X9, conforming to the requirements of IAS 7, in so far as this is possible from the information given.

Solution

Y Plc Statement of cash flows for the year ended 30 September 20X9.

Cash flows from operating activities	£000
Cash receipts from customers (W1)	438
Rental income	18
Cash payments to suppliers (W2)	(228)
Cash payments to employees	(72)
Cash payments for expenses	(12)
	___
Cash generated from operations	144
	___

(W1)
Cash receipts from customers

Opening receivables	42
Revenue	444
Closing receivables	(48)
	___
Cash received from customers	438
	___

(W2)
Cash payments to suppliers

Opening inventories	24
Purchases (bal figure)	240
Closing inventories	(42)
	___
Cost of materials used	222
	___
Opening payables	18
Purchases (above)	240
Closing Payables	(30)
	___
Payments to suppliers	228
	___

The remaining parts of the cash flow will be the produced in the same way as shown in the previous example.

Activity 1

Extracts from the accounts of Deuce showed balances as follows:

	20X9	20X8
Share capital £1	300,000	120,000
Share premium	260,000	100,000

During 20X9 loan notes of £300,000 were issued at par. Interest of £12,000 was also paid during the year. What is the net cash inflow from financing activities?

A £480,000

B £605,000

C £617,000

D £640,000

 Activity 2

A draft statement of cash flows contains the following:

	£m
Profit before tax	22
Depreciation	8
Increase in inventories	(4)
Decrease in receivables	(3)
Increase in payables	(2)
Net cash inflow from operating activities	21

Which of the following corrections needs to be made to the calculations?

(1) Depreciation should be deducted, not added.

(2) Increase in inventories should be added, not deducted.

(3) Decrease in receivables should be added, not deducted.

(4) Increase in payables should be added, not deducted.

A (1) and (2)

B (1) and (3)

C (2) and (4)

D (3) and (4)

4 More complex areas

4.1 Introduction

In many cases the figures for the statement of cash flow can be found simply by comparing the opening and closing statement of financial positions. However in other instances a slightly more involved approach is required.

4.2 Interest paid

Care must be taken as the interest charge in the income statement may not always be the amount of cash paid in interest. If there are accruals for interest payable in the statement of financial position then either a ledger account working will be required in order to determine the interest paid or the alternative working shown.

Example

The interest charge in a company's income statement is £300.The statement of financial position shows the following figures under current liabilities.

	Opening statement of financial position £	Closing statement of financial position £
Interest payable	120	150

What is the amount of interest paid in the year?

Solution

Interest payable

	£
Opening liability	120
Income statement charge	300
Closing liability	(150)
	———
Interest paid (bal fig)	270
	———

4.3   Tax paid

A similar method is used in order to determine the amount of tax paid during a year.

A ledger account is opened for tax. The opening and closing payables for tax and are entered together with the relevant income statement figures and the amount of cash paid is the balancing figure.

If you see a deferred tax balance in the statement of financial position then the opening and closing balance must also be included in your ledger account working. Usually, this is a liability so is shown in the same way as the corporation tax payable.

Example

Given below are extracts from the income statement and statement of financial positions for a business.

Income statement

	£000
Profit before tax	1,300
Tax	(400)
Profit after tax	900

	Opening statement of financial position	Closing statement of financial positions
	£	£
Current liabilities		
Taxation	360	500

What figures should appear in the statement of cash flow for tax paid?

Tax payable

	£
Opening liability	360
Income statement charge	400
Closing liability	(500)
Tax paid (bal fig)	260

4.4 Non-current assets and depreciation

Further calculation problems can arise when trying to find the relevant figures for non-current assets and depreciation.

The depreciation charge for the year is required in order to add back to operating profit. Any additions to non-current assets are also cash outflows and they may also have to be calculated.

Again the technique is to use either a ledger account for non-current assets at cost and for accumulated depreciation and to enter into these accounts all of the relevant figures from the question or to use the alternative working shown.

Example

Given below are extracts from the opening and closing statement of financial positions for a company.

	Opening statement of financial position £000	Closing statement of financial positions £000
Non-current assets at cost	1,000	1,100
Accumulated depreciation	(400)	(480)
Carrying value	600	620

You are also told that an asset which had cost £150,000 and on which £90,000 of accumulated depreciation had been charged was sold during the year for £50,000.

What are the figures for depreciation, profit or loss on disposal and additions to non-current assets for the statement of cash flow?

Solution

Purchase of PPE

	£000
PPE at start	1,000
Less disposal	(150)
PPE at end	(1,100)
PPE additions	250

Now to find the depreciation charge for the year by using the same technique.

Depreciation charge

	£000
Accumulated depreciation at start	400
Less depreciation on disposal	(90)
Accumulated depreciation at end	(480)
Charge in the year	170

Therefore the depreciation charge for the year is £170,000 to be added back to operating profit.

Finally any profit or loss on disposal can be found as follows:

Loss on disposal

	£000
PPE cost	150
Less accumulated depreciation	(90)
Less cash proceeds	(50)
Loss on disposal	10

4.5 Non-current assets at carrying value

In some tasks you are only given the carrying value of the non-current assets rather than separate cost and accumulated depreciation information.

In such questions you may need to find either the depreciation charge for the year or the additions. Again this is done in a similar fashion to before but you must now combine the cost and accumulated depreciation workings, as follows:

	£
PPE CV at start	X
Revaluations during year	X
CV of disposals	(X)
Depreciation charge	(X)
PPE CV at end	(X)
PPE additions	X

Example

Given below is an extract from the opening and closing statement of financial positions of a company.

	Opening statement of financial position	Closing statement of financial positions
	£000	£000
Non-current assets carrying value	3000	3,200

During the year assets with a carrying value of £100,000 were sold and assets costing £650,000 were purchased. What is the depreciation charge for the year?

Solution

Purchase of PPE

	£000
PPE at start	3,000
Additions	650
Less disposal	(100)
PPE at end	(3,200)
	———
PPE depreciation charge	350
	———

4.6   Provisions

In some tasks you might find a provision in the statement of financial position. Any increase or decrease in a provision is not a cash flow and therefore the increase or decrease should be dealt with by adjusting the operating profit. An increase in provision will be added back to profit and a decrease will be deducted.

Activity 3

Fallen plc

Fallen plc has prepared the following draft accounts for the year ended 31 December 20X8.

Income Statement	£000
Revenue	11,019
Cost of sales	(5,502)
Gross profit	5,517
Distribution costs	(402)
Administrative expenses	(882)
Profit from operations	4,233
Finance costs	(152)
Profit before tax	4,081
Taxation	(1,531)
Profit after tax	2,550

Statement of financial positions	31 December	
	20X8	20X7
	£000	£000
ASSETS		
Non-current assets		
Property plant and equipment (CV)	11,640	9,480
Current assets		
Inventories	2,880	1,986
Trade receivables	2,586	1,992
Short-term investments at cost	2,406	2,208
Bank	–	576
	7,872	6,762
Total assets	**19,512**	**16,242**

EQUITY AND LIABILITIES
Equity

Share capital (25p ordinary)	2,280	1,800
Share premium	2,112	1,800
Retained earnings	9,498	6,948
Total equity	13,890	10,548
Non-current liabilities		
Debentures (10%)	1,240	1,800
	1,240	1,800
Current liabilities		
Trade and other payables	2,228	1,718
Overdraft	222	0
Taxation	1,932	2,176
	4,382	3,894
Total liabilities	5,622	5,694
Total equity and liabilities	**19,512**	**16,242**

The following data is relevant.

1   The 10% debentures redeemed during the year were redeemed at par.

2   Plant and equipment with a carrying value of £276,000 was sold for £168,000 giving a loss on disposal of £108,000. New plant was purchased for £2,500,000.

3   Depreciation charged for the year was £1,364,000.

4   Leasehold premises costing £1,300,000 were acquired during the year.

Required:

Prepare the statement of cash flow for 20X8 in accordance with IAS 7.

5 Interpretation of a cash flow

5.1 Introduction

A common exam question is to be asked to prepare a statement of cash flows and then have to comment on what it tells us about a company's performance.

This is relatively straightforward to do and is a way the Examiner can be sure that candidates understand what the cash flow shows.

The best approach to take when interpreting a cash flow is to work through each of the headings in the cash flow in turn. You need to look for large changes in the balances compared to the previous year or any figure that seems to stand out.

5.2 Net cash from operating activities

Operating cash flow is very important to a business as this reflects how well it is generating cash from its day to day activities. A negative operating cash flow is not good and would suggest that the business is not operating efficiently. This would lead you to look at the cash flow from working capital – inventories, receivables and payables.

Also, compare the operating cash flow to the profit from operations to establish the quality of profits. The higher the cash from operations in relation to profit from operations, the better quality of profits as most of it is being converted into cash.

5.3 Working capital

Another easy comment to make is the effect of working capital on the company's cash position. If a company has moved from being cash positive in the previous period to cash negative in the current period then look at the movements on working capital.

For example, you may see that inventories have risen as the company has increased inventory levels, thus spending cash. It may be that receivables have increased which suggests potential inefficiency in credit control procedures. If trade payables have increased then this suggests that the company has not paid its suppliers which is good for cash flow but potentially harmful for supplier relations.

5.4   Purchase of non-current assets

This section of the cash flow deals with the company's investments for the long term. A cash outflow now may bring benefits in the future.

If a company has made an investment in non-current assets, then they are obviously planning for the future which is a positive move. You must also comment on how they have financed this investment. If they are cash rich they may manage to purchase the assets out of cash. Watch out for an increasing overdraft as this is an expensive form of finance and should not be used in the long term.

Other methods of financing the purchase could be an issue of share capital which is a cheap method of raising finance and encourages new investors into the business. Alternatively, the business may take out a loan. This is a common method of financing assets, but the business will now need to pay the interest on the loan.

5.5   Sale of non-current assets

A company may sell non-current assets because they are old or obsolete. Often the cash flow will show the sale of assets and the purchase of new assets as the business is updating its facilities.

However, if the company's cash flow is looking severely depleted, the sale of non-current assets may be a desperate measure to raise cash. Whilst this will get cash into the business it is not a good idea in the long term as the business will not have the assets to continue operating.

5.6   Financing

In the financing section you can comment on issues of new shares and loan transactions. A share issue is a means of raising finance for expansion of the business. You may be able to relate this to non-current asset purchases in the investing section.

As with the share issue, if you see that there has been increased loan finance, then try and establish why the loan has been taken out. This may point you in the direction of non-current asset purchases or perhaps to fund the expansion of the business. You can also look at the level of interest payable to see the effect of an increase in the income statement.

If debt has decreased then the business may have had surplus cash and decided to reduce interest payments by repaying the debt. This is a strong position to be in.

Dividend payments will also be seen in the financing section of the cash flow. You must ensure that there is sufficient cash available to pay the dividend without the company having to rely on overdrafts. Many companies are not keen on reducing dividend payments to shareholders as it sends a sign that the business is not performing well.

 Activity 4

Oxford Ltd

Oxford Ltd has been trading for five years using a patented recipe for apple sauce. You are given the following information.

	30 June 20X8			30 June 20X7		
	Cost	Depn	CV	Cost	Depn	CV
Assets	£	£	£	£	£	£
Freehold factory	142,000	–	142,000	142,000	–	142,000
Plant and machinery	121,800	(47,500)	74,300	99,000	(48,300)	50,700
Patents	2,000	–	2,000	2,000	–	2,000
	265,800	(47,500)	218,300	243,000	(48,300)	194,700
Current assets						
Inventories		11,100			10,000	
Trade receivables		11,000			7,500	
Short-term investments		13,000			–	
Balance at bank		7,100			2,100	
			42,200			19,600
Total assets			260,500			214,300
Equity						
Share capital			115,000			100,000
Share premium			15,000			10,000
Retained earnings			76,200			51,000
Total equity			206,200			161,000

Non-current liabilities		
(8% debentures)	40,000	40,000
	40,000	40,000
Current liabilities		
Trade payables	13,400	12,600
Taxation	900	700
	14,300	13,300
Total liabilities	54,300	53,300
Total equity and liabilities	260,500	214,300

Summary income statement for the year ended 30 June 20X8

	£
Revenue	244,400
Cost of sales	(160,900)
Gross profit	83,500
Administrative expenses	(53,800)
Profit from operations	29,700
Finance costs	(3,200)
Profit before taxation	26,500
Taxation	(1,300)
Profit after taxation	25,200

During the year the company disposed of five apple-bashing machines for a total of £4,200 and replaced them with more modern machinery.

The old machines were standing in the books at a cost of £14,000 with accumulated depreciation of £12,600.

The profit made on the sale has been credited to the income statement.

All purchases and disposals of plant and machinery were settled in cash during the year.

The short-term investment is a one-month bank deposit.

Required:

Prepare a statement of cash flow for the year ended 30 June 20X8.

Activity 5

Springwell Ltd

You have been asked to prepare the statement of cash flows and statement of changes in equity for Springwell Ltd for the year ended 31 May 20X8.

The most recent statement of comprehensive income and statement of financial position (with comparatives for the previous year) of Springwell Ltd are set out below.

Springwell Ltd – Statement of comprehensive income for the year ended 31 May 20X8

Continuing operations	£000
Revenue	89,600
Cost of sales	(49,280)
Gross profit	40,320
Dividends received	240
Gain on disposal of property, plant and equipment	896
Distribution costs	(18,816)
Administrative expenses	(8,960)
Profit from operations	13,680
Finance costs	(210)
Profit before tax	13,470
Taxation	(5,768)
Profit for the period from continuing operations	7,702

Springwell Ltd – Statement of financial position as at 31 May 20X8

Statement of financial positions	31 December	
	20X8	20X7
	£000	£000
ASSETS		
Non-current assets		
Property plant and equipment (CV)	55,780	42,680
Current assets		
Inventories	11,828	9,856
Trade and other receivables	8,960	10,752
Cash and cash equivalents	560	0
	21,348	20,608
Total assets	**77,128**	**63,288**
EQUITY AND LIABILITIES		
Equity		
Share capital	9,000	6,000
Share premium	6,000	4,000
Retained earnings	48,432	41,284
Total equity	**63,432**	**51,284**
Non-current liabilities		
Bank loans	3,000	1,000
	3,000	1,000
Current liabilities		
Trade payables	4,928	8,870
Tax liabilities	5,768	1,774
Bank overdraft	0	360
	10,696	11,004
Total liabilities	**13,696**	**12,004**
Total equity and liabilities	**77,128**	**63,288**

Further information:

1   The total depreciation charge for the year was £8,916,000.

2   Property, plant and equipment costing £1,756,000 with accumulated depreciation of £668,000 was sold in the year.

3   All sales and purchases were on credit. Other expenses were paid for in cash.

4   A dividend of £554,000 was paid during the year.

6 Summary

A statement of cash flow provides information additional to that contained in the statement of comprehensive income and statement of financial position. It is an obligatory disclosure for all except small companies.

The content of a statement of cash flow is governed by IAS 7.

Answers to chapter activities

Activity 1

Answer is D

	£
Issue of shares (560,000 – 220,000)	340,000
Issue of loan notes	300,000
	640,000

Interest paid is included within the 'operating activities' heading of the cash flow.

Activity 2

Answer is D

Depreciation is a non-cash expense and should therefore be added back to profit.

An increase in assets (inventory and receivables) means that less cash is available (as it has been used to fund assets), hence an increase in assets is shown as a deduction in the statement of cashflow.

An increase in liabilities (payables) means that more cash is available (i.e. it has not been used to pay liabilities), hence an increase in liabilities is shown as an addition in the statement of cashflow.

Activity 3

Fallen plc

Statement of cash flow for the year ended 31 December 20X8

Cash from operating activities	£000	£000
Profit from operations	4,233	
Adjustments for:		
Depreciation charges (note 3 from question)	1,364	
Loss on disposal (note 2 from question)	108	
	5,705	
Increase in inventories (2,880 – 1,986)	(894)	
Increase in trade receivables (2,586 – 1,992)	(594)	
Increase in trade payables (2,228 – 1,718)	510	
Cash generated from operations	4,727	
Interest paid	(152)	
Tax paid (W1)	(1,775)	
Net cash from operating activities		2,800
Cash flows from investing activities		
Purchase of property, plant and equipment (note 2 and 4 from question)	(3,800)	
Proceeds from sale of equipment (note 2 from question)	168	
Net cash used in investing activities		(3,632)
Cash flows from financing activities		
Proceeds from issue of shares (4,392 -3,600)	792	
Redemption of loan (1,240 – 1,800)	(560)	
Net cash used in financing activities		232
Net decrease in cash and cash equivalents		(600)
Cash and cash equivalents at beginning of period		2,784
Cash and cash equivalents at end of period		2,184

Tax payable

	£
Opening liability	2,176
Income statement charge	1,531
Closing liability	(1,932)
Tax paid (bal fig)	1,775

Activity 4

Oxford Ltd

Statement of cash flow for the year ended 30 June 20X8

Cash from operating activities	£000	£000
Profit from operations	29,700	
Adjustments for:		
Depreciation charges (W1)	11,800	
Profit on disposal (W2)	(2,800)	
	38,700	
Increase in inventories (£11,100 – £10,000)	(1,100)	
Increase in trade and other receivables (£11,000 – £7,500)	(3,500)	
Increase in trade payables (£13,400 – £12,600)	800	
Cash generated from operations	34,900	
Tax paid (W3)	(1,100)	
Finance costs (Note 1)	(3,200)	
Net cash from operating activities		30,600
Cash flows from investing activities		
Purchase of property, plant and equipment (W4)	(36,800)	
Proceeds from sale of equipment	4,200	
Net cash used in investing activities		(32,600)
Cash flows from financing activities		
Proceeds from issue of shares (W5)	20,000	
Net cash used in financing activities		20,000
Net decrease in cash and cash equivalents		18,000
Cash and cash equivalents at beginning of period		2,100
Cash and cash equivalents at end of period (13,000 + 7,100)		20,100

Workings

(W1) Depreciation charge

	£000
Accumulated depreciation at start	48,300
Less depreciation on disposal	(12,600)
Accumulated depreciation at end	(47,500)
Charge in the year	11,800

(W2) Profit or loss on disposal

	£000
Plant and machinery at cost	14,000
Less accumulated depreciation	(12,600)
Less cash proceeds	(4,200)
Profit on disposal	2,800

(W3) Tax paid

	£000
Tax payables b/d	700
Tax charge for year	1,300
Tax payables c/d	(900)
Tax paid	1,100

(W4) Plant and machinery

	£000
Plant and machinery at start	99,000
Less disposal	(14,000)
Plant and machinery at end	(121,800)
Plant and machinery additions	36,800

(W5) Issue of shares for cash

	£ 20X8	£ 20X7	£ Increase
Share capital	115,000	100,000	15,000
Share premium	15,000	10,000	5,000
Proceeds of share issue			20,000

Note 1:

As there is no opening or closing interest (finance cost) payable, the interest paid must equal the expense for the year recognised in the income statement.

Activity 5

Springwell Ltd

Statement of cash flow for the year ended 30 June 20X8

	£000	£000
Cash from operating activities		
Profit from operations	13,680	
Adjustments for:		
Depreciation charges	8,916	
Gain on disposal of property, plant and equipment	(896)	
Dividends received	(240)	
	21,460	
Increase in inventories (11,828-9,856)	(1,972)	
Decrease in trade receivables (8,960-10,752)	1,792	
Decrease in trade payables (4,928-8,870)	(3,942)	
Cash generated from operations	17,338	
Tax paid (W1)	(1,774)	
Interest paid	(210)	
Net cash from operating activities		15,354
Cash flows from investing activities		
Purchase of property, plant and equipment (W3)	(23,104)	
Proceeds from disposal of property, plant and equipment (W2)	1,984	
Dividends received	240	
Net cash used in investing activities		(20,880)
Cash flows from financing activities		
Proceeds from issue of shares (W4)	5,000	
New bank loans raised	2,000	
Dividends paid	(554)	
Net cash used in financing activities		6,446
Net increase/(decrease) in cash and cash equivalents		920
Cash and cash equivalents at beginning of period		(360)
Cash and cash equivalents at end of period		560

Workings

(W1) Tax paid

	£000
Tax payables b/d	1,774
Tax charge for year	5,768
Tax payables c/d	(5,768)
	———
Tax paid	1,774
	———

(W2) Disposal proceeds

	£000
PPE at cost	1,756
Less accumulated depreciation	(668)
Add gain on disposal	896
	———
Cash proceeds	1,984
	———

(W3) Plant and machinery additions CV

	£000
Plant and machinery at start	42,680
Less disposal	(1,088)
Less Depreciation charge	(8,916)
Plant and machinery at end	(55,780)
	———
Plant and machinery additions	23,104
	———

(W4) Issue of shares for cash

	£ 20X8	£ 20X7	£ Increase
Share capital	9,000	6,000	3,000
Share premium	6,000	4,000	2,000
			———
Proceeds of share issue			5,000
			———

Springwell Ltd

Statement of changes in equity

	Share capital £000	Share premium £000	Retained earnings £000	Total £000
At 1 June 20X7	6,000	4,000	41,284	51,284
Profit for the year			7,702	7,702
Dividends paid			(554)	(554)
Issue of share capital	3,000	2,000		5,000
At 31 May 20X8	9,000	6,000	48,432	63,432

7 Test your knowledge

Workbook Activity 6

The financial statements of Flyingdales Ltd for the year ended 31 March 20X1 include:

Statement of comprehensive income	
	£000
Revenue	205,000
Cost of sales	(191,250)
Profit from operations	13,750
Finance costs	(2,150)
Profit before taxation	11,600
Taxation	(2,850)
Profit after tax	8,750

Note: The depreciation charge for the year was £6.5m. There had been no disposals of non-current assets in the year.

Statement of financial position at 31 March		
	20X1	20X0
ASSETS	£000	£000
Property, plant and equipment	73,000	70,500
Current assets		
Inventories	27,500	25,500
Trade receivables	37,500	33,000
Cash and cash equivalents	4,250	1,250
	69,250	59,750
Total Assets	142,250	130,250

EQUITY AND LIABILTIES

Equity:

Share capital	11,610	10,000
Retained earnings	74,790	66,040
	86,400	76,040
Non-current liabilities		
10% debenture	21,500	20,000
	21,500	20,000
Current liabilities		
Trade payables	31,500	31,950
Taxation	2,850	2,260
	34,350	34,210
Total liabilities	55,850	54,210
Total equity and liabilities	142,250	130,250

Task 1

Provide a reconciliation of profit from operations to net cash from operating activities for Flyingdales Ltd for the year ended 31 March 20X1.

Task 2

Using the proforma below prepare the statement of cash flow for Flyingdales Ltd for the year ended 31 March 20X1.

Flyingdales Ltd

Company statement of cash flow for the year ended 31 March 20X1.

	£000
Net cash from operating activities	
Investing activities	
	_____
Net cash used in investing activities	
	_____
Financing activities	
	_____
Net cash from financing activities	
	_____
Net increase/(decrease) in cash and cash equivalents	
Cash and cash equivalents at beginning of year	
	_____
Cash and cash equivalents at end of year	
	_____

Workings

(W1) **Purchase of property, plant and equipment:**

	£000

Workbook Activity 7

Data

You have been asked to prepare the statement of cashflow for Eigg Ltd for the year ended 31 March 2008.

The most recent income statement and statements of financial position of Eigg Ltd for the past two years are set out below.

Eigg Ltd –income statement for the year ended 31 March 2008

	£000
Continuing operations	
Revenue	44,800
Cost of sales	(24,640)
Gross profit	20,160
Dividends received	120
Gain on the disposal of plant and equipment	448
Distribution costs	(9,408)
Administrative expenses	(4,480)
Profit from operations	6,840
Finance costs	(105)
Profit before taxation	6,735
Tax	(2,884)
Profit for the period from continuing operations	3,851

Eigg Ltd – Statement of financial position at 31 March

	2008 £000	2007 £000
ASSETS		
Non-current assets		
Property, plant and equipment	27,890	21,340
Current assets		
Inventories	5,914	4,928
Trade and other receivables	4,480	5,376
Cash and cash equivalents	280	
Total assets	38,564	31,644
Equity and Liabilities		
Equity		
Share capital	4,500	3,000
Share premium	3,000	2,000
Retained earnings	24,216	20,642
Total equity	31,716	25,642
Non-current liabilities		
Bank loans	1,500	500
Current liabilities		
Trade and other payables	2,464	4,435
Tax liability	2,884	887
Bank overdraft	0	180
Total equity and liabilities	38,564	31,644

You have been given the following further information:

- The total depreciation charge for the year was £4,458,000.

- Property, plant and equipment costing £878,000 with accumulated depreciation of £334,000 was sold in the year.

- All sales and purchases were on credit. Other expenses were paid for in cash.

- A dividend of £277,000 was paid during the year.

Task 1

Prepare a reconciliation of profit from operations to net cash from operating activities for Eigg Ltd for the year ended 31 March 2008.

Task 2

Using the proforma below prepare the statement of cash flow for Eigg Ltd for the year ended 31 March 2008.

Eigg Ltd

Company statement of cash flow for the year ended 31 March 2008.

£000

Net cash from operating activities

Investing activities

————

Net cash used in investing activities

————

Financing activities

————

Net cash (used in)/from financing activities

————

Net increase/(decrease) in cash and cash equivalents

Cash and cash equivalents at beginning of year

————

Cash and cash equivalents at end of year

————

Workings

(W1) **Proceeds of property, plant and equipment:**

	£000
	————
Proceeds	

(W2) **Purchase of property, plant and equipment:**

	£000
	————
PPE Additions	

Workbook Activity 8

Data

You have been asked to prepare a statement of cash flows for Adlington Ltd for the year ended 31 October 20X9.

The most recent income statement and statements of financial position of the company for the past two years are set out below.

Adlington Ltd
Income statement for the year ended 31 October 20X9

	£000
Continuing operations	
Revenue	45,500
Cost of sales	(27,300)
Gross profit	18,200
Gain on disposal of property, plant and equipment	455
Distribution costs	(6,825)
Administrative expenses	(5,005)
Profit from operations	6,825
Finance costs	(595)
Profit before tax	6,230
Tax	(1,757)
Profit for the period from continuing operations	4,473

Adlington Ltd
Statement of financial position at 31 October

	20X9	20X8
	£000	£000
ASSETS		
Non-current assets		
Property, plant and equipment	31,989	22,246
Current assets		
Inventories	6,552	4,914
Trade and other receivables	4,550	4,641
Cash and cash equivalents	450	0
Total assets	43,541	31,801
EQUITY AND LIABILITIES		
Equity		
Share capital	10,000	8,000
Share premium	4,000	3,000
Retained earnings	15,462	10,989
Total equity	29,462	21,989
Non-current liabilities		
Bank loans	8,500	3,500
Current liabilities		
Trade and other payables	3,822	4,368
Tax liability	1,757	658
Bank overdraft	0	1,286
Total liabilities	14,079	9,812
Total equity and liabilities	43,541	31,801

Further information:

- The total depreciation charge for the year was £4,398,000.

- Property, plant and equipment costing £568,000 with accumulated depreciation of £226,000 was sold in the year.

- All sales and purchases were on credit. Other expenses were paid for in cash.

Task 1

Prepare a reconciliation of profit from operations to net cash from operating activities for Adlington Ltd for the year ended 31 October 20X9.

Task 2

Using the proforma below prepare the statement of cashflow for Adlington Ltd for the year ended 31 October 20X9.

Adlington Ltd

Company statement of cash flow for the year ended 31 October 20X9.

	£000
Net cash from operating activities	
Investing activities	
	———
Net cash used in investing activities	
	———
Financing activities	
	———
Net cash (used in)/from financing activities	
	———
Net increase/(decrease) in cash and cash equivalents	
Cash and cash equivalents at beginning of year	
	———
Cash and cash equivalents at end of year	
	———

Workings

(W1) **Proceeds of property, plant and equipment:**

	£000
	———
Proceeds	

(W2) **Purchase of property, plant and equipment:**

	£000
	———
PPE Additions	

Interpretation of accounts

Introduction

It is likely that every exam will include some task which asks you to apply ratio analysis to company financial statements and analyse and interpret the results.

KNOWLEDGE

Explain how to calculate accounting ratios – profitability, liquidity, efficiency, financial position (4.2)

Explain the inter relationships between ratios (4.3)

Explain the purpose of the interpretation of ratios (4.4)

Describe how the interpretation and analysis of accounting ratios is used in a business environment (4.5)

SKILLS

Calculate and interpret the relationship between the elements of the financial statements with regard to profitability, liquidity, efficient use of resources and financial position (3.1)

Draw valid conclusions from the information contained within the financial statements (3.2)

Present clearly and concisely issues, analysis and conclusions to the appropriate people (3.3)

CONTENTS

1 Profitability ratios

1.1 Introduction

Ratios calculated from financial statements help to interpret the information they present. Various users may use these ratios to analyse financial statements.

We can break down the ratios into categories to make our discussion more structured. To begin with we look at ratios relating to profitability.

1.2 Return on capital employed (ROCE)

Capital employed is normally measured as non-current assets plus current assets less current liabilities or total equity + non-current liabilities and represents the long-term investment in the business, or owners' capital plus long-term liabilities. Return on capital employed is frequently regarded as the best measure of profitability, indicating how successful a business is in utilising its assets. The ratio is only meaningful when the true values of assets are known and used in the formula.

$$\text{Return on capital employed} = \frac{\text{Profit from operations}}{\text{Total equity} \pm \text{Non-current liabilities}} \times 100$$

A low return on capital employed (assets used) is caused by either a low profit margin or a low asset turnover or both.

This can be seen by breaking down the primary ROCE ratio into its two components operating profit percentage and asset turnover.

1.3 Operating profit percentage

$$\text{Operating profit percentage} = \frac{\text{Profit from operations}}{\text{Revenue}} \times 100$$

A low margin indicates low selling prices or high costs or both. Comparative analysis will reveal the level of prices and costs in relation to competitors.

1.4 Return on total assets

This will show how fully a company is utilising its assets.

$$\text{Return on total assets} = \frac{\text{Profit from operations}}{\text{Total assets}} \times 100$$

A low turnover shows that a company is not generating a sufficient volume of business for the size of the asset base. This may be remedied by increasing sales or by disposing of some of the assets or both.

1.5 Gross profit percentage

$$\text{Gross profit percentage} = \frac{\text{Gross profit}}{\text{Revenue}} \times 100\%$$

The gross profit percentage focuses on the trading account. A low margin could indicate selling prices too low or cost of sales too high.

1.6 Return on equity

$$\text{Return on owners' equity} = \frac{\text{Profit after tax}}{\text{Total equity}} \times 100\%$$

This looks at the return earned for ordinary shareholders. We use the profit after preference dividends and interest (i.e. the amounts that have to be paid before ordinary shareholders can be rewarded).

1.7 Expense/revenue percentage

$$\text{Expense/revenue percentage} = \frac{\text{Specified expense}}{\text{Revenue}} \times 100$$

The expenses/revenue percentage focuses on individual expenses in relation to revenue.

1.8 Earnings per share

This ratio is used primarily by potential investors. It is, however, a very important ratio and it is required that listed companies disclose the figure for earnings per share at the foot of the statement of comprehensive income.

$$\text{Earnings per share} = \frac{\text{Profit after tax}}{\text{Number of issued ordinary shares}}$$

The calculation is regulated by IAS 33 and shows how much profit 'earnings' the ordinary shareholders have made on a pence per share basis.

2 Liquidity ratios

2.1 Current ratio

This is a common method of analysing working capital (net current assets) and is generally accepted as a good measure of short-term solvency. It indicates the extent to which the claims of short-term payables are covered by assets that are expected to be converted to cash in a period roughly corresponding to the maturity of the claims.

$$\text{Current ratio} = \frac{\text{Current assets}}{\text{Current liabilities}}$$

The current ratio should ideally fall between 1:1 and 2:1.

2.2 Acid test ratio (quick ratio)

This is calculated in the same way as the current ratio except that inventories are excluded from current assets.

$$\text{Acid test ratio} = \frac{\text{Current assets} - \text{Inventories}}{\text{Current liabilities}}$$

This ratio is a much better test of the immediate solvency of a business because of the length of time necessary to convert inventories into cash (via revenue and receivables).

Contrary to what might be expected, this ratio may fall in a time of prosperity since increased activity may lead to larger inventories but less cash; conversely, when trade slows down inventories may be disposed of without renewal and the ratio will rise.

Although increased liquid resources more usually indicate favourable trading, it could be that funds are not being used to their best advantage (e.g. large cash balance).

3 Use of resources

3.1 Trade receivables collection period

This is computed by dividing the trade receivables by the average daily sales to determine the number of days sales held in receivables. It is usually calculated as:

$$\text{Average collection period} = \frac{\text{Trade receivables}}{\text{Revenue}} \times 365 \text{ days}$$

A long average collection period probably indicates poor credit control, but it may be due to other factors such as overseas sales where the collection period will be much longer, or a deliberate decision to extend the credit period to attract new customers.

3.2 Trade payables payment period

This is computed by dividing the trade payables by the average daily purchases to determine the number of days purchases held in payables.

$$\text{Average payment period} = \frac{\text{Trade payable}}{\text{Cost of sales}} \times 365 \text{ days}$$

If only cost of sales rather than purchases is available in the information given this can be used as an approximation to purchases. If the payables period is very low, then the business might not be making the best use of its cash by paying suppliers early. If the period is very long then this is a free source of credit but the business must be careful not to harm relations with suppliers.

3.3 Inventory turnover

This ratio indicates whether inventory levels are justified in relation to cost of sales. The higher the ratio, the healthier the cash flow position, but with the qualification that the profit margin must also be acceptable.

$$\text{Inventory turnover} = \frac{\text{Cost of sales}}{\text{Inventories}}$$

It is usual to calculate this ratio using the closing inventories. A limitation on this ratio is that in a seasonal business inventories may fluctuate considerably during the year. The level of inventory turnover will vary between businesses. A retailer will have a fairly fast inventory turnover as goods are bought and sold fairly quickly. A manufacturing company will have a much slower inventory turnover as inventory is held in the business much longer as it goes through the production process.

3.4 Inventory holding period in days

Inventory turnover can also be calculated in days like receivables and payables.

$$\text{Inventory turnover period} = \frac{\text{Inventories}}{\text{Cost of sales}} \times 365 \text{ days}$$

3.5 Asset turnover

$$\text{Asset turnover (total assets)} = \frac{\text{Revenue}}{\text{Total assets}}$$

OR

$$\text{Asset turnover (net assets)} = \frac{\text{Revenue}}{\text{Total assets} - \text{current liabilities}}$$

This is a measure of how fully a company is utilising its assets.

A low turnover shows that a company is not generating a sufficient volume of business for the size of the asset base. This may be remedied by increasing sales or by disposing of some of the assets or both.

3.6 Working capital cycle

Inventory days + Receivable days – Payable days

This is the length of time between paying out cash for inventory and receiving the cash for goods or services supplied.

4 Financial position

4.1 Gearing

Gearing measures the extent to which a business is dependent on non-equity funds, as opposed to equity funding. A high gearing ratio means that the business has a high proportion of borrowed funds in its total capital.

Gearing gives an indication of long-term liquidity and the financial risk inherent within the business. Highly geared companies have to meet large interest commitments before paying dividends and may have problems raising further finance if expansion is necessary.

$$\text{Gearing} = \frac{\text{Non-current liabilities}}{\text{Total equity} + \text{Non-current liabilities}} \times 100$$

4.2 Interest cover

$$\text{Interest cover} = \frac{\text{Profit from operations}}{\text{Finance costs}}$$

Interest on debt has to be paid before shareholders can receive dividends. Therefore a good measure of risk is to compare available profit with the amount of interest to be paid.

 Example

Fieldsomer Ltd

Data

Maurice Sun plans to invest in Fieldsomer Ltd.

This is a chain of shops. He is to meet his consultants to discuss the profitability of the company.

To prepare for the meeting he has asked you to comment on the change in profitability and the return on capital of the company.

He also has some questions about the company's statement of financial position.

He has given you Fieldsomer's statement of comprehensive income statements and the summarised statement of financial position for the past two years prepared for internal purposes. These are set out below.

Fieldsomer Ltd
Summary Statement of Comprehensive Income
for the year ended 31 March

	20X4 £000	20X3 £000
Continuing operations		
Revenue	8,420	7,595
Cost of sales	(3,536)	(3,418)
Gross profit	4,884	4,177
Distribution costs	(1,471)	(1,016)
Administrative expenses	(1,224)	(731)
Profit from operations	2,189	2,430
Finance costs	(400)	(480)
Profit before tax	1,789	1,950
Tax	(465)	(569)
Profit for the period from continuing operations	1,324	1,381

Fieldsomer Ltd
Summary Statement of Financial Position as at 31 March

	20X4 £000	20X3 £000
ASSETS		
Non-current assets		
Property, plant and equipment	15,132	13,880
Current assets	4,624	3,912
Total assets	**19,756**	**17,792**
EQUITY AND LIABILITIES		
Equity		
Ordinary shares of £1 each	6,000	5,000
Share premium	2,000	1,000
Retained earnings	4,541	3,937
Total equity	12,541	9,937
Non-current liabilities		
Long term loan	5,000	6,000
Current liabilities	2,215	1,855
Total liabilities	7,215	7,855
Total equity and liabilities	**19,756**	**17,792**

Prepare a report for Maurice Sun that includes:

(a) a calculation of the following ratios of Fieldsomer Ltd for each of the two years:

    (i) return on capital employed

    (ii) operating profit percentage

    (iii) gross profit percentage

    (iv) asset turnover (based on net assets).

(b) an explanation of the meaning of each ratio and a comment on the performance of Fieldsomer Ltd as shown by each of the ratios

(c) a conclusion on how the overall performance has changed over the two years.

Solution

REPORT

To: Maurice Sun **Subject:** Interpretation of financial statements

From: A Student **Date:** June 20X4

This report has been prepared to assist in the interpretation of the financial statements of Fieldsomer Ltd. It considers the profitability and return on capital of the business over 20X3 and 20X4.

(a) **Calculation of the ratios**

	20X4	20X3
Return on capital employed	$\dfrac{2,189}{17,541} \times 100 = 12.5\%$	$\dfrac{2,430}{15,937} \times 100 = 15.2\%$
Operating profit percentage	$\dfrac{2,189}{8,420} \times 100 = 26\%$	$\dfrac{2,430}{7,595} \times 100 = 32\%$
Gross profit percentage	$\dfrac{4,884}{8,420} \times 100 = 58\%$	$\dfrac{4,177}{7,595} \times 100 = 55\%$
Asset turnover	$\dfrac{8,420}{17,541} = 0.48$	$\dfrac{7,595}{15,937} = 0.48$

(b) **Explanation and comment**

Return on capital employed

- This ratio shows in percentage terms how much profit is being generated by the capital employed in the company.

- The company is showing a lower return on capital employed in 20X4 compared to 20X3 and hence is generating less profit per £ of capital employed in the business.

Operating profit percentage

- This ratio shows in percentage terms how much net profit is being generated from revenues.

- The ratio has decreased over the two years.

- This could be explained either by a decrease in the gross profit margin or by an increase in expenses, or both.

- In fact, the ratio of distribution costs and admin expenses as a percentage of revenue has increased from 23% in 20X3 to 32% in 20X4.

20X4:

(1,471 + 1,224)/8,420 × 100

= 32%

20X3:

(1,016 + 731)/7,595 × 100

= 23%

Gross profit percentage

- This ratio shows in percentage terms how much gross profit is being generated from the company's revenues and thus indicates the gross profit margin on sales.

- The ratio has improved over the two years with an increase in the percentage from 55% to 58%.

- The company is increasing its revenue without significantly cutting its margins.

- This may be due to increasing its sales price or reducing the cost of sales or both.

Asset turnover

- This ratio shows how efficient the company is in generating revenue from the available capital employed/net assets.

- The ratio has stayed the same between the two years and so a similar level of revenue has been generated from the available capital employed/net assets in 20X4 than in 20X3.

- The new investment that has been made in property, plant and equipment and current assets in 20X4 has generated a proportional increase in sales

(c) *Overall*

The ratios show that the return on capital employed has deteriorated in 20X4 and that the company is thus generating less profit from the capital employed/net assets. Although there are increased margins there is less control over expenses and this has contributed to the deteriorating position. Control of expenses needs to be addressed by management. The efficiency in the use of assts has remained the same in 20X4 and the increased investment in assets that has taken place in 20X4 has yielded benefits in terms of increased sales.

Regards

AAT Student

5 Answering an exam question

5.1 Introduction

The first stage of answering questions on interpretation is to calculate the ratios; the second is to draw conclusions about the company based on those ratios. It is important to remember that there are limitations to the use of ratios, not the least of which is that a study of the trend of ratios for several years is desirable before drawing firm conclusions about many aspects of a company's position.

The usual question format is to be given two years of statement of comprehensive income and statement of financial position from a company or to compare two different companies. You are then usually asked to:

(i) select the correct formulae for different ratios

(ii) calculate the ratios

(ii) comment on your own calculations or you will be given a separate set of pre-calculated ratios to comment upon

(iii) reach a conclusion based upon your commentary.

When practising calculating the ratios you should produce a table (similar to the one above showing the formulae and the calculation for each year/company).

You must then comment on each ratio in turn giving one sentence on what the ratio shows, one sentence relating the ratio to the user and one sentence that links the ratio to other ratios or absolute figures. You must use this methodical approach in your CBA. This part of the assessment requires human assessment.

When looking for comments review the statement of financial position and the income statement and look for significant movements. For example, if revenue has increased, check that gross profit has increased in line with the increase in revenue. Then you can check receivables, inventories and payables to see what effect the increased trade has had. Often with ratio questions the company has poor working capital management so look for significant worsening in the working capital and liquidity ratios.

Finally if the question asks for a conclusion you must make a sensible assessment based on the points you have made.

6 General points about financial ratios

There are some more points on ratio analysis which should be particularly noted.

6.1 Caution in interpretation

Dogmatic conclusions should be avoided. For example, a reduction in the inventory holding period may be a good thing, but if it is likely to cause loss of customer goodwill or production dislocations due to inventory shortages, it may not be such an advantage. Ratios rarely answer questions but they can highlight areas where questions might usefully be asked.

6.2 Statement of financial position figures

Many of the ratios considered in this chapter involve the use of statement of financial position figures. These ratios should be interpreted with caution since the statement of financial position shows the position at a specific moment only and this may not be typical of the general position.

This point is particularly important where the ratio is derived from a statement of financial position figure in conjunction with a figure from the statement of comprehensive income.

This is because the first figure relates to a moment in time whereas the second is a total for a period. A sensible way to try to avoid possible distortions here is to use the average figure for the statement of financial position figure. So, for example, the receivables collection period would relate credit sales to the average of the trade receivables figures at the beginning and at the end of the year.

However in many industries the existence of recurrent seasonal factors may mean that averaging beginning and end of year figures will not solve the problem.

It may be for example, that the date up to which a business draws up its final accounts has been selected because it is a time when inventory levels are always low, so that inventory is relatively easy to value.

In such cases, averaging the inventory figures for two consecutive year end dates would simply be averaging two figures which were totally untypical of inventory levels throughout the rest of the year. Averaging monthly figures would usually be the solution to this problem. However, outsiders would not typically have access to such information.

6.3 Other financial ratios

There are an almost infinite number of ratios which can be calculated from a set of final accounts. The ones shown above are those most commonly used in practice and include those which have been specifically identified by the FNST study guide. It should be noted, however, that there are many other ratios which could be useful in particular contexts.

6.4 Partial sightedness of ratios

It is usually unwise to limit analysis and interpretation only to information revealed by ratios. For example, revenue for a business could double from one year to the next.

This would be a dramatic and important development, yet none of the ratios whose use is advocated in most textbooks would reveal this, at least not directly.

However, this significant increase in turnover would be fairly obvious from even a superficial glance at the final accounts. There is the danger that excessive reliance on ratios in interpretation and analysis can lead to a 'blinkered' approach.

7 The working capital cycle

7.1 Introduction

The working capital cycle can be illustrated by the following set of activities which underpin the process of manufacture and trade:

- a company acquires inventories on credit;

- inventories are held until sold (or used in production);

- the sale is usually made on credit;

- trade payables need to be paid and cash needs to be collected from trade receivables;

- more inventories are then acquired and the cycle starts again.

The working capital cycle

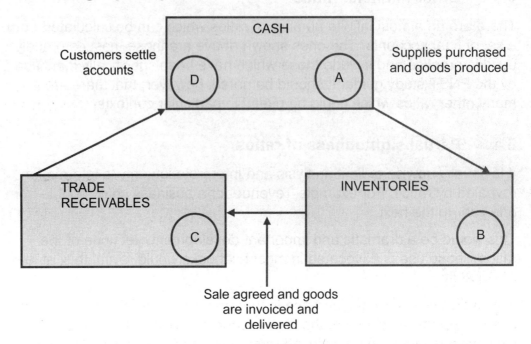

7.2 Effect on cash flows

All of these activities affect cash flows:

- acquisition of inventories on credit helps cash flow temporarily;

- when trade payables are paid cash flows out;

- while inventories are held, and until customers settle, cash is 'tied up', i.e. cash inflow is deferred;

- when customers settle, cash flows in.

The longer the period over which cash is tied up, the greater is the exposure of the firm to exceptional demands for cash. In terms of cash management:

- a working cash balance must be retained at the bank to avoid the bank imposing bank interest and charges;

- any surplus cash in excess of the working balance could be invested in higher interest earning accounts.

The longer the period of time that cash is tied up in working capital the more cost that is incurred by companies either directly, by virtue of bank interest, or indirectly, as a result of the inability to invest cash surpluses into higher interest yielding accounts.

7.3 Working capital management

The company must therefore ensure that inventory levels are watched very carefully and that trade receivables are collected on a timely basis whilst simultaneously monitoring the cash balance to ensure that sufficient funds are held for short-term requirements. Any genuinely surplus funds in excess of a working cash balance should be reinvested in higher interest accounts.

8 Summary

Many ratios can be calculated from a set of financial statements. By comparison with the ratios of other businesses, or of the same business in previous years, it is possible to interpret the messages conveyed by the accounts.

To give structure to your solutions in an assessment it is helpful to analyse ratios under a number of categories. In this chapter we have used the following categories:

* profitability
* liquidity and asset utilisation
* investor ratios
* ratios relating to risk.

Activity 1

Falcon Ltd

The draft accounts of Falcon Ltd for the years ended 30 June 20X8 and 30 June 20X7 are as follows.

Summary statement of financial position

	20X8		20X7	
	£	£	£	£
ASSETS				
Non-current assets				
Freehold premises at cost		125,000		75,000
Plant at cost		130,000		70,000
		255,000		145,000
Current assets				
Inventories		120,000		100,000
Trade receivables		80,000		60,000
		200,000		160,000
Total assets		455,000		305,000
EQUITY AND LIABILITIES				
Equity				
£1 ordinary shares		100,000		50,000
Retained earnings		135,000		120,000
Share premium account		90,000		35,000
Total equity		325,000		205,000
Non-current liabilities				
7% debentures		50,000		50,000
		50,000		50,000
Current liabilities				
Trade payables		45,000		30,000
Bank overdraft		15,000		5,000
Current taxation		20,000		15,000
		80,000		50,000
Total liabilities		130,000		100,000
Total equity and liabilities		455,000		305,000

Statements of comprehensive income extracts

	20X8 £	20X7 £
Continuing operations		
Revenue	525,000	425,000
Cost of sales	(446,500)	(364,000)
Gross profit	78,500	61,000
Administration expenses	(25,000)	(20,000)
Profit from operations	53,500	41,000
Debenture interest	(3,500)	(3,500)
Profit before tax	50,000	37,500
Tax	(20,000)	(15,000)
Profit after tax	30,000	22,500

Note:

Dividends paid (shown in SOCE)	15,000	10,000

Required:

Calculate the following ratios:

- Return on capital employed
- Operating profit percentage
- Asset turnover (net assets)
- Inventory turnover
- Current ratio
- Acid test ratio
- Trade receivables collection period

A comment on the relative performance of the company for the two years based on the ratios calculated and what this tells you about the company.

Activity 2

Big Brother plc

Big Brother plc serves the growing market for electronic security systems and equipment. The accounts for the year ended 31 December 20X8 are summarised below.

Statements of comprehensive income	20X8	20X7
	£000	£000
Revenue	51,882	43,217
Cost of sales	(21,705)	(18,221)
Gross profit	30,177	24,996
Expenses	(17,020)	(14,235)
Profit from operations	13,157	10,761
Finance costs	(4,695)	(3,574)
Profit before tax	8,462	7,187
Taxation	(3,071)	(2,694)
Profit after tax	5,391	4,493

Statement of financial position	20X8		20X7	
	£000	£000	£000	£000
ASSETS				
Non-current assets		62,247		51,457
Current assets				
Inventories	8,159		7,181	
Trade receivables	10,021		8,715	
Cash	3,609	21,789	1,924	17,820
Total assets		84,036		69,277
EQUITY AND LIABILITIES				
Equity				
Called up share capital (see note)		10,000		10,000
Share premium account		11,095		10,217
Retained earnings		9,360		4,669
		30,455		24,886

Non-current liabilities		
Loans	30,105	27,419
Rentals in advance	8,261	4,357
	38,366	31,776
Current liabilities	15,215	12,615
Total liabilities	53,581	44,391
Total equity and liabilities	84,036	69,277

Note 1: Called up share capital

	£000
Authorised	
40,000,000 Ordinary shares of 50p each	20,000
10,000,000 6% Preference shares of £1 each	10,000
	30,000

Issued (all fully paid)	
10,000,000 Ordinary shares of 50p each	5,000
5,000,000 6% Preference shares of £1 each	5,000
	10,000

Note 2: The directors have paid dividends of £700,000 in 20X8 (£600,000 in 20X7)

The directors have asked for your comments about the profitability, liquidity and financial position of the company and have provided you with the following typical industry statistics which have been independently assimilated from the statutory accounts of companies in the security systems and equipment sector.

Gross profit percentage	50%
Operating profit percentage	25%
Current ratio	1.20
Quick ratio	0.90
Gearing	50%
Inventory turnover	3.5
Trade receivables turnover	5.0
Return on capital employed	17%

Required:

In your capacity as a financial advisor write a report for submission to the directors of Big Brother plc.

Activity 3

1   What is the numerator of the formula for return on capital employed?

2   What is the numerator for return on owners' equity?

3   What is the difference between the current ratio and the acid test ratio?

4   What does interest cover measure?

Answers to chapter activities

Activity 1

Falcon Ltd

As a first step, produce a table which shows your ratio calculations.

	20X4	20X3
Return on capital employed	$\frac{53,500}{375,000} \times 100 = 14.27\%$	$\frac{41,000}{255,000} \times 100 = 16.08\%$
Operating profit percentage	$\frac{53,500}{525,000} \times 100 = 10.19\%$	$\frac{41,000}{425,000} \times 100 = 9.65\%$
Asset turnover	$\frac{525,000}{375,000} = 1.4$	$\frac{425,000}{255,000} = 1.67$
Inventory turnover rate	$\frac{446,500}{120,000} = 3.72$	$\frac{364,000}{100,000} = 3.64$
Current ratio	$\frac{200,000}{80,000} = 2.5$	$\frac{160,000}{50,000} = 3.2$
Acid test ratio	$\frac{80,000}{80,000} = 1.0$	$\frac{60,000}{50,000} = 1.2$
Trade receivables collection period	$\frac{80,000}{525,000} \times 365 = 56$ days	$\frac{60,000}{425,000} \times 365 = 52$ days

Comments

Profitability

The return on capital employed has worsened and this is as a result of less efficient use of assets. (The asset turnover has deteriorated whereas the operating profit percentage has improved.)

If we look at the assets individually the inventory turnover and the trade receivables collection period should not have caused any substantial reduction of the asset turnover.

The major change appears to have occurred in the non-current assets where at some point during the year, extra capital has been raised for a major investment in non-current assets.

If these assets were purchased towards the end of the year then this would have made the figure for assets at the year-end unrepresentative of the assets used throughout the year. If we take the average of the beginning and year end assets, the return on capital employed is 16.98%.

Therefore, before we can draw any firm conclusions about the performance of the company, we need further information about the purchase of the non-current assets.

Liquidity

The ratios used to measure liquidity have also worsened during the year.

This is mostly due to a large increase in the overdraft, perhaps to part finance the purchase of the non-current assets.

Once again, it is necessary to establish whether the year-end picture is really representative of the year as a whole before coming to any firm conclusions.

Inventory turnover has remained fairly stable which is good. The receivables collection period has worsened slightly so this is an area the company need to keep under control. This is likely to lead to a further increase in the overdraft if the collection period is allowed to get longer.

Finance

The gearing ratio has been reduced over the year owing entirely to the large amount of share capital raised to finance the purchase of the non-current assets.

There has been no change in the level of the debenture loan so the company has managed to finance the new assets wholly from equity.

KAPLAN PUBLISHING

Activity 2

Big Brother plc

REPORT

To   The Directors, Big Brother plc

From   AN Accountant

Date   20 July 20X9

Subject Big Brother plc – Profitability, liquidity and solvency of the group

(a) **Terms of reference**

This report examines the profitability, liquidity and solvency of Big Brother in 20X7 and 20X8, and recommends necessary action. It is based on financial statements and industry statistics provided. Ratios calculated from the statutory accounts are included in Appendix 1.

(b) **Executive summary**

The group is under-capitalised, highly geared, and approaching a liquidity crisis. It has, however, earned more than sufficient profits in both 20X7 and 20X8 to cover both interest charges and dividends, which suggests that there will be no immediate concerns from lenders or shareholders.

(c) **Profitability**

The gross profit percentage has exceeded the industry norm at the same time as the net margin remained at industry levels. This discrepancy is probably due to non-standard cost allocations between cost of sales and other categories. This would also explain the low inventory turnover ratio.

It is possible that the gross profit percentage are genuinely high, in which case overheads are also high, and savings may be available. A comparison of Big Brother's and the industry's usual cost allocation methods would allow more conclusive analysis.

Return on capital has improved in the year, and is well above industry levels. The apparent improvement is due mainly to the lack of extra long-term finance referred to below, and is not an underlying strength.

(d) **Liquidity**

Liquidity has deteriorated in the period, and the company is exhibiting signs of overtrading, its expansion not being financed by long-term methods.

The company is financing its increased working capital requirements out of rentals in advance. The low industry quick ratio indicates that some reliance on short-term finance is usual, but Big Brother's is excessive.

Unless further long-term finance (e.g. by a rights issue) is raised soon, the company will have liquidity problems.

(e) **Financial position**

The company is highly geared compared to the industry average, although a slight improvement occurred in the year. The gearing ratios referred to in the Appendix exclude any overdrafts and loans included within current liabilities, and it is likely that underlying gearing is substantially higher.

The high level of gearing, allied to poor liquidity, casts doubt over the company's continued stability.

Appendix 1: Ratios

	Big Brother plc		Industry average
	20X8	20X7	
Gross profit percentage	58.2%	57.8%	50%
Operating profit percentage	25.4%	24.9%	25%
Current ratio (including rentals in advance)	0.93	1.05	1.20
Quick ratio (including rentals in advance)	0.58	0.63	0.90

Big Brother

20X8	20X7	Industry

Gearing

$$\frac{30,105 + 5,000}{30,455 + 30,105} \times 100 = 58\% \qquad \frac{27,419 + 5,000}{24,886 + 27,419} \times 100 = 62\% \qquad 50\%$$

Inventory turnover

$$\frac{21,705}{8,159} = 2.66 \qquad\qquad \frac{18,221}{7,181} = 2.54 \qquad\qquad 3.5$$

Receivables turnover

$$\frac{51,882}{10,021} = 5.2 \qquad\qquad \frac{43,217}{8,715} = 5.0 \qquad\qquad 5.0$$

ROCE

$$\frac{13,157}{30,455 + 30,105} \times 100 = 21.7\% \qquad \frac{10,761}{24,886 + 27,419} \times 100 = 20.6\% \qquad 17\%$$

Appendix 2

A rights issue could bring in fresh long-term funds and bring the company's gearing down to the industry average level.

Assuming that £10 million is raised from a rights issue.

Gearing $\qquad \dfrac{5,000 + 30,105}{30,455 + 30,105 + 10,000} \times 100 \quad = 49.8\%$

Quick ratio $\qquad \dfrac{10,021 + 3,609 + 10,000}{15,215 + 8,261} \qquad = 1.01 : 1$

(including rentals in advance)

 Activity 3

1   Profit from operations.

2   Profit after tax.

3   The current ratio includes inventories in the numerator, while the acid test ratio excludes inventories.

4   The risk that profits might be insufficient to pay the interest payments due.

9 Test your knowledge

📝 Workbook Activity 4

Fylingdales Quarries Ltd is a medium sized business which supplies a variety of products to the civil engineering sector of industry.

The following is an extract from its accounts for the year ended 31 December 20X1. The company contributes to an inter-firm comparison scheme through the Quarrying Trade Association and a summary of performance indicators are also shown below.

Income statement	£m
Revenue	6.90
Cost of sales	(6.08)
Operating profit before tax	0.82
Taxation	(0.24)
Profit after tax	0.58

Statement of financial position	
Assets	£m
Property, plant and equipment	2.90
Current assets	
Inventories	0.60
Trade receivables	1.84
Bank	0.05
Total assets	5.39
Equity and liabilities	
Equity	3.49
Current liabilities	1.90
Total equity and liabilities	5.39

Note: The finished goods valuation included in inventories was £0.40m. Distribution and administration costs included in cost of sales were £0.88m.

Quarrying Trade Association performance indicators – year ended 31 December 20X1

Return on capital employed	25.60%
Asset turnover	1.80
Net profit before tax to sales	14.22%
Current ratio	1.50 : 1
Liquidity ratio (acid test)	1.02 : 1
Receivables collection period	82 days
Cost of sales to finished goods	8.10
Operating costs % of sales	72.1%
Distribution and admin costs as % of sales	14.12%

NB: Operating costs are defined as cost of sales excluding distribution and administration costs.

Task

(a) Calculate for Fylingdales Quarries Ltd the ratios listed in the Trade Association data based on the accounts for the year ended 31 December 20X1.

(b) Compare the performance of Fylingdales Quarries with the performance for the sector as a whole based on the data from the Trade Association.

Workbook Activity 5

Wodehouse

Your firm has been asked by Wodehouse plc, a company owning a chain of hardware shops, to carry out a preliminary investigation with a view to the possible acquisition of two smaller companies in the same trade, Pelham Ltd and Grenville Ltd.

You are not yet able to visit either of the companies' premises, but have obtained copies of their latest accounts, both for the year ended 31 March 20X8. The income statements and statement of financial positions are set out below.

	Income statements	
	Pelham Ltd	Grenville Ltd
	£000	£000
Revenue	840	762
Cost of sales	(610)	(505)
Gross profit	230	257
Distribution costs	(115)	(56)
Administrative expenses	(30)	(57)
Profit from operations	85	144
Finance costs	(10)	(6)
Net profit before taxation	75	138
Taxation	(30)	(40)
Profit for the financial year	45	98

Statement of financial positions		
	Pelham Ltd	*Grenville Ltd*
	£000	£000
ASSETS		
Non-current assets	216	268
Current assets		
Inventories	104	80
Trade receivables	38	86
Cash at bank	205	3
Total assets	563	437
EQUITY AND LIABILITIES		
Equity		
Share capital -£1 ordinary shares	100	100
Retained earnings	182	149
Total equity	282	249
Non-current liabilities		
10% debentures	150	–
Bank loan (secured)	–	56
Current liabilities		
Trade and other payables	101	92
Taxation payable	30	40
Total equity and liabilities	563	437

Task

Write notes for a meeting with the directors of Wodehouse plc to discuss your findings.

Include in your notes the following:

(a) Appropriate accounting ratios indicating the profitability and liquidity of the two companies.

(b) Brief comments on these ratios.

(c) An indication of the reasons for which one company might be preferable to the other as an investment.

Workbook Activity 6

Data

Magnus Carter has recently inherited a majority shareholding in a company, Baron Ltd. The company supplies camping equipment to retail outlets. Magnus wishes to get involved in the management of the business, but until now he has only worked in not-for-profit organisations.

He would like to understand how the company has performed over the past two years and how efficient it is in using its resources. He has asked you to help him to interpret the financial statements of the company which are set out below.

Baron Ltd – Summary income statement for the year ended 31 March

	20X1	20X0
Continuing activities	£000	£000
Revenue	1,852	1,691
Cost of sales	(648)	(575)
Gross profit	1,204	1,116
Expenses	(685)	(524)
Profit from operations	519	592
Tax	(125)	(147)
Profit for the period from continuing operations attributable to equity holders	394	445

Baron Ltd – Summary statement of financial positions as at 31 March

	20X1	20X0
Assets	£000	£000
Non-current assets	1,431	1,393
Current assets		
Inventories	217	159
Trade receivables	319	236
Cash	36	147
Total assets	2,003	1,935
Equity and liabilities		
Equity		
Share capital	500	500
Retained earnings	1,330	1,261
	1,830	1,761
Current liabilities		
Trade payables	48	44
Taxation	125	130
	173	174
Total equity and liabilities	2,003	1,935

Task 1

Prepare a report for Magnus Carter that includes:

(a)   A calculation of the following ratios for the two years:

   (i)   gross profit percentage.

   (ii)   net profit percentage.

   (iii) receivable turnover in days

   (iv)   payable turnover in days (based on cost of sales)

   (v)   inventory turnover in days (based on cost of sales)

(b)   For each ratio calculated:

   (i)   a brief explanation in general terms of the meaning of the ratio.

   (ii)   comments on how the performance or efficiency in the use of resources has changed over the two years.

Task 2

Prepare brief notes to answer the following questions asked by Magnus:

(a) How can the accounting equation in a company balance, when, unlike a not-for-profit organisation, there are no funds to balance with net assets on its statement of financial position?

(b) Can you give me two examples of users outside of the company, other than myself and the other shareholders, who may be interested in the financial statements of Baron Ltd. For each user can you tell me for what purpose they would use them?

(c) A statement, with reasons, identifying the areas that could be improved over the next year as indicated by the ratios and analysis performed.

 Workbook Activity 7

Data

Jonathan Fisher is intending to invest a substantial sum of money in a company. A colleague has suggested to him that he might want to invest in a private company called Carp Ltd which supplies pond equipment to retail outlets. You have been asked to assist him in interpreting the financial statements of the company which are set out below.

Carp Ltd – Summary income statement for the year ended 30 September 20X9

	20X9	20X8
Continuing operations	£000	£000
Revenue	3,183	2,756
Cost of sales	(1,337)	(1,020)
Gross profit	1,846	1,736
Expenses	(1,178)	(1,047)
Profit from operations	668	689
Finance costs	(225)	(92)
Profit before tax	443	597
Taxation	(87)	(126)
Profit for the period from continuing operations attributable to equity holders	356	471

Carp Ltd – Summary statement of financial positions at 30 September

	20X9 £000	20X8 £000
Assets		
Non-current assets	4,214	2,030
Current assets		
Inventories	795	689
Trade receivables	531	459
Cash	15	136
Total assets	5,555	3,314
Equity and Liabilities		
Equity		
Share capital	700	500
Retained earnings	1,517	1,203
Total equity	2,217	1,703
Non-current liabilities		
Long term loan	2,500	1,000
Current liabilities		
Trade payables	751	485
Taxation	87	126
Total liabilities	3,338	1,611
Total equity and liabilities	5,555	3,314

Task

Prepare notes for Jonathan Fisher covering the following points:

(a) Explain what a 'statement of financial position' is and what an 'income statement' is and identify the elements that appear in each statement.

(b) Explain the 'accounting equation' and demonstrate that the statement of financial position at 30 September of Carp Ltd as at 30 September 20X9 confirms to it.

(c)   Calculate the following ratios for the two years:

(i) gearing.

(ii) net profit percentage.

(iii) current ratio.

(iv) return on equity (after tax).

(d)   Using the ratios calculated, comment on the company's profitability, liquidity and financial position and consider how these have changed over the two years.

(e)   Using only the calculation of the ratios and the analysis of the changes over the two years, state whether the company is a better prospect for investment in 20X9 than it was in 20X8. Give reasons for your answer.

 Workbook Activity 8

Bimbridge Hospitals Trust has just lost its supplier of bandages. The company that has been supplying it for the last five years has gone into liquidation.

The Trust is concerned to select a new supplier which it can rely on to supply it with its needs for the foreseeable future. You have been asked by the Trust managers to analyse the financial statements of a potential supplier of bandages.

You have obtained the latest financial statements of the company, in summary form, which are set out below.

Patch Ltd – Summary income statement for the year ended 30 September 20X8		
	20X8	20X7
	£000	£000
Revenue	2,300	2,100
Cost of sales	(1,035)	(945)
Gross profit	1,265	1,155
Expenses	(713)	(693)
Net profit from operations	552	462

Patch Ltd – Summary statement of financial positions at 30 September

	20X8	20X7
	£000	£000
Assets		
Non-current assets	4,764	5,418
Current assets		
Inventories	522	419
Trade receivables	406	356
Cash	117	62
Total assets	5,809	6,255
Equity and Liabilities		
Equity		
Share capital	1,100	1,000
Share premium	282	227
Retained earnings	2,298	2,073
	3,680	3,300
Non-current liabilities		
Long-term loan	1,654	2,490
Current liabilities		
Trade payables	305	254
Taxation	170	211
Total liabilities	2,129	2,955
Total equity and liabilities	5,809	6,255

You have also obtained the relevant industry average ratios which are as follows:

	20X8	20X7
Return on capital employed	9.6%	9.4%
Net profit percentage	21.4%	21.3%
Quick ratio/acid test	1.0 : 1	0.9 : 1
Gearing (debt/capital employed)	36%	37%

Task

Prepare a report for the managers of Bimbridge Hospitals Trust recommending whether or not to use Patch Ltd as a supplier of bandages. Use the information contained in the financial statements of Patch Ltd and the industry averages supplied.

Your answer should:

- Comment on the company's profitability, liquidity and financial position.

- Consider how the company has changed over the two years.

- Include a comparison with the industry as a whole.

The report should include calculation of the following ratios for the two years:

(i)   Return on capital employed.

(ii)   Net profit percentage.

(iii)   Quick ratio/acid test.

(iv)   Gearing.

 Workbook Activity 9

Youngernst Ltd

Data

A colleague has asked you to take over an assignment. He has been helping a shareholder of Youngernst Ltd to understand the financial statements of the company for the past two years.

The shareholder is interested in finding out how well the company has managed working capital.

Your colleague has obtained the financial statements of Youngernst Ltd for the past two years and has calculated the following ratios:

Ratio	20X3	20X2
Current ratio	2.8 : 1	2.3 : 1
Quick ratio	0.6 : 1	1.1 : 1
Receivables turnover in days	48 days	32 days
Payables turnover in days	27 days	30 days
Inventory turnover in days (inventory turnover period based on cost of sales)	84 days	67 days

Task

Prepare notes for a meeting with the shareholder that includes the following:

(a)   the formulas used to calculate each of the ratios

(b)   an explanation of the meaning of each of the ratios

(c)   your comments on the change in the ratios of Youngernst Ltd over the two years, including an analysis of whether the change in each of the ratios shows that the management of the components of working capital has improved or deteriorated.

Consolidated accounts: statement of financial position

Introduction

For this unit you may have to draft a consolidated statement of financial position using the financial statements of a parent and a subsidiary undertaking.

KNOWLEDGE

Describe the key components of a set of consolidated financial statements – parent, subsidiary, non-controlling interest, goodwill, fair values, pre and post acquisition profits and equity (3.1)

Explain the process of basic consolidation for a parent and subsidiary (3.2)

Describe the effect of consolidation on each of the key elements – parent, subsidiary, non-controlling interest, goodwill, fair values, pre and post acquisition profits and equity (3.3)

Explain the key features of a parent/associate relationship (3.4)

SKILLS

Draft a consolidated statement of financial position for a parent company with one partly owned subsidiary (2.2)

Apply current standards to accurately calculate and appropriately deal with the accounting treatment of goodwill, non-controlling interest and post acquisition profits, in the group financial statements (2.3)

CONTENTS

1 Group accounts
2 The consolidation process
3 Non-controlling interest
4 Accounting for reserves
5 Fair values
6 Intra-group balances
7 Provisions for unrealised profits
8 Other considerations

1 Group accounts

1.1 Introduction

Until now, we have only dealt with the accounts of a single company. In this and the following chapters, we cover the major topic of group accounts.

In this chapter, we meet the basic principles of consolidation whilst preparing a consolidated statement of financial position. This will provide us with the foundation for studying the area in more detail in later chapters. In studying these chapters, you should always keep in mind these basic principles.

1.2 Groups

A group comprises a parent company and the undertakings (usually companies) under its control, which are called subsidiaries. The full legal definitions of a parent and subsidiaries are dealt with later and are not important at this stage.

For now, we shall assume that a parent has control of another company if it holds more than 50% of that company's ordinary shares.

1.3 Group accounts

In the UK, the Companies Act 2006 requires a parent company to produce group accounts which show a true and fair view of the group to the parent's shareholders. The group accounts provide the parent's shareholders with information about the parent and the investments which it has made. Group accounts are intended for the parent's shareholders and are therefore prepared from the perspective of the parent company.

The parent's own individual statement of financial position shows the investment in the subsidiary, usually at cost, and its income statement shows dividend income from the subsidiary in investment income. Where the investing company has a controlling interest in another company, it is not sufficient merely to show the investment in this way as this does not reflect the substance of the relationship between a parent and its subsidiaries.

1.4   Control

As the parent has control, it can decide how a subsidiary's assets are used to generate income in the same way that it can decide how to manage its own resources. Hence, the Companies Act requires group accounts to be in the form of consolidated accounts, which combine the results and net assets of the group members into a single set of figures.

Group accounts comprise the following:

- a consolidated statement of financial position, which is presented in addition to the parent's own statement of financial position as an individual company

- a consolidated income statement, which is usually presented instead of the parent's own individual income statement, although the parent may choose to publish its own individual income statement as well

- a consolidated statement of cash flow and statement of changes in equity (preparation of these for group accounts is beyond the scope of this Unit)

- notes to the accounts, including accounting policies.

The requirement to produce group accounts is subject to exemptions, which are dealt with later.

Note that, although the parent does not need to publish its own statement of comprehensive income as an individual company since it is publishing a consolidated income statement instead, it must still publish its own individual statement of financial position, in addition to the consolidated statement of financial position.

1.5   Single entity concept

Group accounts consolidate the results and net assets of the individual group members to present the group to the parent's shareholders as a single economic entity.

This contrasts with the legal form that each company is a separate legal person. This is called the single entity concept and is an example of reflecting economic substance in financial statements rather than strict legal form.

Single entity concept

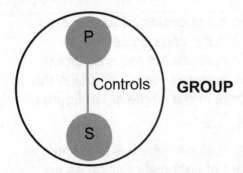

The group is viewed as a single entity.

2 The consolidation process

2.1 Introduction

A standard group accounting examination task will present you with the accounts of the parent company and the accounts of the subsidiary and will require you to prepare consolidated accounts.

The basic process is to add together the parent's and the subsidiary's accounts (e.g. revenues, expenses, assets and liabilities) on a line-by-line basis. However, there are a number of adjustments that need to be made, namely: goodwill; non-controlling interests; retained earnings; fair values; inter-group transactions and balances; and unrealised profit.

To tackle tasks of this kind we will use a formal pattern of workings required for the exam. These are detailed in the following pages.

2.2 The basic workings

We are going to use a formal pattern of basic workings to illustrate the approach to group questions and gradually build in complications.

The first step is to establish percentage ownership and control. The percentage ownership is calculated by dividing the number of shares owned by the parent in the subsidiary by the total number of shares the subsidiary has in issue and multiplying by 100. (**Note:** The number of shares is not shown on the statement of financial position. The SoFP shows the value of shares in issue).

Unless other information is provided it is assumed that a parent has control over another company if it owns more than 50% of the shares in issue. In these circumstances consolidated financial statements should be prepared.

Working 1: Goodwill

Goodwill is the difference between the price paid for a subsidiary and the fair value of the net assets acquired. It represents the premium paid over and above the value of the assets in the business.

Goodwill is capitalised on the consolidated statement of financial position. It is subject to an annual impairment review and this is adjusted in the working below as well as in W4.

Goodwill	£
Price paid	X
Share capital acquired (W1)	(X)
Retained earnings acquired (W2)	(X)
Other reserves acquired (W3)	(X)
Goodwill at acquisition	X
Impairment	(X)
Goodwill in SoFP	X

Workings

(1)   Parent's percentage ownership (P%) × subsidiary's (S's) share capital at the date of acquisition

(2)   P% × S's retained earnings at the date of acquisition

(3)   P% × S's other reserves (e.g. revaluation) at the date of acquisition

Note: Impairment may either be given as a percentage of goodwill at acquisition or in monetary terms.

Working 2: Non-controlling interests (NCI)

The non-controlling interest represents the shareholders that are not part of the group. For example, if the parent owns 80% of a subsidiary's shares the NCIs would own the remaining 20% of the shares.

The mechanics of a consolidation require that 100% of the subsidiary's revenues, expenses, assets and liabilities are added to the parent's in the consolidated statement of comprehensive income and statement of financial position. This is performed regardless of the parent's % shareholding. If the parent owns less than 100% of the shares then an amount is calculated for both the SoCI and the SoFP as attributable to the NCIs.

Non-controlling interest

Statement of financial position:

	£
Share Capital attributable to NCI (W1)	X
Retained Earnings attributable to NCI (W2)	X
Revaluation attributable to NCI (W3)	X
	___
Total	X
	___

Statement of comprehensive income:

NCI% × subsidiary's profit after tax	X
	___

Workings

(1) NCI percentage ownership (NCI%) × subsidiary's (S's) share capital at the period-end

(2) NCI% × S's retained earnings at the period-end

(3) NCI% × S's other reserves (e.g. revaluation) at the period-end

Working 3: Group retained earnings

In order to calculate group profits you cannot add together the retained earnings of the parent and the subsidiary because some of the retained earnings may have been earned before they were purchased by the parent company. The parent has no right to recognise profits earned before they controlled the subsidiary. You therefore need to work out the profit attributable to the parent after they gained control of the subsidiary.

Retained earnings	£
100% of the parent's retained earnings	X
Parent's share of the subsidiary's retained earnings (W1)	X
Impairment of goodwill (as per goodwill working)	(X)
Total	X

Workings

(1)   P% × (S's retained earnings at the period-end – S's retained earnings at the date of acquisition).

2.3   Buying shares in another company

When one company buys shares in another company the cash paid is recorded as an investment in the acquiring company's statement of financial position (DR Investment CR Cash). When the consolidated statement of financial position is prepared this investment is substituted by the net assets of the subsidiary, which are included in the consolidated statement of financial position on a line by line basis.

Example

Draft statements of financial position of Polar and Squirrel on 31 December.

	Polar Ltd	Squirrel Ltd
Assets	£000	£000
Property, plant and equipment	90	80
Investment in Squirrel at cost	110	
Current assets	50	30
Total assets	250	110
Equity		
Share capital	100	100
Retained earnings	120	–
	220	100
Current liabilities	30	10
	30	10
Total equity and liabilities	250	110

Polar Ltd has just bought 100% of the shares of Squirrel on the statement of financial position date.

Required:

Prepare a consolidated statement of financial position as at 31 December 20X1.

Solution

Step 1

- Set up a proforma for the answer, in this case the consolidated statement of financial position.

- Set up a separate proformas for the workings.

- Start with the workings then use these to construct the statement of financial position.

Step 2

Establish the percentage ownership and control. We are told that Polar owns 100% of Squirrel:

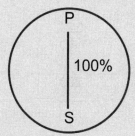

In the absence of any other information we can assume that P controls S by virtue of its 100% shareholding.

Step 3

Calculate the goodwill.

Step 4

Calculate non-controlling interests.

As Polar owns 100% of the share capital of Squirrel there are **NO NCIs** to calculate in this question.

Step 5

Calculate group retained earnings.

As Polar owns 100% of Squirrel, there is no non-controlling interest. Squirrel has no retained earnings so there is no need for that working either.

Note:

- Do not include the investment in Squirrel in the consolidation.

- Do not consolidate the share capital of Squirrel.

Polar Group consolidated statement of financial position as at 31 December 20X1

	£000
Goodwill (W1)	10
Property, plant and equipment (90 + 80)	170
	180
Current assets (50 + 30)	80
Total Assets	**260**
Equity	
Share capital (P only)	100
Retained earnings (W2)	120
	220
Current Liabilities (30 + 10)	40
Total Equity and Liabilities	**260**

Workings

(W1) Goodwill

	£000
Purchase consideration	110
Share capital acquired (100% × £100,000)	(100)
Retained earnings acquired	0
Goodwill	10

(W2) Retained earnings

	£000
100% Polar	120
Polar's share of Squirrel's retained earnings	0
Impairment of goodwill	0
	120

Note: Squirrel has no retained earnings to consolidate

Activity 1

Puffin (I)

Draft statement of financial position of Puffin and Seagull on
31 December 20X1 are as follows:

	Puffin Ltd £000	Seagull Ltd £000
Property, plant and equipment	146	35
Investment in Seagull at cost	90	
Current assets	24	15
Total Assets	260	50
Equity		
Share capital	100	40
Retained earnings	130	–
	230	40
Current liabilities	30	10
Total equity and liabilities	260	50

Puffin Ltd has just bought 100% of the shares of Seagull on the
statement of financial position date.

Required:

Prepare a consolidated statement of financial position as at
31 December 20X1.

3 Non-controlling interest

3.1 Control

We said earlier that we can 'control' a company without necessarily
owning it 100%. In fact any holding of more than 50% of the equity shares
is usually sufficient to give control. If we own more than 50%, but less than
100%, of the equity shares of another company we need an additional
working: (W3) non-controlling interest. This calculation is necessary to
reflect the third-party ownership in the net assets of the subsidiary.

Example

Suppose that Polar's investment in Squirrel represents only 80% of Squirrel's equity, not 100%. All other details remain the same.

Required:

Prepare a consolidated statement of financial position as at 31 December 20X1.

Solution

We use exactly the same technique as before, following our standard pattern of workings.

Polar Group consolidated statement of financial position as at 31 December 20X1

	£000
ASSETS	
Non-current assets	
Goodwill (W1)	30
Property, plant and equipment (90 + 80)	170
	200
Current assets (50 + 30)	80
Total Assets	280
EQUITY AND LIABILITIES	
Equity	
Share capital (100% P only)	100
Retained earnings (W3)	120
Non-controlling interest (W2)	20
Total equity	240
Current liabilities (30 + 10)	40
Total equity and liabilities	280

Note: Even though Polar only owns 80% of the share capital of Squirrel we still add together 100% of Polar's and 100% of Squirrel's revenues, expenses, assets and liabilities.

(W1) Goodwill

	£000
Purchase consideration	110
Share capital acquired (80% × £100,000)	(80)
Retained earnings acquired	0
	____
Goodwill	30
	____

(W2) Non-controlling interests

	£000
Share Capital attributable to NCI (20% × £100,000)	20
Retained Earnings attributable to NCI	0
	____
	20
	____

(W2) Retained earnings

	£000
100% Polar	120
Polar's share of Squirrel's retained earnings	0
Impairment of goodwill	0
	____
	120
	____

Note: Squirrel has no retained earnings to consolidate.

 Activity 2

Puffin (II)

Using Activity 1, facts as before, but now assume that Puffin's investment in Seagull represents only a 90% interest.

Required:

Prepare a consolidated statement of financial position as at 31 December 20X1.

4 Accounting for reserves

4.1 Pre and post acquisition reserves

The reserves which exist in a subsidiary company at the date when it is acquired are called its 'pre-acquisition' reserves. These are capitalised at the date of acquisition by including them in the goodwill calculation.

To see what this means, remember that we calculate the value of net assets acquired not by totalling the value of individual assets, but instead (as a short cut) by referring to the other side of the statement of financial position – Equity.

Thus the value of net assets acquired is the value of share capital acquired plus the value of (pre-acquisition) profits acquired. By comparing this total with the amount of the purchase consideration we arrive at the value of goodwill.

In the previous examples the parent acquired its shares in the subsidiary on the reporting date. However in the case when the parent made the purchase some months or years prior to the reporting date, the subsidiary reserves must be split out into pre and post acquisition.

The parent has influenced any change in reserves since the date of acquisition only.

Example

Draft statement of financial positions of Piper and Swans on 31 December 20X1 are as follows.

	Piper Ltd £000	Swans Ltd £000
ASSETS		
Property, plant and equipment	90	100
Investment in Swans at cost	110	
Current assets	50	30
Total Assets	250	130

EQUITY AND LIABILITIES
Equity

Share capital	100	100
Retained earnings	120	20
	220	120
Current liabilities	30	10
Total Equity and Liabilities	250	130

Piper Ltd had bought 80% of the shares of Swans on 1 January 20X1 when the retained earnings of Swans had stood at £15,000.

Required:

Prepare a consolidated statement of financial position as at 31 December 20X1.

Solution

We use our standard workings as before, but when we calculate net assets at the date of acquisition in W2 we include share capital and reserves at the date of acquisition.

If we follow our standard workings our answer will be as follows.

Piper Group consolidated statement of financial position as at 31 December 20X1

	£000
ASSETS	
Non-current assets	
Goodwill (W1)	18
Property, plant and equipment (90 + 100)	190
	208
Current assets (50 + 30)	80
Total Assets	288

Equity

£1 shares (100% P only)	100
Retained earnings (W3)	124
Equity attributable to holders of the parent	224
Non-controlling interest (W2)	24
Total equity	248
Current Liabilities (30 + 10)	40
Total equity and liabilities	288

Workings

(W1) **Goodwill**

	£000
Purchase consideration (price paid)	110
Share capital acquired (80% × £100,000)	(80)
Retained earnings acquired (80% × £15,000)	(12)
Goodwill	18

(W2) **Non-controlling interests**

Share capital attributable to NCIs (20% × £100,000)	20
Retained earnings attributable to NCIs (20% × £20,000)	4
	24

(W3) **Group retained earnings**

Profits earned by the subsidiary after the date of acquisition are called 'post-acquisition reserves'. At the date of acquisition Swans had retained earnings of £15,000. At the year-end they have retained earnings of £20,000. Therefore, Swans have earned £5,000 of profit post acquisition.

Piper includes their share of the post acquisition profits in group retained earnings, as calculated below.

	£000
100% Piper's retained earnings	120
Piper's share of Swans' retained earnings	
(80% × £5,000)	4
	124

If the subsidiary had other reserves (e.g. a revaluation reserve or a general reserve) we would use the same basic calculation for each one separately.

 Activity 3

Pluto

Draft statement of financial positions of Pluto and Snoopy on 31 December 20X8 are as follows.

	Pluto Ltd £000	Snoopy Ltd £000
ASSETS		
Property, plant and equipment	120	150
Investment in Snoopy at cost	140	–
Current assets	40	50
Total Assets	300	200
EQUITY AND LIABILITIES		
Equity		
Share capital	100	100
Retained earnings	160	70
Total equity	260	170
Current liabilities	40	30
Total equity and liabilities	300	200

Pluto purchased 75% of the shares of Snoopy on 1 January 20X7, when the retained earnings of Snoopy stood at £40,000.

Required:

Prepare a consolidated statement of financial position as at 31 December 20X8.

Activity 4

Dublin

The following are the summarised statement of financial positions of Dublin and Shannon at 31 December 20X9.

	Dublin Ltd £	Shannon Ltd £
ASSETS		
Non-current assets		
Property, plant and equipment	100,000	60,000
Investments:		
24,000 shares in Shannon Ltd	50,000	
Current assets	215,000	50,000
Total Assets	365,000	110,000
EQUITY AND LIABILITIES		
Equity		
Called up share capital (£1 ordinary)	190,000	40,000
Retained earnings	25,000	50,000
	215,000	90,000
Current liabilities	150,000	20,000
Total equity and Liabilities	365,000	110,000

Dublin Ltd purchased 60% of its shares in Shannon Ltd on 1 January 20X9, when Shannon's retained earnings were £40,000.

Required:

Prepare the consolidated statement of financial position as at 31 December 20X9.

5 Fair values

5.1 Introduction

Goodwill is determined by comparing the value of the business as a whole with the aggregate of the fair values of its identifiable net assets. In our consolidation examples to date we have assumed that the fair value of the subsidiary's assets was equal to their carrying values. This approach is fine for assessment tasks where you are not given any information about the fair values.

If the fair value of the subsidiary's net assets, at the date of acquisition, is different from their carrying value, the book amounts should be adjusted to fair value on consolidation. The fair value is the amount the asset could be exchanged or sold in an arm's length transaction.

Example

Hardy Ltd acquired 80% of the share capital of Woolf Ltd for £54,000 on 31 December 20X7. The draft statement of financial positions of the two companies have been drawn up on that date.

	Hardy Ltd £	Woolf Ltd £
ASSETS		
Non-current assets		
Property, plant and equipment	75,000	35,000
Investment in Woolf Ltd	54,000	
Current assets	35,000	39,500
Total assets	164,000	74,500
EQUITY AND LIABILITIES		
Equity		
Share capital – £1 ordinary shares	60,000	20,000
Retained Earnings	62,000	38,500
	122,000	58,500
Current liabilities	42,000	16,000
Total equity and liabilities	164,000	74,500

You are given the following additional information:

The fair value of the net assets of Woolf Ltd, on 31 December 20X7, was £66,000. This increase in value over the carrying value of the assets can be attributed to freehold land.

Required:

Prepare the consolidated statement of financial position of Hardy Ltd as at 31 December 20X7.

Solution

Fair value adjustment

Looking at the net assets of Woolf Ltd:

	£
Fair value at 31 December 20X7	66,000
Carrying value at 31 December 20X7	58,500
	———
Revaluation to fair value	7,500
	———

We must increase the carrying value of Woolf Ltd's freehold land by £7,500. The necessary journal entry is:

	£	£
Dr Non-current assets – freehold land	7,500	
Cr Pre acquisition revaluation reserve		7,500

Putting through this adjustment Woolf Ltd's statement of financial position becomes:

Woolf Ltd: Statement of financial position at 31 December 20X7

	£
ASSETS	
Property, plant and equipment at valuation	42,500
Current assets	39,500
	———
Total assets	82,000
	———

EQUITY AND LIABILITIES
Equity

Share capital – £1 ordinary shares	20,000
Revaluation reserve	7,500
Retained earnings	38,500
	66,000
Current liabilities	16,000
Total equity and liabilities	82,000

The increase in the value of Woolf Ltd's land occurred over time up to the date of takeover.

The revaluation reserve is therefore a pre-acquisition reserve and is treated in the same way as pre-acquisition profits.

This revaluation reserve will not be included in the group statement of financial position.

We will now prepare the consolidated statement of financial position.

Hardy Ltd: Consolidated statement of financial position at 31 December 20X7

	£
ASSETS	
Non-current assets	
Goodwill (W1)	1,200
Property, plant and equipment (75,000 + 42,500)	117,500
Current assets (35,000 + 39,500)	74,500
Total assets	193,200
EQUITY AND LIABILITIES	
Equity	
Share capital – £1 ordinary shares	60,000
Retained earnings (W3)	62,000
Equity attributable to equity holders of the parent	122,000
Non-controlling interests (W2)	13,200
Total equity	135,200
Current liabilities (42,000 + 16,000)	58,000
Total equity and liabilities	193,200

Consolidated workings

(W1) Goodwill

	£
Cost of shares in Woolf	54,000
Share capital acquired (80% × 20,000)	(16,000)
Retained earnings acquired (80% × 38,500)	(30,800)
Revaluation adjustment (80% × 7,500)	(6,000)
	1,200

(W2) Non-controlling interests

	£
Share capital attributable to NCIs (20% × 20,000)	4,000
Retained earnings attributable to NCIs (20% × 38,500)	7,700
Revaluation adjustment (20% × 7,500)	1,500
	13,200

(W3) Retained earnings

	£
100% Hardy Ltd	62,000

(Note that there are no post-acquisition retained earnings for the subsidiary, since the consolidation is being performed immediately after acquisition.)

6 Intra-group balances

6.1 Introduction

Intra group balances must be eliminated in full, since the group as a single entity cannot owe balances to/from itself.

Intra-group balances may arise in the following situations:

- P and S trade with each other, resulting in current account balances i.e. receivables and payables

- Intra-group loans, resulting in an investment and loan balance

Adjust:

* Face of CSFP

Current account balances may disagree. This is most likely to be due to cash in transit or goods in transit.

6.2 Cash in transit

Cash has been sent by one group company, but has not been received and so is not recorded in the books of the other group company. The following adjustment will be required:

CR   Receivables
DR   Bank
DR   Payables

6.3 Goods in transit

Goods have been sent by one company, but have not been received and so are not recorded in the books of the other group company. The following adjustment will be required:

DR   Inventory
CR   Payables
DR   Payables
CR   Receivables

💡 Example

The following extracts are provided from the statements of financial position of P and S at the year-end:

	P Ltd £000	S Ltd £000
Current assets		
Inventory	100	50
Receivables	270	80
Cash	120	40
Current liabilities		
Payables	160	90

P's statement of financial position includes a receivable of £40,000 being due from S.

Shortly before the year-end, S sent a cheque for £4,000 to P, P did not receive this cheque until after the year-end.

Also P had dispatched goods to S with a value of £6,000 but S had not received them by the year end.

Required:

Prepare a consolidated statement of financial position as at 31 December 20X1.

Solution

If we follow our standard workings our answer will be as follows.

P Group consolidated statement of financial position as at 31 December 20X1

	£000
Current Assets	
Inventory (100 + 50 + 6)	156
Receivables (270 + 80 – 40 –6)	304
Cash (120 + 40 + 4)	164
Current Liabilities	
Payables (160 + 90 – 36)	214

Start by adding across P and S's assets and liabilities for the consolidated statement of financial position.

For the cash in transit, neither entity is recording the cash so this needs to be amended i.e. add £4,000 to cash. Then eliminate the remaining intra group balances i.e. £40,000 from receivables and £36,000 from payables.

CR Receivables £40
DR Bank £ 4
DR Payables £36

The goods in transit have also not been recorded in the receiving entity's books. The £6,000 must be added to inventory and recorded in payables.

DR Inventory £6
CR Payables £6

It is then deducted both from receivables and payables as an intercompany balance.

7 Provisions for unrealised profits

7.1 Introduction

The Parent and/or the subsidiary may sell goods to each other, resulting in a profit being recorded in the selling company's financial statements. If these goods are still held by the purchasing company at the year-end, the goods have not been sold outside the group. The profit is therefore unrealised from the group's perspective and should be removed.

The adjustment is also required to ensure that inventory is stated at the cost to the group.

 Example

P sells goods to S for £400 at cost plus 25%. All goods remain in the inventory of S at the end of the year.

Mark up on cost

	%	£
Selling price	125	400
Cost of goods	100	320 (400 × 100/125)
Profit	25	80 (400 × 25/125)

Individual FS

P records profit	80
S records inventory	400

Group financial statements should show:

Profit	0
Inventory	320

Provision for unrealised profit adjustment

Dr	Group profit reserves (W4)	80
Cr	Group inventory (CSFP)	80

The group profit figure for the parent will be reduced as it is the parent that recorded the profit in this case.

Example

Sat Ltd acquired 100% of the share capital of Shindo Ltd when the balance on Shindo's retained earnings stood at £250,000.

The draft statement of financial positions of the two companies, have been drawn up as at 30 June 2009.

During the year, Sat Ltd sold goods to Shindo Ltd for £120,000 at a mark up of 20%. Half of these goods still remain in inventory at the year end.

Required:

Prepare the consolidated statement of financial position of Sat Ltd as at 30 June 2009.

	£000	£000
ASSETS		
Non-current assets		
Property, plant and equipment	4,000	2,000
Investment in Shindo Ltd	3,400	
Current assets		
Inventory	500	100
Other current assets	100	300
Total assets	8,000	2,400
EQUITY		
Equity		
Share capital – £1 ordinary shares	6,000	1,500
Retained Earnings	1,600	700
	7,600	2,200
Current liabilities	400	200
Total equity and liabilities	8,000	2,400

Solution

We will now prepare the consolidated statement of financial position.

Sat Ltd: Consolidated statement of financial position at 30 June 2009

	£000
ASSETS	
Non-current assets	
Goodwill (W1)	1,650
Property, plant and equipment (4,000 + 2,000)	6,000
Current assets	
Inventory (500 + 100 – 10)(W4)	590
Other current assets (100 + 300)	400
Total assets	8,640
EQUITY AND LIABILITIES	
Share capital – £1 ordinary shares	6,000
Retained earnings (W3)	2,040
	8,040
Current liabilities (400 + 200)	600
Total equity and liabilities	8,640

Consolidated workings (all in £000)

(W1) **Goodwill**

Cost of shares in Shindo Ltd	3,400
Share capital acquired (100% × 1,500)	(1,500)
Retained earnings acquired (100% × 250)	(250)
	1,650

(W2) **Non-controlling interests**

There are no NCIs: Sat owns 100% of the shares of Shindo.

(W3) **Retained earnings**

Sat Ltd	1,600
PUP adjustment (W5)	(10)
Shindo Ltd (100% × (700 – 250) (post acquisition reserves)	450
	2,040

(W4) PUP

	£
Selling price	120
Cost of goods (120 × 100/120)	(100)
Profit on sale	20

Half of these goods were sold outside, therefore only half remain. We adjust the unrealised profit for the half of the goods remaining within the group. Therefore 10 will be adjusted in (W3) and against inventory.

8 Other considerations

8.1 Other reserves

In many cases, there is only one reserve, retained earnings, in the subsidiary's statement of financial position. The pre-acquisition retained earnings are taken to the goodwill computation and the parent's share of the subsidiary's post acquisition retained earnings are included in the group retained earnings calculation.

A subsidiary may have other reserves in its statement of financial position, such as a revaluation reserve. On consolidation, we treat these in exactly the same way as retained earnings. Hence, the parent's reserves at acquisition are taken to the goodwill computation and the parent's share of any post-acquisition reserves is added to the parent's own reserves.

However, it is important not to mix up the different categories of reserve. Therefore, if a subsidiary has a post acquisition revaluation reserve, for example, the parent's share goes in the consolidated statement of financial position under 'revaluation reserve' not 'retained earnings'.

8.2 Accounting policies

All balances included in consolidated accounts should be based on the same accounting policies. If a subsidiary uses different accounting policies in preparing its own accounts from those adopted by the group as a whole (e.g. regarding development costs), the subsidiary's accounts should be adjusted prior to consolidation for consistency. We should make any necessary adjustment to the subsidiary's retained earnings in a working prior to calculating goodwill, non-controlling interests and group reserves.

Activity 5

1 P Ltd acquires 90% of S Ltd for £100,000 on a date when S Ltd's net assets total £80,000. What is the goodwill arising on consolidation?

2 P Ltd owns 80% of S Ltd. S Ltd's net assets total £100,000 on the statement of financial position date. What figure for non-controlling interests will appear in the consolidated statement of financial position?

3 What accounting treatment does IAS 36 require for purchased goodwill?

4 S Ltd has net assets of £60,000 at the date of acquisition. However the Land of S Ltd has been revalued by £30,000. This has not been included on S Ltd's statement of financial position. What is the fair value of S Ltd's net assets?

9 Summary

In this chapter, we have met the basic principles of preparing a consolidated statement of financial position. Make sure that you understand the concept of the group as a single entity and the distinction between control and ownership.

To reflect the fact that the parent controls the subsidiary and its operating policies, all of the subsidiary's assets and liabilities are consolidated in to the group statement of financial position. Even if the parent only holds say 60% of the shares, this is enough to give it control and all of the assets and liabilities are consolidated.

To reflect the ownership of the subsidiary in the group statement of financial position, in the equity section of the statement of financial position the share capital and reserves are effectively split into reserves of the group and the non-controlling interest. The group can only take its share of the post acquisition reserves, whilst the non-controlling interest shows its share of net assets. This reflects the fact that whilst the group controls all of the assets and liabilities it does not own them all.

This last point is summarised in the following proforma:

Consolidated statement of financial position

	£
Net assets	X
P + S (100%)	
CONTROL	X
OWNERSHIP:	
Equity:	
Share capital (P only)	X
Reserves (P + P% × S post-acq)	X
Owned by P's shareholders	X
Non-controlling interest	X
(NCI% × S's net assets consolidated)	
Total equity	X

Key

P	= parent
S	= subsidiary
P%	= parent share of subsidiary
NCI%	= Non-controlling interest share of subsidiary

If you remember the single entity concept and use the standard workings then exam tasks should be achievable.

Answers to chapter activities

Activity 1

Puffin (I)

Consolidated statement of financial position as at 31 December 20X1

	£000
ASSETS	
Non-current assets	
Goodwill (W1)	50
Property plant and equipment (146 + 35)	181
Current assets (24 + 15)	39
Total Assets	270
EQUITY AND LIABILITIES	
Equity	
Share capital	100
Retained earnings	130
	230
Current liabilities (30 + 10)	40
Total Equity and Liabilities	270

Workings

(W1) Goodwill

	£000
Purchase consideration	90
Share capital acquired (100% × £40,000)	(40)
Retained earnings	(0)
Goodwill	50

Activity 2

Puffin (II)

Consolidated statement of financial position as at 31 December 20X1

	£000
ASSETS	
Non-current assets	
Goodwill (W1)	54
Property plant and equipment (146 + 35)	181
Current assets (24 + 15)	39
Total Assets	274
EQUITY AND LIABILITIES	
Equity	
Share capital	100
Retained earnings	130
Non-controlling interest (W2)	4
Total equity	234
Current liabilities (30 + 10)	40
Total equity and Liabilities	274

Workings

(W1) Goodwill

	£000
Purchase consideration	90
Share capital acquired (90% × £40,000)	(36)
Goodwill	54

(W2) Non-controlling interests

Share capital acquired (10% × £40,000)	4

Activity 3

Pluto

Consolidated statement of financial position as at 31 December 20X8

	£000
ASSETS	
Non-current assets	
Goodwill (W1)	35
Property plant and equipment (120 + 150)	270
Current assets (40 + 50)	90
Total assets	395
EQUITY AND LIABILITIES	
Equity	
Share capital	100
Retained earnings (W3)	182.5
Equity attributable to equity holders of the parent	282.5
Non-controlling interest (W2)	42.5
Total equity	325
Current liabilities (40 + 30)	70
Total equity and liabilities	395

Workings

(W1) Goodwill

	£000
Purchase consideration	140
Share capital acquired (75% × £100,000)	(75)
Retained earnings acquired (75% × 40,000)	(30)
Goodwill	35

(W2) **Non-controlling interest**

	£000
Share capital attributable to NCIs (25% × £100,000)	25
Retained earnings attributable to NCIs (25% × 70,000)	17.5
	42.5

(W4) **Group retained earnings**

	£000
100% Pluto Ltd	160
Pluto's share of Snoopy's retained earnings (75% × 30)	22.5
	182.5

Snoopy's retained earnings were £40,000 at acquisition and £70,000 at the year-end. Therefore post acquisition profits were £30,000.

Activity 4

Dublin

Consolidated financial statement of financial position as at 31 December 20X9

	£
ASSETS	
Non-current assets	
Goodwill (W1)	2,000
Property, plant and equipment (100,000 + 60,000)	160,000
	162,000
Current assets (215,000 + 50,000)	265,000
Total assets	427,000

EQUITY AND LIABILITIES
Equity

Called up share capital	190,000
Retained earnings (W3)	31,000
Non-controlling interest(W2)	36,000
Total equity	257,000
Current liabilities (150,000 + 20,000)	170,000
Total equity and liabilities	427,000

Workings

(W1) **Goodwill**

	£
Purchase consideration	50,000
Share capital acquired (60% × 40,000)	(24,000)
Retained earnings acquired (60% × 40,000)	(24,000)
Goodwill	2,000

(W2) **Non-controlling interest**

	£
Share capital attributable (40% × 40,000)	16,000
Retained earnings attributable (40% × 50,000)	20,000
	36,000

(W3) **Group reserves**

	£
100% Dublin	25,000
Dublin's share of Shannon's retained earnings (60% × £10,000)	6,000
	31,000

Shannon's retained earnings at acquisition were £40,000 and at the year-end were £50,000. Therefore post acquisition profits were £10,000.

Activity 5

1   Goodwill = £100,000 − (90% × £80,000) = £28,000.

2   Non-controlling interests = 20% × £100,000 = £20,000.

3   Purchased goodwill should be capitalised as a non-current asset and reviewed for impairment annually.

4   £90,000.

10 Test your knowledge

 Workbook Activity 6

The following are the statement of financial positions of Dunsley Ltd and its subsidiary undertaking Ravenscar Ltd as at 31 December 20X1.

	Dunsley Ltd £000	Ravenscar Ltd £000
ASSETS		
Non-current assets	5,210	1,250
Investment in Ravenscar Ltd	1,800	
	7,010	1,250
Current assets		
Inventories	1,520	610
Trade receivables	1,120	520
Cash	120	85
	2,760	1,215
Total assets	9,770	2,465
EQUITY AND LIABILITIES		
Equity		
Share capital	3,000	500
Share premium	1,000	100
Retained earnings	4,160	1,155
Total equity	8,160	1,755
Current liabilities	1,610	710
Total equity and liabilities	9,770	2,465

Additional information:

- The share capital of both companies consists of ordinary shares of £1 each.
- Dunsley Ltd acquired 60% of the shares in Ravenscar Ltd on 31 December 20X1.
- The fair value of the property, plant and equipment of Ravenscar Ltd at 31 December 20X1 was £1,750,000.

Task

Prepare a consolidated statement of financial position for Dunsley Ltd and its subsidiary undertaking as at 31 December 20X1.

Consolidated statement of financial position, Dunsley Ltd as at 31 December 20X1

£000

ASSETS
Non-current assets

Property, plant and equipment
Current assets

—————

—————

Total assets

—————

EQUITY AND LIABILITIES
Equity

—————

Total equity

—————

Current liabilities

—————

Total equity and liabilities

—————

Workings

(W1) **Goodwill**

£000

_____

_____

(W2) **Non-controlling interest**

£000

_____

_____

(W3) **Retained earnings**

£000

_____

_____

Workbook Activity 7

Shireoaks Ltd acquired a 60% holding in Harkhill Ltd on 1 January 20X1.

The statement of financial positions as at 31 December 20X1 showed the following:

	Shireoaks Ltd £000	Harkhill Ltd £000
ASSETS		
Non-current assets		
Property, plant and equipment	17,500	5,750
Investment in Harkhill	5,100	
Current assets	4,750	1,520
Total assets	27,350	7,270
EQUITY AND LIABILITIES		
Equity		
Share capital	8,000	1,000
Share premium	1,500	500
Retained earnings	11,500	3,830
Non-current liabilities		
Debentures	4,100	1,000
Current liabilities	2,250	940
Total equity and liabilities	27,350	7,270

Additional information:

- The share capital of both companies comprises ordinary shares of £1 each and there have been no changes during the year.

- Shireoaks acquired 60% of the shares in Harkhill Ltd.

- At 1 January 20X1 the balance of retained earnings of Harkhill Ltd was £3,000,000.

- The fair value of freehold land at Harkhill Ltd as at 1 January 20X1 was £3,500,000 as compared with a carrying value of £3,100,000. This revaluation has not been reflected in the books.

Task

Prepare a consolidated statement of financial position as at 31 December 20X1.

Consolidated statement of financial position as at 31 December 20X1

	£000
ASSETS	
Non-current assets	
Property, plant and equipment	
Current assets	
	_____
Total assets	
	_____
EQUTY AND LIABILITIES	
Equity	
	_____
	_____
Non-current liabilities	
Current liabilities	
	_____
Total equity and liabilities	
	_____

Workings

(W1) **Goodwill**

	£000
	_____
	_____

(W2) Non-controlling interest

£000

_____

_____

(W3) Retained earnings

£000

_____

_____

Workbook Activity 8

Data

The managing director of Tolsta plc has asked you to prepare the Statement of financial position for the group.

Tolsta has one subsidiary undertaking, Balallan Ltd. The statement of financial position of the two companies as at 31 October 2008 are set out below.

Statement of Financial Positions as at 31 October 2008

	Tolsta Ltd £000	Balallan Ltd £000
ASSETS		
Property, plant and equipment	47,875	31,913
Investment in Balallan Ltd	32,000	
	79,875	31,913
Current assets		
Inventories	25,954	4,555
Trade receivables	14,343	3,656
Cash	1,956	47
	42,253	8,258
Total assets	122,128	40,171
EQUITY AND LIABILITIES		
Equity		
Share capital	45,000	12,000
Share premium	12,000	6,000
Retained earnings	26,160	11,340
Total equity	83,160	29,340
Non-current liabilities		
Long term loans	20,000	7,000
Current liabilities		
Trade and other payables	14,454	3,685
Tax liabilities	4,514	146
Total equity and liabilities	122,128	40,171

Further information:

* The share capital of Balallan consists of ordinary shares of £1 each. Ownership of these shares carries voting rights in Balallan Ltd. There have been no changes to the balances of share capital and share premium during the year. No dividends were paid or proposed by Balallan Ltd during the year.

* Tolsta Ltd acquired 70% of the shares in Balallan Ltd on 1 November 2007.

* At 1 November 2007 the balance of retained earnings of Balallan Ltd was £9,750,000.

* The fair value of the non-current assets of Balallan Ltd at 1 November 2007 was £31,100,000. The carrying value of the non-current assets at 1 November 2007 was £26,600,000.

   The revaluation has not been recorded in the books of Balallan Ltd (ignore any effect on the depreciation for the year).

* Included in trade and other receivables for Tolsta plc and in trade and other payables for Balallan Ltd is an inter company transaction for £2,000,000 that took place in early October 2008.

* The directors of Tolsta plc have concluded that goodwill has been impaired by 20% during the year.

Task

Using the proforma which follows, draft a consolidated statement of financial position for Tolsta plc and its subsidiary undertaking as at 31 October 2008.

Proforma consolidated statement of financial position	
	£000
ASSETS	
Non-current assets	
	_____
	_____
Current assets	
	_____
	_____
Total assets	_____
EQUITY AND LIABILITIES	
Equity	
Non-controlling interest	_____
Total equity	_____
Non-current liabilities	
Current liabilities	
	_____
Total equity and liabilities	_____

(W1) Goodwill

£000

_____

_____

Goodwill impairment 20%

_____

Goodwill on CSoFP

_____

(W2) Non-controlling interest

£000

_____

_____

(W3) Retained earnings

£000

_____

_____

Consolidated accounts: statement of comprehensive income

Introduction

For this unit you may have to draft a consolidated statement of comprehensive income from the financial statements of a parent and a subsidiary undertaking. In this chapter therefore we will build on the consolidation principles from the previous chapter and prepare a consolidated statement of comprehensive income.

KNOWLEDGE

Describe the key components of a set of consolidated financial statements – parent, subsidiary, non-controlling interest (minority interest), goodwill, fair values, pre-post acquisition profits and equity (3.1)

Explain the process of basic consolidation for a parent and subsidiary (3.2)

Describe the effect of consolidation on each of the key elements – parent, subsidiary, non-controlling interest (minority interest), goodwill, fair values, pre and post acquisition profits and equity (3.3)

Explain the key features of a parent/associate relationship (3.4)

SKILLS

Draft a consolidated income statement for a parent company with one partly owned subsidiary (2.1)

Apply current standards to accurately calculate and appropriately deal with the accounting treatment of goodwill, non-controlling interest (minority interest) and post acquisition profits, in the group financial statements (2.3)

CONTENTS

1 Basic principles
2 Inter-company trade and unrealised profits

1 Basic principles

1.1 Introduction

In this chapter, we switch our attention to the consolidated statement of comprehensive income. This is prepared on the same basis as the consolidated statement of financial position and thus most of the key principles will already be familiar.

In particular, the single entity concept and the distinction between control and ownership are as important to the consolidated statement of comprehensive income as they are to the consolidated statement of financial position.

The parent's own statement of comprehensive income as an individual company will show dividend income from the subsidiary. The consolidated statement of comprehensive income shows the incomes generated from the group's resources. Those resources are shown by the net assets in the consolidated statement of financial position.

1.2 Control and ownership

When we prepared the consolidated statement of financial position, we added together the net assets of the parent and subsidiary line by line to show the resources under the parent's control.

We apply exactly the same principle in preparing the consolidated statement of comprehensive income by adding together the parent's and subsidiary's income and expenses line by line from revenue down to profit after tax. This will give us the profit after tax generated from the resources under the group's control.

In the consolidated statement of financial position, we showed the ownership of the group's net assets on the equity side, where we showed the non-controlling interests separately from the equity attributable to the parent's shareholders.

In the consolidated statement of comprehensive income, the parent's and non-controlling interest's share of the profit after tax is shown in a note beneath the statement of comprehensive income.

KAPLAN PUBLISHING

1.3   Intra-group items

We need to cancel out any intra-group trading i.e. sales from the parent to the subsidiary and vice versa and also intra group interest e.g. if the parent has made a loan to the subsidiary and is charging interest. If we are showing the results of the group as a single entity, then we cannot include transactions between the companies. If allowed, group companies might make sales between them in order to generate profit which would not give a true and fair view of the results. Therefore, we show the results of transactions which the group as a whole has made with third parties.

The journal to cancel out intra group trading is therefore:

Dr   Revenue   X

       Cr   Cost of sales   X

with the value of inter-company sales.

We shall now see in more detail how to prepare the consolidated statement of comprehensive income.

1.4   Proforma consolidated statement of comprehensive income

Work your way through the tutorial notes, which are referenced by letters in brackets in the pro forma that follows:

Tutorial notes:

(a)   Intra-group sales must be eliminated from both the revenue of the selling company and the cost of sales of the buying company.

(b)   Any intra-group interest must be eliminated from interest receivable and interest payable respectively (single entity concept).

(c)   Similarly, dividends from subsidiaries must be eliminated since the profits of those subsidiaries are being consolidated and it would be double counting to include the dividends as well.

(d)   Profit after taxation – Up to this point, 100% of all items for the parent company and all subsidiaries have been aggregated (subject to intra group adjustments). It is now necessary to compute the amount of the profit after taxation that is attributable to outside (non-controlling interests) shareholders.

(e)   Non-controlling interest – This is calculated by taking the non-controlling interest's share of the subsidiary's profit after tax.

Consolidated income statement for the year ended....

	£
Revenue (a)	X
Cost of sales (a)	(X)
Gross profit	X
Distribution costs	(X)
Administrative expenses	(X)
Other income(b)(c)	X
Profit /(loss) from operations	X
Finance costs (b)	(X)
Profit /(loss) before tax	X
Tax	(X)
Profit /(loss) for the period (d)	X
Attributable to:	
Equity holders of the parent	X
Non-controlling interest (e)	X
	X

1.5 Key exam workings

(*Note:* The percentage of ownership will be given in the exam).

(W1) **Revenue**

	£000
P Ltd	X
S Ltd	X
Intercompany transaction	(X)
Total	X

(W2) **Cost of sales**

	£000
P Ltd	X
S Ltd	X
Intercompany transaction	(X)
Total	X

Example

Set out below are the draft statements of comprehensive income of Smiths plc and its subsidiary company Flowers Ltd for the year ended 31 December 20X7.

On 31 December 20X5 Smiths plc purchased 75% of the ordinary shares and £10,000 10% debentures in Flowers Ltd. At that date the retained earnings of Flowers Ltd were £3,000.

The issued share capital of Flowers Ltd is 100,000 £1 ordinary shares, and it had £30,000 10% debentures outstanding on 31 December 20X7. Flowers Ltd pays its debenture interest on 31 December each year.

During the year Smiths plc sold goods to Flowers Ltd for £20,000, making a profit of £5,000. These goods were all sold by Flowers Ltd before the end of the year.

	Smiths plc	Flowers Ltd
	£	£
Revenue	600,000	300,000
Cost of sales	(427,000)	(232,000)
Gross profit	173,000	68,000
Distribution costs	(41,000)	(14,000)
Administrative expenses	(52,000)	(31,000)
Income from shares in subsidiary	7,500	–
Income from other fixed asset investments (dividends from UK quoted companies)	3,000	1,000
Other interest receivable – from group companies	1,000	–
Finance costs	–	(3,000)
Profit before tax	91,500	21,000
Tax	(38,500)	(8,000)
Profit for the period	53,000	13,000

Required:

Prepare the consolidated statement of comprehensive income for Smiths PLC and its subsidiary undertaking for the year ended 31 December 20X7.

Solution

Following through the pro forma, we will deal with the issues one at a time.

Where you are uncertain of the treatment, refer back to the earlier tutorial notes.

Step 1

Revenue and cost of sales

The total revenue is £900,000 but the intra-group sale of £20,000 has been included as part of Smiths plc's revenue. It must be eliminated, leaving £880,000 (600,000 + 300,000 – 20,000).

Similarly, total cost of sales is £659,000 but the intra-group purchase of £20,000 has been included in cost of sales for Flowers Ltd. Eliminating it leaves £639,000 (427,000 + 232,000 – 20,000).

Step 3

Investment income and interest payable

- **Income from shares in group companies** of £7,500 represents the dividend receivable from the subsidiary (75% × £10,000). It must be excluded from the consolidated statement of comprehensive income.

- **Interest receivable from group companies** of £1,000 is Smiths plc's share of the debenture interest paid by Flowers Ltd (10% × £10,000). It must be cancelled against the finance cost in Flowers Ltd's income statement to leave the net finance cost to people outside the group of £2,000.

Step 4

Non-controlling interest

The non-controlling interest is 25% of Flowers Ltd's profit after tax figure (25% × £13,000 = £3,250).

Step 5

Prepare the consolidated statement of comprehensive income.

Smiths plc

Consolidated statement of comprehensive income for the year ended 31 December 20X7

	£
Revenue (600,000 + 300,000 –20,000)	880,000
Cost of sales (427,000 + 232,000– 20,000)	(639,000)
Gross profit	241,000
Distribution costs (41,000 + 14,000)	(55,000)
Administrative expenses (52,000+ 31,000)	(83,000)
Income from other NC asset investments (3,000 + 1,000)	4,000
Finance costs(3,000 – 1,000)	(2,000)
Profit before taxation	105,000
Tax (38,500 + 8,000)	(46,500)
Profit for the period	58,500
Attributable to:	
Equity holders of the parent	55,250
Non-controlling interest (25% × 13,000)	3,250
	58,500

Key exam style workings are below:

(W1) Establish the group structure

The percentage of ownership will be given in the exam

Smiths plc

75%

Flowers Ltd

(W2) Revenue

	£000
Smiths plc	600,000
Flowers Ltd	300,000
Intercompany transaction	(20,000)
Total	880,000

(W3) Cost of sales

	£000
Smiths plc	427,000
Flowers Ltd	232,000
Intercompany transaction	(20,000)
Total	639,000

Activity 1

Pulp plc

Given below are the draft statements of comprehensive income of Pulp plc and Saxon Ltd for the year ending 31 March 20X2. Pulp plc purchased 60% of the share capital of Saxon Ltd on 1 April 20X0 at which date Saxon Ltd had a balance on its retained earnings of £20,000.

	Pulp plc £000	Saxon Ltd £000
Revenue	650	380
Cost of sales	(320)	(180)
Gross profit	330	200
Distribution costs and administrative expenses	(190)	(90)
Dividend from Saxon Ltd	24	–
Profit before tax	164	110
Tax	(50)	(30)
Profit for the period	114	80

During the year Pulp plc sold goods costing £80,000 to Saxon Ltd and all of these had been sold outside the group by the end of the year.

You are required to prepare the consolidated statement of comprehensive income for the Pulp plc group for the year ending 31 March 20X2.

Activity 2

Aswall plc

Statement of Comprehensive Income for the year ended 31 March 20X4

	Aswall plc £000	Unsafey Ltd £000
Revenue	32,412	12,963
Cost of sales	(14,592)	(5,576)
Gross profit	17,820	7,387
Distribution costs	(5,449)	(1,307)
Administrative expenses	(3,167)	(841)
Dividends received from Unsafey Ltd	1,500	–
Profit from operations	10,704	5,239
Finance costs	(1,960)	(980)
Profit before taxation	8,744	4,259
Tax	(2,623)	(1,063)
Profit for the year	6,121	3,196

Further information:

• Aswall plc owns 75% of the ordinary share capital of Unsafey Ltd.

• During the year Unsafey Ltd sold goods which had cost £1,200,000 to Aswall plc for £1,860,000. All of these goods had been sold by Aswall plc by the end of the year.

• All operations are continuing operations.

Required:

Draft a consolidated statement of comprehensive income for Aswall plc and its subsidiary undertaking for the year ended 31 March 20X4.

2 Inter-company trade and unrealised profits

2.1 Inter-company trade and unrealised profit

Earlier we cancelled out trade between group companies. The whole amount of the intercompany trade was deducted from both sales and purchases (cost of sales). An additional problem can arise if some of this inventory is unsold at the year end.

The provision for unrealised profit is calculated in the same way for both the income statement and statement of financial position.

The effect on the income statement is that the reduction in the value of closing inventory will increase the cost of sales, and thereby reduce the group profits.

When the group reserves are calculated the reserves of the selling company will be reduced by the provision for unrealised profit.

If the subsidiary sold the goods then the non-controlling interest will also be reduced in respect of their share of the provision for unrealised profit.

This section will look at the impact this has on the statement of comprehensive income.

Example

Sat Plc acquired 90% of the issued share capital of Shindo Ltd on 1 January 20X7.

Set out below are the extracts from their statements of comprehensive income for the year ended 31 December 20X7.

	Sat Plc	Shindo Ltd
	£000	£000
Continuing operations		
Revenue (W1)	81,600	37,200
Cost of sales (W2)	(48,400)	(14,600)
Gross profit	33,200	22,600
Other income – dividend from Shindo Ltd	(3,600)	–
Distribution costs and administrative expenses	(5,000)	(3,200)
Profit before tax	24,600	19,400

The following additional information is relevant:

During the year Shindo Ltd sold goods which had cost £200,000 to Sat Plc for £960,000.

Half of these goods still remain in inventory at the end of the year.

Required:

Prepare the consolidated statement of comprehensive income for Sat PLC and its subsidiary undertaking up to and including the profit before tax line for the year ended 31 December 20X7.

Solution

Following through the pro forma, we will take the issues one at a time. Where you are uncertain of the treatment, refer back to the earlier tutorial notes. All workings are in £000.

Step 1

Group structure

Sat plc

90%

Shindo Ltd

Step 2

Revenue, cost of sales and provision for unrealised profits (PUP)

The total revenue is £118,800 but the intra-group sale of £960 has been included as part of Shindo Ltd's revenue.

It must be eliminated, leaving £117,840 (81,600 + 37,200 – 960).

Similarly, total cost of sales is £63,000 but the intra-group purchase of £960 has been included in cost of sales for Sat Plc.

Eliminating it leaves £62,040 (48,400 + 14,600 – 960).

The cost of sales needs to be adjusted for the unrealised profit. Shindo Ltd sold goods to Sat Plc, so closing inventory will need to be adjusted by £380 because half of the goods have not been sold outside the group, the provision for unrealised profit is calculated below.

	£
Selling price (960/2)	480
Cost of goods (200/2)	100
Unrealised profit	380

Step 3

Investment income

Income from shares in group companies

Dividends from Shindo Ltd of £3,600 must be excluded from the consolidated statement of comprehensive income.

Step 4

Non-controlling interest

The non-controlling interest is 10% of Shindo Ltd's profit after tax figure, this does not need to be calculated in this question as the information for profit after tax is not been given.

Step 5

Prepare the consolidated statement of comprehensive income extracts.

Sat plc

Consolidated statement of comprehensive income for the year ended 31 December 20X7

	£
Revenue (W1)	117,840
Cost of sales (W2)	(62,420)
Gross profit	55,420
Other income – dividend from Shindo Ltd	–
Distribution costs and administrative expenses (5,000+3,200)	(8,200)
Profit before tax	47,220

(W1) Revenue

	£000
Sat Ltd	81,600
Shindo Ltd	37,200
Intercompany transaction	(960)
Total	117,840

(W2) Cost of sales

	£000
Sat Ltd	48,400
Shindo Ltd	14,600
Intercompany transaction	(960)
PUP adjustment (W3)	380
Total	62,420

(W3) PUP workings

	£000
Selling price	960
Cost of goods sold	(200)
Profit	760
Provision for unrealised profit (760 × ½)	380

Half the goods remain in inventory and therefore half the profit remains in the books. This unrealised profit needs to be eliminated.

Activity 3

1   P Ltd owns 80% of S Ltd. During 20X4, P Ltd reported revenue of £100,000 while S Ltd reported revenue of £50,000. What revenue will be reported in the consolidated statement of comprehensive income?

2   What is the journal entry for the consolidation adjustment to eliminate intra-group sales?

3   P Ltd owns 80% of S Ltd. S Ltd has profit after tax of £60,000. What is the non-controlling interest reported in the consolidated statement of comprehensive income?

3   Summary

The key thing to remember is that the consolidated statement of comprehensive income gives the results of the group trading with third parties.

Therefore the following adjustments are necessary:

* Eliminate any intra-group sales from revenue and cost of sales.

* Exclude dividends and interest received from the subsidiary.

* Include non-controlling interest, being the non-controlling interest's share of the subsidiary company's profit after tax.

* Eliminate unrealised profit on inventory.

Answers to chapter activities

📝 Activity 1

Pulp plc

Consolidated income statement for the year ending 31 March 20X2

	£000
Revenue (650 + 380 – 80)	950
Cost of sales (320 + 180 – 80)	(420)
Gross profit	530
Expenses (190 + 90)	(280)
Profit before tax	250
Tax (50 + 30)	(80)
Profit for the period	170
Attributable to:	
Equity holders of the parent	138
Non-controlling interest (40% × 80)	32
	170

Activity 2

Aswall plc

Consolidated statement of comprehensive income for the year ended 31 March 20X4

	£000
Revenue (W1)	43,515
Cost of sales (W2)	(18,308)
Gross profit	25,207
Distribution costs (5,449 + 1,307)	(6,756)
Administrative expenses (3,167 + 841)	(4,008)
Profit from operations	14,443
Finance costs (1,960 + 980)	(2,940)
Profit before taxation	11,503
Tax (2,623 +1,063)	(3,686)
Profit for the year	7,817
Attributable to:	
Equity holders of the parent	7,018
Non-controlling interest (W3)	799
	7,817

Workings

(W1) **Revenue**

	£000
Aswall plc sales	32,412
Unsafey Ltd sales	12,963
Less Inter-company sale	(1,860)
	43,515

(W2) Cost of sales:

	£000
Aswall plc cost of sales	14,592
Unsafey Ltd cost of sales	5,576
Less Inter-company purchase	(1,860)
	18,308

(W3) Non-controlling interest:

25% × 3,196 =	799

 Activity 3

1   £100,000 + £50,000 = £150,000.

2   Debit group turnover, Credit group cost of sales.

3   NCI = 20% × £60,000 = £12,000

4 Test your knowledge

Workbook Activity 4

You work as an accounting technician for Malton Ltd which has a single subsidiary, Whitby Ltd.

The income statements for the two companies for the year ended 31 December 20X1 were:

	Malton Ltd £000	Whitby Ltd £000
Revenue	14,100	5,100
Cost of sales	(7,150)	(2,750)
Gross profit	6,950	2,350
Distribution costs	(1,600)	(450)
Admin costs	(1,450)	(375)
Dividends received from Whitby Ltd	360	
Profit from operations	4,260	1,525
Finance costs	(760)	(125)
Profit before tax	3,500	1,400
Taxation	(1,200)	(400)
Profit for the year	2,300	1,000

Additional information:

- Malton Ltd acquired 80% of the ordinary share capital of Whitby Ltd on 1 January 20X1.

- During the year Whitby Ltd sold goods which had cost £500,000 to Malton Ltd for £800,000. All the goods had been sold outside the group by the end of the year.

Task

Draft a consolidated income statement for Malton Ltd and its subsidiary for the year ended 31 December 20X1. Ignore goodwill.

Consolidated income statement for the year ended 31 December 20X1

	£000
Revenue	
Cost of sales	
	_____
Gross profit	
Distribution costs	
Admin costs	
	_____
Profit from operations	
Finance costs	
	_____
Profit before tax	
Tax	
	_____
Profit for the year	
	_____
Attributable to:	
Equity holders of the parent	
Non-controlling interest (W3)	
	_____
	_____

Workings

(W1) **Revenue**

	£000
	_____
	_____

(W2) Cost of sales

£000

_____

_____

(W3) Non-controlling interest

_____

 Workbook Activity 5

Data

The Managing Director of Wraymand plc has asked you to prepare the income statement for the group. The company has one subsidiary undertaking, Blonk Ltd. The income statements for the two companies prepared for the year ended 31 March 2007 are set out below.

Income statements for the year ended 31 March 2007

	Wraymand plc £000	Blonk Ltd £000
Continuing operations		
Revenue	38,462	12,544
Cost of sales	(22,693)	(5,268)
Gross profit	15,769	7,276
Other income – dividend from Blonk Ltd	580	–
Distribution costs	(6,403)	(2,851)
Administrative expenses	(3,987)	(2,466)
Profit from operations	5,959	1,959
Finance costs	(562)	(180)
Profit before taxation	5,397	1,779
Tax	(1,511)	(623)
Profit for the period from continuing operations attributable to equity holders	3,886	1,156

Additional information:

- Wraymand plc acquired 75% of the ordinary share capital of Blonk Ltd on 1 April 2006.

- During the year Blonk Ltd sold goods which had cost £1,100,000 to Wraymand plc for £1,600,000. Half of these goods remain in inventory at the end of the year.

Task

Using the proforma provided, draft a consolidated income statement for Wraymand plc and its subsidiary undertaking for the year ended 31 March 20X7.

Wraymand plc
Consolidated income statement for the year ended
31 March 20X7

	£000
Continuing operations	
Revenue	
Cost of sales	_____
Gross profit	
Distribution costs	
Administrative expenses	_____
Profit from operations	
Finance costs	_____
Profit before taxation	
Tax	_____
Profit for the period from continuing operations	_____
Attributable to:	
Equity holders of the parent	
Non-controlling interest	_____
	_____

Workings

(W1) **Revenue:**

£000

———

———

(W2) **Cost of sales:**

£000

———

———

(W3) **Non-controlling interest:**

£000

———

(W4) **PUP adjustment:**

£000

———

———

Consolidated accounts: parents, subsidiaries and associates

Introduction

For this Unit you need to have an awareness of the legal factors and the IFRSs that affect the preparation of consolidated accounts, namely IFRS 3 *Business Combinations,* IAS 27 *Consolidated and Separate Financial Statements* and *IAS 28 Investments in Associates.* In this final chapter on consolidated accounts we will cover the areas that are required knowledge.

KNOWLEDGE
Explain the key features of a parent/associate relationship (3.4)

CONTENTS

1 IFRS 3 *Business Combinations*
2 IAS 27 *Consolidated and Separate Financial Statements*
3 IAS 28 *Investments in Associates*

1 IFRS 3 *Business Combinations*

1.1 Definition of a business combination

IFRS 3 defines a business combination as the bringing together of separate entities into one reporting entity. In most cases, when this occurs, one entity (the parent or acquirer) acquires control of the other entities (subsidiaries or acquirees).

There are different ways a business combination can be effected. In the examples we have seen so far, one company purchases the shares in another company. Other ways a business combination can occur include the purchase of the net assets of a business rather than the equity, or a reorganisation where a new company is created to control the newly acquired subsidiaries. However they are arranged, all business combinations are accounted for using the purchase method of accounting which is the method we have already seen in the previous two chapters.

1.2 Definition of parent and subsidiary

When a parent acquires a subsidiary it is said to control that subsidiary once more than 50% of the share capital has been acquired. Control is defined in IFRS 3 as:

'the power to govern the financial and operating policies of an entity so as to obtain benefits from its activities'.

However, IFRS 3 allows for situations where a parent may not own more than half of a entity's share capital but does exercise control (as demonstrated by the list below).In this case if the parent exercises control then it should consolidate the entity as a subsidiary regardless of the shareholding. Therefore the definition of control is the key factor when determining group structure.

An undertaking is the parent of another (a subsidiary) if any of the following apply:

- It holds a majority of voting rights.

- Power over the majority of voting rights through agreement with other investors.

- Power to govern the financial or operating policies of the entity under statute or an agreement.

- Power to appoint/remove the majority of members of the board of directors or equivalent governing body.

- Power to cast the majority of votes at meetings of the board of directors or equivalent.

2 IAS 27 *Consolidated and Separate Financial Statements*

2.1 Requirement to prepare group accounts

A company must prepare group accounts if it is a parent company at its reporting date (i.e. it has one or more subsidiaries, unless it qualifies for exemption from this requirement). The consolidated accounts must include all of the subsidiaries of the parent.

2.2 Other points

IAS 27 details the consolidation procedures that we have already seen in the previous chapters, such as the requirement to eliminate inter-company trading.

IAS 27 also states that uniform accounting policies should be used for amounts included in the group accounts. All companies within the group need to follow the same policies otherwise the group accounts will be prepared with many differing policies which would not be useful to the users of those accounts.

3 IAS 28 *Investments in Associates*

3.1 Introduction

We have seen that, if a company has an investment in another company, the accounting treatment of that investment depends upon whether or not that investment gives control.

- If the investment gives control, the investment is treated as a subsidiary and group accounts are prepared.

- If the investment does not give control, it is treated as a simple investment.

3.2   Significant influence

In practice, there is a third possibility.

An associate is an entity (usually a company) over which the group exerts significant influence but not control. A holding of 20% to 50% usually indicates significant influence. Significant influence involves active participation in management, not simply a passive role, as would be the case with a simple trade investment.

We need to distinguish an associate from a subsidiary and from a simple trade investment because, whilst the group does not have control over the associate, it does have more than a passive interest. Hence, we need a treatment in between full consolidation and leaving the investment at cost in the group accounts.

3.3   Relationship with group

As we saw in the first chapter on group accounts, a group comprises a parent and its subsidiaries. As an associate is neither a parent nor a subsidiary, it is not part of the group. Instead, the group has an investment in the associate. When we identify the group structure, we include the associate, even though it is not part of the group, as this helps us to identify its status and the actual percentage interest which, as we shall see, is important.

For example:

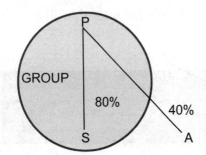

The associate is not part of the group.

3.4   Treatment in investing company's own accounts

In the statement of financial position the investment in an associate is included under non-current assets as an investment, usually at cost which is the same way a subsidiary is dealt with.

In the individual company income statement we include dividend income from the associate which is also the same way a subsidiary is dealt with.

3.5 Treatment in group accounts

In the group accounts, we use a technique called equity accounting for an associate.

As we do not control an associate we cannot bring all of the associate's net assets and profits into the group accounts. Instead, we only include the group share of the associate's net assets and profits.

3.6 Statement of financial position

In non-current asset investments, we replace the investment as shown in the investing company's own individual statement of financial position with the group share of the associate's net assets at the statement of financial position date, in one line, Investment in associate.

In group reserves, we include the parent's share of the associate's post-acquisition reserves (calculated in the same way as for a subsidiary).

We cancel the investment in the associate as shown in the investing company's own individual statement of financial position against the group share of the associate's net assets at the date of acquisition (at fair value).

The difference is the premium i.e. the equivalent of goodwill for a subsidiary which is included in the consolidated statement of financial position under the heading 'Investment in associate' as the carrying value for the associate.

The premium relative to the investment in the associate is part of the net carrying value on the consolidated statement of financial position.

Example

P Ltd owns 80% of S Ltd and 40% of A Ltd. Statement of financial positions of the three companies at 31 December 20X8 are:

	P Ltd £	S Ltd £	A Ltd £
Investment: Shares in S Ltd	800	–	–
Investment: Shares in A Ltd	600	–	–
Sundry net assets	3,600	3,800	4,400
	5,000	3,800	4,400
Share capital	1,000	400	800
Retained earnings	4,000	3,400	3,600
	5,000	3,800	4,400

P Ltd acquired its shares in S Ltd when S Ltd's retained earnings were £520 and P Ltd acquired its shares in A Ltd when A Ltd's retained earnings were £400.

Required:

Prepare the consolidated statement of financial position at 31 December 20X8.

Solution

P Ltd: Consolidated statement of financial position as at 31 December 20X8

	£
Goodwill (W1)	64
Investment in associate (W4)	1,880
Sundry net assets (3,600 + 3,800)	7,400
	9,344
Share capital	1,000
Retained earnings (W3)	7,584
	8,584
Non-controlling interest (W2)	760
	9,344

Workings

Note: Group structure

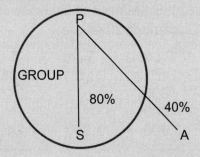

(W1) Goodwill

S Ltd

	£
Cost of investment	800
Share capital acquired (80% × 400)	(320)
Retained earnings (80% × 520)	(416)
Goodwill in subsidiary on the consolidated statement of financial position	64

A Ltd

	£
Cost of investment	600
Share capital acquired (40% × 800)	(320)
Retained earnings (40% × 400)	(160)
Premium in associate include in investment in associate on the consolidated statement of financial position	120

(W2) Non-controlling interests

	£
S Ltd only	
Share capital attributable (20% × 400)	80
Retained earnings attributable (20% × 3,400)	680
	760

(W3) Retained earnings

	£
P Ltd – from question	4,000
Share of S Ltd [80% × (3,400 – 520)]	2,304
Share of A Ltd [40% × (3,600 – 400)]	1,280
	7,584

(W4) Investment in associate

	£
Cost of investment	600
Share of A Ltd [40% × (3,600 – 400)]	1,280
	1,880

Activity 1

A, B and C Ltd

Given below are the statements of financial positions of three companies at 31 March 20X2. A Ltd owns 60% of the share capital of B Ltd and 30% of the share capital of C Ltd.

	A Ltd £	B Ltd £	C Ltd £
Investment: Shares in B Ltd	1,000		
Investment: Shares in C Ltd	750		
Other net assets	5,250	4,000	3,000
	7,000	4,000	3,000
Share capital – £1 ordinary shares	3,000	1,000	1,000
Retained earnings	4,000	3,000	2,000
	7,000	4,000	3,000

A Ltd acquired its shares in B Ltd when B Ltd's retained earnings were £400 and acquired its shares in C Ltd when C Ltd's retained earnings were £1,000.

Prepare the consolidated statement of financial position at 31 March 20X2.

3.7 Statement of comprehensive income

The treatment of an associate in the consolidated statement of comprehensive income is consistent with its treatment in the consolidated statement of financial position.

We replace the dividend income from the investment in the associate, as shown in the investing company's own statement of comprehensive income, with the group share of the associate's profit after tax, in one line, as 'Share of profit of associates'.

Do not add in the associate's revenue or expenses line by line.

Dividend income from associates is excluded from the consolidated statement of comprehensive income.

Example

P Ltd has owned 80% of S Ltd and 40% of A Ltd for several years. Income statements for the year ended 31 December 20X8 are:

	£	£	£
Revenue	14,000	12,000	10,000
Cost of sales	(9,000)	(4,000)	(3,000)
Gross profit	5,000	8,000	7,000
Administrative expenses	(2,000)	(6,000)	(3,000)
	3,000	2,000	4,000
Income from associates	400		
Profit before taxation	3,400	2,000	4,000
Tax	(1,000)	(1,200)	(2,000)
Profit after taxation	2,400	800	2,000

Required:

Prepare the consolidated statement of comprehensive income for the year ended 31 December 20X8.

Solution

P Ltd: statement of comprehensive income for the year ending 31 December 20X8

	£
Revenue (14,000 + 12,000)	26,000
Cost of sales (9,000 + 4,000)	(13,000)
Gross profit	13,000
Administrative expenses (2,000 + 6,000)	(8,000)
Profit from operations	5,000
Share of profit of associate (40% × 2,000)	800
Profit before taxation	5,800
Tax (1,000 + 1,200)	(2,200)
Profit for the period	3,600

Attributable to:

Equity holders of the parent (bal fig)	3,440
Non-controlling interest (20% × 800)	160
	3,600

Note: Group structure

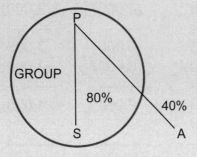

 Activity 2

D, E and F Ltd

Given below are the statements of comprehensive income for D Ltd, its 75% owned subsidiary E Ltd, and F Ltd its 30% owned associate for the year ended 30 June 20X1. Both E Ltd and F Ltd were acquired by D Ltd a number of years ago.

	D Ltd £	E Ltd £	F Ltd £
Revenue	440,000	180,000	250,000
Cost of sales	(210,000)	(80,000)	(160,000)
Gross profit	230,000	100,000	90,000
Administrative expenses	(80,000)	(30,000)	(25,000)
Income from associates	6,000	–	–
Profit before tax	156,000	70,000	65,000
Tax	(46,000)	(20,000)	(18,000)
Profit for the year	110,000	50,000	47,000

Prepare the consolidated statement of comprehensive income for the year ended 30 June 20X1.

4 Summary

The main legal and professional requirements in respect of group accounts are set out in:

- IFRS 3 *Business Combinations*
- IAS 27 *Consolidated and Separate Financial Statements*
- IAS 28 *Investments in Associates*

An undertaking is the parent of another (a subsidiary) if any of the following apply:

- It holds a majority of voting rights.
- Power over majority of voting rights through agreement with other investors.
- Power to govern the financial or operating policies of the entity under statute or an agreement.
- Power to appoint/remove majority of members of the board of directors or equivalent governing body.
- Power to cast the majority of votes at meetings of the board of directors or equivalent.

If a parent company with subsidiaries has an associate then this must be accounted for using the equity accounting method in the consolidated financial statements.

Answers to chapter activities

Activity 1

A, B and C Ltd

Consolidated statement of financial position as at 31 March 20X2

	£
Goodwill in subsidiary (W1)	160
Investment in associate (W4)	1,050
Other net assets (5,250 + 4,000)	9,250
	10,460
Share capital	3,000
Retained earnings (W3)	5,860
	8,860
Non-controlling interest (W2)	1,600
	10,460

Workings

Note: Group structure

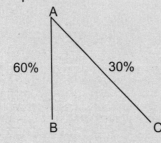

(W1) Goodwill

		£
B Ltd	Cost	1,000
	Share capital acquired (60% × 1,000)	(600)
	Retained earnings acquired (60% × 400)	(240)
		160

		£
C Ltd	Cost	750
	Share capital acquired (30% × 1,000)	(300)
	Retained earnings acquired (30% × 1,000)	(300)
		150

(W2) Non-controlling interest

	£
Share capital attributable (40% × 1,000)	400
Retained earnings attributable (40% × 3,000)	1,200
	1,600

(W3) Retained earnings

	£
A Ltd	4,000
B Ltd 60% × (3,000 – 400)	1,560
C Ltd 30% × (2,000 – 1,000)	300
	5,860

(W4) Investment in associate

	£
Cost of investment	750
C Ltd 30% × (2,000 – 1,000)	300
	1,050

Activity 2

D, E and F Ltd

Consolidated statement of comprehensive income for the year ended 30 June 20X1

	£
Revenue (440,000 + 180,000)	620,000
Cost of sales (210,000 + 80,000)	(290,000)
Gross profit	330,000
Administrative expenses (80,000 + 30,000)	(110,000)
Share of profit of associate (30% × 47,000)	14,100
	234,100
Tax (46,000 + 20,000)	(66,000)
Profit for the year	168,100
Attributable to:	
Equity holders of the parent (bal fig)	155,600
Non-controlling interest (25% × 50,000)	12,500
	168,100

5 Test your knowledge

 Workbook Activity 3

Data

Bell plc owns 60% of its subsidiary undertaking, Clive Ltd, and 25% of its associate company, Grant Ltd. The statement of financial position of Bell plc as at 31 March 20X5 is set out below.

Bell plc
Statement of financial positions as at 31 March 20X5

	£000
ASSETS	
Non-current assets	
Property, plant and equipment	85,386
Investment in Clive Ltd	25,160
Investment in Grant Ltd	5,000
Current assets	24,052
Total assets	139,598
EQUITY AND LIABILITIES	
Equity	
Share capital	35,000
Share premium	25,000
Retained earnings	67,617
Total equity	127,617
Current liabilities	11,981
Total equity and liabilities	139,598

The statements of financial position of Clive Ltd and Grant Ltd as at 31 March 20X5 are set out below.

Statement of financial positions as at 31 March 20X5		
	Clive Ltd £000	Grant Ltd £000
ASSETS		
Non-current assets		
Property, plant and equipment	32,504	18,465
Current assets	11,585	4,852
Total assets	44,089	23,317
EQUITY AND LIABILITIES		
Equity		
Share capital	20,000	10,000
Share premium	5,000	–
Retained earnings	12,930	9,000
Total equity	37,930	19,000
Current liabilities	6,159	4,317
Total equity and liabilities	44,089	23,317

You also have the following information.

• The share capital of Clive Ltd consists of ordinary shares of £1 each. There have been no changes to the balances of share capital and share premium during the year. No dividends were paid by Clive Ltd during the year.

• Bell plc acquired 60% of the shares in Clive Ltd on 1 April 20X4 at a cost of £25,160,000.

• At 1 April 20X4 the balance on the retained earnings of Clive Ltd was £10,600,000.

• The fair value of the non-current assets of Clive Ltd at 1 April 20X4 was £33,520,000. The book value of the non-current assets at 1 April 20X4 was £30,520,000. The revaluation has not been reflected in the books of Clive Ltd. There were no other differences between fair values and book values as at 1 April 20X4.

• The share capital of Grant Ltd consists of ordinary shares of £1 each. There have been no changes to the balance of share capital during the year. No dividends were paid by Grant Ltd during the year.

- Bell plc acquired 25% of the shares in Grant Ltd on 1 April 20X4 at a cost of £5,000,000.

- At 1 April 20X4 the balance on the retained earnings of Grant Ltd was £8,000,000.

- The fair value of the net assets of Grant Ltd at 1 April 20X4 was £18,000,000, the same as the book value as at this date.

- Goodwill on both acquisitions has been impaired by 10% at the statement of financial position date.

Task 1

Calculate the goodwill figure relating to the acquisition of Clive Ltd that will appear in the consolidated statement of financial position of Bell plc as at 31 March 20X5.

Task 2

(a) Calculate the amount of the investment in the associate, Grant Ltd, which will appear in the consolidated statement of financial position of Bell plc as at 31 March 20X5.

(b) Define an 'associate' making reference to relevant accounting standards.

WORKBOOK ACTIVITIES
ANSWERS

Workbook Activities Answers

1-2 The regulatory and conceptual framework of accounting

 Workbook Activity 5

The Framework identifies two fundamental characteristics which make financial information useful:

- Relevance, and

- Faithful representation

Relevant information is capable of influencing the economic decisions of the key users of the financial statements. Thus, if information is not relevant to a user it is unlikely to be useful. For example; the managing director's shoe size is information but it is not relevant to a shareholder's decision regarding whether to retain or sell their shares.

Faithful representation means that financial information must be complete, neutral and free from error.

It is not sufficient to only report some liabilities to users as the debt position of the business is crucial to making decisions. All liabilities must be reported to users.

Neutral information is information that is free of director/manager bias. A good example of this would be with regard to the recognition of provisions (are they probable?) and the useful life of property, plant and equipment. Managers could manipulate these figures to suit their own profit and remuneration targets so they must be (and be perceived to be) neutral when they make estimates.

Finally, information should be free from errors: users need quality information to make quality decisions. If the information is wrong then their decisions may be too.

Workbook Activity 6

The Framework defines an asset as:

'A resource controlled by the entity as a result of past events and from which future economic benefits are expected to flow to the entity'.

The Framework defines a liability as:

'A present obligation of the entity arising from past events, the settlement of which is expected to result in an outflow from the entity of resources embodying economic benefits'.

The Framework defines equity as:

'The residual interest in the assets of the entity after deducting all its liabilities'.

In other words, equity is what is left when all liabilities have been settled. This is essentially the net assets of a business.

Income consists of both revenue and gains. Revenue arises from a business's ordinary activities such as the sale of goods. Gains represent increases in economic benefits such as a gain on disposal of a non-current asset.

Expenses are losses as well as expenses that arise in the normal course of business such as cost of sales, wages and depreciation. Losses represent a decrease in economic benefits such as losses on disposal of non-current assets or disasters such as fire or flood.

Accounting equation

Assets less liabilities = equity interest

 Workbook Activity 7

(a) 'Assets' are resources controlled by the entity as a result of past events and from which future economic benefits are expected to flow to the entity.

'Liabilities' are present obligations of the entity arising from past events, the settlement of which is expected to result in an outflow from the entity of resources embodying economic benefits

'Equity interest' is the residual amount found by deducting all of the entity's liabilities from all of the entity's assets.

(b) The first transaction would increase the assets (inventories) by £120 and increase the liabilities (trade payables) by £120.

The second transaction would decrease the asset (inventories), i.e. inventories at cost, by £120, but increase the asset cash by £180. This would increase net assets by £60 and equity interest, i.e. capital, by £60 (the profit on the transaction).

(c) The accounting equation would then appear as:

Assets £1,380 – Liabilities £920 = Equity Interest £460

(d) A simple income statement would show:

	£
Revenue	180
Cost of sales	(120)
Profit	60

(e) Users identified in the Framework would include shareholders, customers, suppliers, loan payable group, employees, public, government.

For example, existing or potential shareholders would be interested in the business' profitability and its earning potential. They may compare current performance with the previous year's performance. Using such information they may decide to invest or disinvest in the business.

Workbook Activity 8

(a) The elements of assets, liabilities and equity interest are shown in the statement of financial position. The relationship between these elements is shown by the accounting equation as:

Assets – Liabilities = Equity Interest

(b) 'Income' encompasses revenue and gains. Income increases the equity interest.

- Expenses' leads to a decrease in equity interest.
- Both are shown either in the income statement or in the statement of changes in equity.

Workbook Activity 9

(a)   Potential investors are interested in information that is useful to them in taking decisions about potential investment in the company.

   They need information about the entity's potential return to investors and the risk inherent in those returns. Information about the entity's past financial performance helps them to assess its anticipated performance and cash-generation abilities

   Information about its financial position and structure can be useful in assessing how future cash flows will be distributed and whether the company can meets its commitments as they fall due and raise finance in the future.

   Information about its financial adaptability is useful in assessing risk or benefit from unexpected changes.

(b)   Assets are defined by the Framework as 'resources controlled by the entity as a result of past events and from which future economic benefits are expected to flow to the entity'. Inventories are an asset because they give rise to future economic benefits controlled by the company in the form of cash that will be received from the sale of the goods.

   The benefits came about as a result of the past transaction of purchasing the inventories for resale.

3 Limited company financial statements

Workbook Activity 4

(1) C

	£
Trade receivables	19,100
Less irrecoverable debt	(400)
	18,700
5% allowance	935
Existing allowance	(735)
Increase in allowance	200

(2) C

Disposal of asset

	£		£
Asset at cost	3,400	Proceeds	2,150
Profit on sale	750	Accumulated depreciation (bal)	2,000
	4,150		4,150

(3) A

Rent and rates account

	£		£
Balance b/d	2,850	Pre-payment balance c/d	720
Accrual balance c/d	500	Income statement (bal)	2,630
	3,350		3,350
Balance b/d	720	Balance b/d	500

(4) C

Purchase ledger control account

	£		£
Returns	1,100	Balance b/d	15,100
Discounts	4,100	Purchases	96,000
Payments to suppliers	83,200		
Contra offset against ledger	1,560		
Balance c/d	21,140		
	111,100		111,100

(5) (a) D

Cost of goods sold:	£	
Inventories at start	16,200	
Add purchases	94,500	(net of drawings £1,500)
Less returns	(1,100)	
Less closing inventories	(17,220)	
	92,380	

(b) B

	£	
Net sales	130,000	i.e. sales less returns inward
Cost of goods sold	(92,380)	
	37,620	

4 Property, plant and equipment

 Workbook Activity 5

(a) The principal issues are the timing of recognition of assets, the determination of their carrying amounts, and the depreciation charges to be recognised in relation to them.

(b) Items of property, plant, and equipment should be recognised as assets when it is probable that :

- the future economic benefits associated with the asset will flow to the enterprise; and

- the cost of the asset can be measured reliably.

(c) This recognition principle is applied to all property, plant, and equipment costs at the time they are incurred. These costs include costs incurred initially to acquire or construct an item of property, plant and equipment and costs incurred subsequently to add to, replace part of, or service it.

 Workbook Activity 6

Answer B

	£
List price of machinery	600,000
Less: Trade discount (5% × £600,000)	(30,000)
Transportation costs	3,500
Site preparation costs	1,500
Installation costs	3,800
Pre production testing	5,300
Initial measurement value (capitalised cost)	**584,100**

Two year maintenance contract cost, warranty cost and annual insurance should not be capitalised but treated as revenue expenditure.

Workbook Activity 7

Answer D

	£
Land at book value	500,000
Revaluation reserve (gain)	**100,000**
Land valuation	600,000
Buildings at cost	450,000
Buildings – accumulated depreciation	(180,000)
Carrying value	270,000
Revaluation reserve (gain)	**330,000**
Buildings valuation	600,000

Double entry:	£
Dr Land	100,000
Dr Buildings cost (600,000 – 450,000)	150,000
Dr Buildings depreciation	180,000
Cr Revaluation reserve (£330,000 + £100,000)	430,000

KAPLAN PUBLISHING

5 Intangible assets and impairment of assets

 Workbook Activity 4

(a) An intangible asset according to IAS 38?

"an identifiable, non-monetary asset without physical substance" (para 8)

(b) Harris would have to demonstrate:

- the technical feasibility of completing the intangible asset so that it will be available for use or sale

- its intention to complete the intangible asset and use or sell it

- its ability to use or sell the intangible asset

- how the intangible asset will generate future economic benefits

- the availability of adequate technical, financial and other resources to complete the development and to use or sell the intangible asset

---

 Workbook Activity 5

Answer A

Development expenditure must be capitalised if it satisfies the criteria of IAS 38.

All research expenditure should be written off to the income statement.

Development expenditure that is capitalised should be treated as intangible non-current asset.

Workbook Activity 6

Answer B

Impairment arises when the carrying amount exceeds the recoverable amount.

An impairment charge is recorded by debiting the income statement and crediting the asset account.

6   Inventory

 Workbook Activity 4

Answer B

	A	B	Total
Purchase price	£10	£12	
Carriage inwards costs	£2	£3	
Total cost	**£12**	£15	
Estimated selling price	£15	£14	
Sales commission	£(1)	£(6)	
Net selling price	£14	**£8**	
Lower of: cost or net selling price	£12	£8	
× Number of units	x 20	x 25	
Valuation	£240	£200	**£440**

Workbook Activity 5

Answer D

Inventory is valued at the lower of cost or net selling price.

Production overheads should be absorbed at normal production capacity.

LIFO method of valuation of inventory is not an acceptable method under IAS 2.

8 Leases

 Workbook Activity 3

Answer A

The annual **depreciation charge** will be **£17,435** (£69,740/4 years)

The **carrying value** will be **£52,305** (£69,740 – £17,435)

Year ended 31 December	Opening balance	Lease payment	Total	Finance charge 10%	Closing balance
	£	£	£	£	£
20X1	69,740	(20,000)	49,740	**4,974**	54,714 Total obligation
20X2	54,714	**(20,000) Current obligation**	**34,714 Non current obligation**		

9 Events after the reporting period, provisions and contingencies

 Workbook Activity 4

(i) **Outline answer**

- The fire took place after the year end therefore it is an event after the reporting date therefore IAS 10 applies.

- According to IAS 10 this is an example of a non adjusting event.

- The loss of £10 million should therefore be disclosed.

- The expected recovery of £4 million should be disclosed separately.

- Due to the huge losses in the foreseeable future the going concern of the company may be in jeopardy. If this is the case then the fire could be treated as an adjusting event.

- The financial statements for the year ended 30 September should therefore be redrafted and prepared on a liquidation basis.

(ii) **Outline answer**

- The dividend is proposed after the year end therefore it should be treated as a non adjusting event.

- This should be disclosed in the notes to the financial statements.

 Workbook Activity 5

Answer D

The company's solicitor's fees amounting to £3,000 is to be provided for in full.

The claim by the ex-employee of £45,000 may possibly succeed therefore it should be disclosed.

10 Other accounting standards

Workbook Activity 7

Mattesich Ltd
Income statement for the year ended 30 September 20X0

	£000
Continuing operations	
Revenues (W1)	39,235
Cost of sales (W2)	(17,385)
Gross profit	21,850
Distribution costs (5,863 – 234)	(5,629)
Administrative expenses (3,469 – 178)	(3,291)
Profit from operations	12,930
Finance costs	(544)
Profit before taxation	12,386
Tax	(3,813)
Profit for the period from continuing operations	8,573
Discontinued operations	
Loss for the period from discontinued operations (13 – 473)	(460)
Profit for the year	8,113

Workings

(W1) Revenue

	£000
Revenue per ETB	40,448
Less discontinued operations	(1,213)
Revenue from continuing operations	39,235

(W2) Cost of sales

	£000
Opening inventory	12,973
Purchases	18,682
Closing inventory	(13,482)
Less discontinued operations	(788)
	17,385

 ## Workbook Activity 8

Answer C

When there is a change in accounting policy the changes should be applied retrospectively.

When there is a change in an accounting estimate the comparatives must not be restated. The change is applied prospectively.

 ## Workbook Activity 9

Answer D

(4/12 × £240,000 = £80,000)

Workbook Activity 10

Three since the A, B and C's revenue exceed the 75% threshold.

	Revenue	%	Cumulative %
A	186	41.3	41.3
B	140	31.1	72.4
C	86	19.1	91.5
D	24	5.3	
E	14	3.2	
Total	450	100.0	

12 Preparing financial statements

Workbook Activity 2

Task 1

Laxdale Ltd
Income Statement for the year ended 31 October 2008

	£000
Continuing operations	
Revenue (W1)	58,411
Cost of sales (W2)	(42,774)
Gross profit	15,637
Distribution costs (W3)	(5,458)
Administrative expenses	(4,789)
Profit from operations	5,390
Finance costs (W4)	(1,200)
Profit before tax	4,190
Tax	(2,540)
Profit for the period from continuing operations	1,650

Workings

(W1)	Sales		58,975
	Less: Returns in		(564)
			58,411
(W2)	Opening inventories		9,032
	Purchases	42,398	
	Less: Returns out	(778)	41,620
			50,652
	Less closing inventories		(7,878)
			42,774
(W3)	Distribution costs		5,443
	Accrual		15
			5,458
(W4)	Finance costs		600
	Accrual		600
			1,200

Task 2

Laxdale Ltd
Statement of financial position as at 31 October 20X8

	£000
Assets	
Non-current assets	
Property, plant and equipment (W1)	24,237
Current assets	
Inventories	7,878
Trade and other receivables	5,436
Cash and cash equivalents	9,774
Total assets	47,325

Equity and liabilities

Equity

Share capital	16,000
Retained earnings (W3)	9,936
	25,936

Non-current liabilities	
Bank loans	15,000
Current liabilities	
Trade and other payables (W2)	3,849
Tax payable	2,540
Total equity and liabilities	47,325

Workings

(W1)	Property, plant and equipment – Cost	47,652
	Property, plant and equipment – accumulated depreciation	(23,415)
		24,237

(W2)	Per TB	2,798
	Accruals	436
	Interest	600
	Distribution costs (advertising)	15
		3,849

(W3)	Per TB	9,786
	From income statement	1,650
	Final dividend for year ended 31 October 2007	(850)
	Interim dividend for year ended 31 October 2008	(650)
		9,936

Workbook Activity 3

Hightink Ltd
Income statement for the year ended 31 March 20X2

	£000
Revenue (W1)	31,506
Cost of sales (W2)	(14,178)
Gross profit	17,328
Distribution costs	(6,852)
Administrative expenses	(3,378)
Profit from operations	7,098
Finance costs (W3)	(480)
Profit before tax	6,618
Tax	(1,920)
Profit from continuing operations	4,698
Other comprehensive income	
Gain on revaluation	500
Total comprehensive income for the year	5,198

Statement of changes in equity for the year ended 31 March 20X2

	Share capital	Share premium	Revaluation reserve	Retained earnings	Total
Balance at 31 March 20X1	4,000	2,000	–	6,217	12,217
Gain on property revaluation			500		500
Profit for the financial year				4,698	4,698
Dividends				(400)	(400)
Balance at 31 March 20X2	4,000	2,000	500	10,515	17,015

Hightink Ltd
Statement of financial position as at 31 March 20X2

	£000
Property, plant and equipment (W4)	14,105
Current assets	
Inventories	7,878
Trade receivables (5,455 – 204)	5,251
Cash and cash equivalents	304
	13,433
Total assets	27,538
Equity	
Called up share capital	4,000
Share premium	2,000
Revaluation reserve	500
Retained Earnings	10,515
	17,015
Non-current liabilities	
Long term loan	6,000
Current liabilities	
Trade and other payables (2,363 + 240)	2,603
Taxation	1,920
	4,523
Total liabilities	10,523
Total equity and liabilities	27,538

Workings (all figures in £000)

(W1) Revenue

Per TB	31,710
Adjustment for April 20X2 sales	(204)
	31,506

(W2) Cost of Sales

Opening inventory	6,531
Purchases	15,525
Closing inventory	(7,878)
	14,178

(W3) Finance Costs

Interest per TB	240
Interest accrued (6,000 × 8% − 240)	240
	480

(W4) Property, plant and equipment

	Cost or valuation	Accumulated depreciation	CV
Land	5,500	–	5,500*
Buildings	3,832	564	3,268
Fixtures and fittings	2,057	726	1,331
Motor vehicles	3,524	1,283	2,241
Office equipment	2,228	463	1,765
	17,141	3,036	14,105

*Land: 5,000 + 500 = £5,500

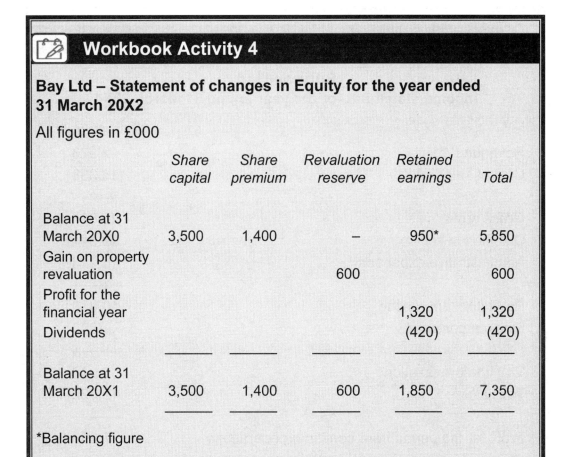

Workbook Activity 4

Bay Ltd – Statement of changes in Equity for the year ended 31 March 20X2

All figures in £000

	Share capital	Share premium	Revaluation reserve	Retained earnings	Total
Balance at 31 March 20X0	3,500	1,400	–	950*	5,850
Gain on property revaluation			600		600
Profit for the financial year				1,320	1,320
Dividends				(420)	(420)
Balance at 31 March 20X1	3,500	1,400	600	1,850	7,350

*Balancing figure

Workbook Activity 5

Burysane Ltd
Income statement for the year ended 31 March 20X4

	£000
Revenue (W1)	42,973
Cost of sales (W2)	(16,338)
Gross profit	26,635
Distribution costs	(9,544)
Administrative expenses	(6,213)
Profit from operations	10,878
Finance costs (W3)	(800)
Profit before taxation	10,078
Tax	(2,822)
Profit for the period from continuing operations	7,256
Other comprehensive income	
Gain on revaluation	1,000
Total comprehensive income for the year	8,256

Workings

(W1) **Revenue**

	£000
Sales per TB	39,773
Plus credit sales omitted	3,200
	42,973

(W2) Cost of sales

	£000
Opening inventories	8,912
Purchases	16,858
Closing inventories	(9,432)
	16,338

(W3) Finance costs

	£000
Interest per TB	400
Accrued interest	400
	800

Burysane Ltd
Statement of financial position as at 31 March 20X4

	£000
Non-current assets	
Property, plant and equipment (W1)	47,024
Current assets	
Inventories	9,432
Trade and other receivables (W2)	4,581
Cash and cash equivalents	463
	14,476
Total assets	61,500
Equity	
Called-up share capital	18,000
Share premium	6,000
Revaluation reserve	1,000
Retained earnings (15,411 + 7,256 – 2,160)	20,507
	45,507
Non-current liabilities – long term loan	10,000

Current liabilities

Trade and other payables (2,409 + 400 + 362)	3,171
Tax liability	2,822
	5,993
Total liabilities	15,993
Total equity and liabilities	61,500

Workings (all £000)

(W1) Property, plant and equipment

	Cost or valuation	Acc. Depn.	CV
Land	15,000	–	15,000
Buildings	12,068	2,603	9,465
Fixtures and fittings	10,217	2,754	7,463
Motor vehicles	18,548	5,621	12,927
Office equipment	3,004	835	2,169
	58,837	11,813	47,024

(W2) Trade and other receivables

Trade receivables per TB	1,359
Adjustment for omitted credit sales	3,200
Less allowance for doubtful receivables	(185)
Prepayments	207
	4,581

Workbook Activity 6

(a)

Moatsart Ltd
Income statement for the year ended 30 September 20X5

	£000
Revenue (W1)	68,241
Cost of sales (W2)	(34,803)
Gross profit	33,438
Distribution costs	(12,386)
Administration expenses	(7,115)
Profit from operations	13,937
Profit on sale of non-current assets (W3)	450
Profit before finance costs	14,387
Finance costs (600 + 600)	(1,200)
Profit before tax	13,187
Tax	(3,948)
Profit for the period	9,239

Workings

(W1) **Revenue**

	£000
Sales revenue per TB	70,613
Less returns inwards	(2,372)
	68,241

(W2) Cost of sales

	£000
Opening inventories	7,454
Purchases	37,543
Less Returns outwards	(1,463)
	43,534
Closing inventories	(8,731)
	34,803

(W3) Profit on disposal

	£000
Cost of asset	2,300
Accumulated depreciation	1,250
Cash proceeds	(1,500)
Profit on disposal	450

(b)

Moatsart Ltd
Statement of financial position as at 30 September 20X5

	£000	£000
Non-current assets (W1)		57,384
Property, plant and equipment		
Investment		4,000
Current assets		
Inventories	8,731	
Trade receivables (W2)	8,475	
Cash (W3)	6,035	23,241
Total assets		84,625
Equity		
Share capital		10,000
Share premium		4,000
Revaluation		2,500
Retained earnings (32,157 + 9,239 – 2,400)		38,996
		55,496

Non-current liabilities		15,000
Current liabilities (W4)		14,129
Total liabilities		29,129
Total equity and liabilities		84,625

Workings (all £000)

(W1) Non-current assets

	Cost	Acc. Depn.	CV
Per ETB	84,856	26,422	58,434
Disposal	(2,300)	(1,250)	(1,050)
	82,556	25,172	57,384

(W2) Trade receivables

Trade receivables	8,754
Less allowance for receivables	(682)
Prepayments	403
	8,475

(W3) Cash

Cash at bank	1,535
Cash from sale of shares	3,000
Cash proceeds from sale of assets	1,500
	6,035

(W4) Current liabilities

Trade payables	8,939
Corporation tax payable	3,948
Accruals	642
Interest payable	600
	14,129

(c) Statement of changes in Equity for the year ended 30 September 20X5

All figures in £000

	Share capital	Share premium	Revaluation reserve	Retained earnings	Total
Balance at 1 October 20X4	8,000	3,000	2,500	32,157	45,657
Profit for the financial year				9,239	9,239
Dividends				(2,400)	(2,400)
Share issue	2,000	1,000			3,000
Balance at 30 September 20X5	10,000	4,000	2,500	38,996	55,496

13 Statement of cash flows

Workbook Activity 6

Task 1

Flyingdales Ltd
Reconciliation of profit from operations to net cash from operating activities

	£000
Profit from operations	13,750
Depreciation charges	6,500
Operating cash flows before working capital changes	20,250
Increase in inventories (27,500 – 25,500)	(2,000)
Increase in trade and other receivables (37,500 – 33,000)	(4,500)
Decrease in trade, and other payables (31,500 – 31,950)	(450)
Cash generated from operations	13,300
Interest paid	(2,150)
Tax paid	(2,260)
	8,890

Task 2

Flyingdales Ltd
statement of cash flow for the year ended 31 March 20X1

	£000
Net cash from operating activities	8,890
Investing activities	
Purchase of property plant and equipment (W1)	(9,000)
Net cash used in investing activities	(9,000)
Financing activities	
Proceeds from issue of shares (11,610 – 10,000)	1,610
Proceeds from long-term borrowing (21,500 – 20,000)	1,500
Net cash from financing activities	3,110
Net increase in cash and cash equivalents	3,000
Cash and cash equivalents at beginning of period	1,250
Cash and cash equivalents at end of period	4,250

Workings

(W1) Purchase of property, plant and equipment:

	£000
CV 20X0	70,500
Less depreciation 20X1	(6,500)
	64,000
CV 20X1	73,000
Purchases	9,000

Workbook Activity 7

Task 1

Eigg Ltd
Reconciliation of profit from operations to net cash from operating activities

	£000
Profit from operations	6,840
Adjustments for:	
Depreciation charges	4,458
Gain on disposal of property, plant and equipment	(448)
Operating cash flows before working capital changes	10,850
Increase in inventories (5,914 – 4,928)	(986)
Decrease in trade and other receivables (4,480 – 5,376)	896
Decrease in trade, and other payables (2,464 – 4,435)	(1,971)
Cash generated from operations	8,789
Tax paid	(887)
Interest paid	(105)
Net cash from operating activities	7,797

Task 2

Eigg Ltd

Statement of cash flow for the year ended 31 March 2008

	£000
Net cash from operating activities	7,797
Investing activities	
Proceeds on disposal of property plant and equipment	992
Purchases of property, plant and equipment	(11,552)
Net cash used in investing activities	(10,560)
Financing activities	
New bank loans raised	1,000
Proceeds of share issue	2,500
Dividends paid during year	(277)
Net cash from financing activities	3,223
Net increase in cash and cash equivalents	460
Cash and cash equivalents at beginning of year	(180)
Cash and cash equivalents at end of year	280

Workings

(W1) **Proceeds of property, plant and equipment:**

	£000
CV (878 – 334)	544
Add profit	448
	992

(W2) **Purchase of property, plant and equipment:**

	£000
PPE at start	21,340
Less depreciation	(4,458)
Less CV of assets sold	(544)
PPE at end	(27,890)
PPE additions (β)	(11,552)

Workbook Activity 8

Task 1

Adlington Ltd
Reconciliation of profit from operations to net cash from operating activities

	£000
Profit from operations	6,825
Adjustments for:	
Depreciation charges	4,398
Gain on disposal of property, plant and equipment	(455)
Operating cash flows before working capital changes	10,768
Increase in inventories (6,552 – 4,914)	(1,638)
Decrease in trade and other receivables (4,550 – 4,641)	91
Decrease in trade, and other payables (3,822 – 4,368)	(546)
Cash generated from operations	8,675
Tax paid	(658)
Interest paid	(595)
Net cash from operating activities	7,422

Task 2

Adlington Ltd
Statement of cash flow for the year ended 31 October 2009

	£000
Net cash from operating activities	7,422
Investing activities	
Proceeds on disposal of property plant and equipment	797
Purchases of property, plant and equipment	(14,483)
Net cash used in investing activities	(13,686)
Financing activities	
New bank loans raised	5,000
Proceeds of share issue	3,000
Net cash from financing activities	8,000
Net increase in cash and cash equivalents	1,736
Cash and cash equivalents at beginning of year	(1,286)
Cash and cash equivalents at end of year	450

Workings

(W1) Proceeds of property, plant and equipment:

	£000
CV (568 – 226)	342
Add profit	455
	797

(W2) Purchase of property, plant and equipment:

	£000
PPE at start	22,246
Less depreciation	(4,398)
Less book value of sold assets	(342)
PPE at end	(31,989)
PPE additions	(14,483)

14 Interpretation of accounts

 Workbook Activity 4

(a) **Return on capital employed**

$$\frac{\text{Profit before interest and tax}}{\text{Total assets less current liabilities}} \times 100\%$$

(If the statement of financial position had included long-term debt then this figure of total assets less current liabilities would comprise 'capital and reserves' plus 'long-term debt'.)

$$\frac{0.82}{3.49} \times 100 \qquad = \qquad 23.50\%$$

Asset turnover

$$\frac{\text{Revenues}}{\text{Total assets less current liabilities}}$$

$$\frac{6.90}{3.49} \qquad = \qquad 1.98 \text{ times}$$

% net profit before tax to revenue

$$\frac{0.82}{6.90} \times 100 \qquad = \qquad 11.88\%$$

Current ratio

Current assets : current liabilities

2.49 : 1.90   =   1.31 : 1

Liquidity ratio/acid test

Current assets less inventories : current liabilities

1.89 : 1.90   =   0.99 : 1

Receivables collection period

$$\frac{\text{Receivables}}{\text{Revenues}} \times 365$$

$$\frac{1.84}{6.90} \times 365 \qquad = \qquad 97 \text{ days}$$

Cost of sales to finished goods

6.08 : 0.40 = 15.2

Operation costs as % of revenue

$$\frac{6.08 - 0.88}{6.90} \times 100 = 75.36\%$$

Distribution and admin costs % of revenue

$$\frac{0.88}{6.90} \times 100 = 12.75\%$$

(b) **Comparison of Flyingdales Quarries Ltd with sector as a whole**

Ratio	Flyingdales	Sector	Comment
Return on capital employed	23.50%	25.60%	Marginally less than sector as a whole but still giving a more than adequate return on investment.
Asset turnover	1.98	1.80	The company is generating more volume of output per '£' worth of investment than its competitors.
% net profit to revenue	11.88%	14.22%	The company is less profitable than the sector as a whole. It seems to be achieving volume at the expense of profitability.
Current ratio	1.31 : 1	1.50 : 1	The company has a sound level of liquidity, but marginally less than the sector.
Acid test	0.99 : 1	1.02 : 1	An ideal ratio here would be 1 : 1, the company has almost achieved this desired level of liquidity; again marginally less than the sector.
Trade receivables collection period	97 days	82 days	Tighter controls are required here.

The collection period is typically high for the sector but the company needs to review is position. There is always the danger of the incidence of irrecoverable debts. |

Cost of sales to finished goods	15.2	8.10	The company is turning over its finished goods inventories faster than the industry as a whole. It is holding approx 0.8 months compared with 1.48 month for the sector.
Operating costs % of revenue	75.36%	72.10%	The lack of profitability is highlighted here. Costs may need review and control or selling prices may need revising.
Distribution and admin cost % of revenue	12.75%	14.12%	More favourable than the sector as a whole

Overall the company performance is marginally worse than the average performance for the sector.

The lack of profitability as highlighted in the % of operating costs to revenue is the significant factor which affects the return on capital. The company is achieving a good level of activity but is marginally less profitable.

Workbook Activity 5

Wodehouse

(a) Accounting

Profitability

Ratios			Pelham Ltd	Grenville Ltd
(i)	Gross profit margin	$\dfrac{GP}{\text{Revenues}}$	$\dfrac{230}{840} \times 100 = 27.4\%$	$\dfrac{257}{762} \times 100 = 33.7\%$
(ii)	Net profit margin	$\dfrac{\text{Op profit}}{\text{Revenues}}$	$\dfrac{85}{840} \times 100 = 10.1\%$	$\dfrac{144}{762} \times 100 = 18.9\%$
(iii)	ROCE	$\dfrac{\text{Op profit}}{\text{Cap employed}}$	$\dfrac{85}{432} \times 100 = 19.7\%$	$\dfrac{144}{305} \times 100 = 47.2\%$
(iv)	Asset turnover	$\dfrac{\text{Revenue}}{\text{Cap employed}}$	$\dfrac{840}{432} = 1.9$	$\dfrac{762}{305} = 2.5$
(v)	Inventory turnover	$\dfrac{\text{Cost of sales}}{\text{Inventory}}$	$\dfrac{610}{104} = 5.9$	$\dfrac{505}{80} = 6.3$

Liquidity

(i)	Current ratio	$\dfrac{\text{CA}}{\text{CL}}$	$\dfrac{347}{131} = 2.65$	$\dfrac{169}{132} = 1.28$
(ii)	Quick ratio	$\dfrac{\text{CA - Inventory}}{\text{CL}}$	$\dfrac{243}{131} = 1.85$	$\dfrac{89}{132} = 0.67$
(iii)	Receivables collection period (days)	$\dfrac{\text{Receivables}}{\text{Revenues}} \times 365$	$\dfrac{38}{840} \times 365 = 16\tfrac{1}{2}$	$\dfrac{86}{762} \times 365 = 41.2$

(b) **Comments**

Profitability

(1) Fairly large difference in both GP and NP margins between two companies in same retailing sector. Grenville is much better than Pelham.

Possible reasons:

Grenville may have shops in better positions than Pelham.

Pelham may have a higher proportion of cash sales or prompt payment discounts.

Grenville may simply be more effective in its control of costs.

Pelham's comparatively low CV of non-current assets could indicate a need for high maintenance costs.

(2) ROCE much lower for Pelham: high cash balance may point to under-use of resources. With a lower gross margin, Pelham's asset turnover should be considerably higher than Grenville's to compensate. This is not the case so more revenue volume is needed by Pelham.

Liquidity

(1) Pelham's large cash balance makes its current ratio unnecessarily high: it could afford an increase in capital expenditure, leading potentially to increased production and revenue.

(2) Grenville's liquidity looks alarming but may not be if the amount of the bank loan can be increased and if trade receivables will pay promptly. Its credit period of 41 days is somewhat high, and there could be a problem here. Further information needed as to the ageing of receivables and the terms of the bank loan.

(c) **Comparison of two companies as investments**

Pelham: could be said to be ripe for a takeover as it appears to be under-using its assets. A safe but unexciting performance which could be improved with more dynamic management.

Grenville: more of a risk. Needs an injection of cash for security, but given a state of continued solvency it has the potential to make high profits and a good return on investment.

 Workbook Activity 6

Task 1

REPORT

To: Magnus Carter
From: A Student
Subject: Interpretation of financial statements
Date: 23 June 20X1

This report has been prepared to support the interpretation of the financial statements of Baron Ltd and to compare and contrast the company performance over the two year period.

(a) **Calculation of the ratios**

	20X1		20X0	
Gross profit percentage	$\dfrac{1{,}204}{1{,}852}$	= 65%	$\dfrac{1{,}116}{1{,}691}$	= 66%
Net profit percentage	$\dfrac{519}{1{,}852}$	= 28%	$\dfrac{592}{1{,}691}$	= 35%
Receivables collection period in days	$\dfrac{319}{1{,}852} \times 365$	= 63 days	$\dfrac{236}{1{,}691} \times 365$	= 51 days
Payables payment period in days	$\dfrac{48}{648} \times 365$	= 27 days	$\dfrac{44}{575} \times 365$	= 28 days
Inventory turnover in days	$\dfrac{217}{648} \times 365$	= 122 days	$\dfrac{159}{575} \times 365$	= 101 days

(b) **Explanation and comment**

- *Gross profit percentage*

  This measure of profitability shows the percentage of gross profit in relation to revenue, it is often termed the gross margin.

  The ratio has remained fairly constant over the two year period with only a marginal decrease from 66% to 65%. It is expressed as:

  $$\frac{\text{Gross profit}}{\text{Revenues}} \times 100\%$$

  The company has achieved a greater volume of business without having to reduce its margins.

- *Net profit percentage*

  This measure of profitability shows the percentage of net profit in relation to revenue. It is influenced by the gross margin and the level of other costs in relation to revenue. There has been a significant fall in the net return over the period. The gross margin has only fallen marginally, however the expenses in relation to revenue have increased from 31% to 37% over the period and this has had an adverse effect on the performance.

  This indicates that the company is generating less net profit per '£' of revenue than previously achieved.

- *Receivables collection period*

  This is a measure of management control as it relates to the effectiveness of the credit control policy.

  The ratio shows the average number of days it takes to collect debts. It is expressed as:

  $$\frac{\text{Receivables}}{\text{Revenues}} \times 365 \text{ days}$$

  The collection period has increased over the two year period and it is taking 12 days longer to collect debts than previously experienced. This may be due to either customer cash flow problems or poor and less effective credit control.

- *Payables payment period*

  This ratio shows the average days it takes for the company to pay its suppliers. This period has remained similar over the two years. It indicates that the company can meet its demands from trade payables on a timely and regular basis.

- *Inventory turnover*

  This is a measure of the effectiveness of the inventory control policy. It shows the average number of days it takes to turn over inventories.

  There has been a deterioration in this control over the two years as it is taking a further 21 days to turn over inventories than previously experienced.

Task 2

(a) The accounting equation is:

$$\text{Assets} = \text{Equity} + \text{Liabilities}$$

In a not-for-profit entity, funds given to the organisation by donors and those generated from within are utilised to meet the entity's objective. Such funds are equivalent to the equity interest element of the accounting equation.

In a company's statement of financial position the equity interest of the shareholders is represented by the share capital and reserves of the company.

(b) Examples of outside users and uses (only two required):

User	Uses
Potential investors	To decide whether to invest in the company.
Bank	To decide whether to grant a loan to the company.
Payables	To decide whether to supply goods or services to the company.

Other reasonable examples of outside users are also acceptable.

(c) **Areas for improvement**

The measures of performance and other ratios indicate that Baron Ltd should focus on the control of expenses, trade receivables and inventories.

The gross margin and payables payment periods have remained similar to the previous year, but there has been a decline in the net profit percentage due to a more than proportional increase in the level of expenses to revenue, which suggests controls are needed.

The credit control policy and procedures need review and there is also the danger of irrecoverable debts occurring. The inventory holding policy needs considering with a full analysis of both moving and slow moving inventories.

Workbook Activity 7

Notes to Jonathan Fisher

(a) A statement of financial position shows the financial position of an entity at a point in time. It lists the assets, liabilities and equity interest at the statement of financial position date.

 An income statement shows the financial performance of an entity over a specific period of time. It shows income and expenditure, the difference between these elements being profit over the accounting period.

(b) The accounting equation is:

Assets = Equity + Liabilities

Figures in £000 at 30 September 20X9

The accounting equation is: £5,555 = £2,217 + £3,338

(c) **Calculation of ratios**

 The following ratios for the company have been computed:

		20X9		20X8	
(i)	*Gearing* Debt/cap. employed	$\frac{2,500}{4,717}$	× 100 = 53%	$\frac{1,000}{2,703}$	× 100 = 37%
	or				
	Debt/equity	$\frac{2,500}{2,717}$	× 100 = 92%	$\frac{1,000}{1,703}$	× 100 = 59%
(ii)	*Net profit percentage*	$\frac{668}{3,183}$	× 100 = 21%	$\frac{689}{2,756}$	× 100 = 25%
(iii)	*Current ratio*	$\frac{1,341}{838}$	= 1.6:1	$\frac{1,284}{611}$	= 2.1:1
(iv)	*Return on equity*	$\frac{356}{2,217}$	× 100 = 16%	$\frac{471}{1,703}$	× 100 = 28%

(d) • *Gearing ratio*: This measure represents the company's reliance on debt in relation to total equity. The gearing has increased over the two years and the company is now a 'high geared' organisation. There is a greater reliance on borrowed funds in the second year. This increases shareholder risk as when profits reduce, interest payments must still be met.

- *Net profit percentage:* The net return to revenue has fallen over the period. This is a result of a fall in the gross margin from 63% to 58%, the level of expenses to revenue remaining fairly constant.

- *Current ratio:* There has been a reduction in this measure of liquidity over the period, there has been a deterioration in the cash position and the acid test ratio has fallen significantly from 0.97 to 0.65. The business now has less current assets per '£' of current liabilities than previously.

- *Return on equity:* The return has fallen over the two year period which has been influenced by the overall reduction in profitability as shown in the net profit percentage to revenue.

  The company is not generating as much profit for each '£' worth of equity investment as it did in the previous year.

(e) The decrease in both profitability and liquidity indicates that the company is a worse prospect for investment than it was in the previous year.

 ## Workbook Activity 8

To: Managers of Bimbridge Hospitals Trust
From: AAT Student
Date: 3 December 20X8
Re: Analysis of Patch Ltd's financial statements

Introduction

The purpose of this report is to analyse the financial performance of Patch Ltd for 20X8 and 20X7 to consider it as a major supplier of bandages and dressings to the Trust.

The following are key financial ratios together with industry benchmarks.

	Patch Ltd 20X8	Industry average 20X8	Patch Ltd 20X7	Industry average 20X7
Return on capital employed	$\frac{552}{5,334} = 10.3\%$	9.6%	$\frac{462}{5,790} = 8.0\%$	9.4%
Net profit percentage	$\frac{552}{2,300} = 24\%$	21.4%	$\frac{462}{2,100} = 22\%$	21.3%

Quick ratio/acid test	$\frac{523}{475} = 1.1:1$	1.0:1	$\frac{418}{465} = 0.9:1$	0.9:1
Gearing: Debt/capital employed	$\frac{1,654}{5,334} = 31\%$	36%	$\frac{2,490}{5,790} = 43\%$	37%

Comment and analysis

Overall company profitability has improved over the two years with return on capital employed strengthening from 8% to 10.3%.

The company is generating more net profit per '£' of investment in 20X8 than in the previous year.

Compared with the sector average their performance was adverse in 20X7 but more favourable in 20X8.

The percentage of net profit to revenue also increased over the period increasing from 22% to 24%.

The company is therefore more profitable in the current year and is performing more favourably than the sector as a whole and a good indicator for the future.

Company liquidity has shown an improvement with a slightly stronger acid test ratio than the sector as a whole.

The company currently has £1.10 worth of liquid assets for each '£' worth of current liabilities. This appears to be a sound liquidity position.

There has been a reduction in gearing over the two year period, with a much less reliance on debt than previously experienced.

High geared companies increase shareholder risk in times of profit decline. The company is moving to a 'lower' geared structure and to a position less than the industry average.

The company is considered to be a lower risk than previously.

Conclusion

Based on this assessment of the financial statements provided, it is recommended that Patch Ltd can be used as a supplier to the Trust.

Its profitability, liquidity and gearing suggest that the company is financially sound.

Workbook Activity 9

Youngernst Ltd

Notes for a meeting

(a) **Formulas used in calculating the ratios:**

Current ratio $= \dfrac{\text{Current assets}}{\text{Current liabilities}}$

Quick ratio $= \dfrac{\text{Current assets less inventories}}{\text{Current liabilities}}$

Receivables turnover $= \dfrac{\text{Trade receivables}}{\text{Revenue}} \times 365$

Payables turnover $= \dfrac{\text{Trade payables}}{\text{Cost of sales (or purchases)}} \times 365$

Inventories turnover $= \dfrac{\text{Inventories}}{\text{Cost of sales}} \times 365$

(b) Explanation of the meaning of the ratios

Current ratio:

- this ratio measures the extent to which the company has sufficient current assets to meet its current liabilities

- it gives an indication of the liquidity of the company, but can also show that too much is invested in current assets such as inventories and trade receivables and cash in relation to current liabilities

Quick ratio/Acid test:

- this ratio measures the extent to which the company has sufficient current assets that are quickly convertible into cash to meet its current liabilities

- it also gives an indication of the liquidity of the company, but can also indicate whether too much is invested in trade receivables and cash in relation to current liabilities

Receivable turnover:

- this ratio shows the average number of days it takes to collect trade receivables

Payable turnover:

- this ratio shows the average number of days it takes for the company to pay its trade payables

Inventory turnover

- this ratio shows the average number of days that it takes to sell the inventories of the company

(c) **Comment on change in ratios**

Current ratio:

- this ratio has increased during the year suggesting that the company has more current assets to meet its current liabilities than in previous years and hence better liquidity

- however, this might be because inventories or trade receivable balances have increased rather than cash balances and these may not be readily convertible to cash to pay off trade payables and so does not necessarily mean more liquidity and may indicate problems in selling inventories or collecting trade receivables

Quick ratio/Acid test:

- this ratio has deteriorated during the year which means that there are less current assets that are quickly convertible into cash to meet its current liabilities which suggests decreased liquidity

- the fact that this ratio has decreased even though the current ratio has increased suggests that the reason why the current ratio has increased is due to increases in the amount of inventories held in relation to current liabilities rather than any genuine improvement in liquidity

- because the quick assets include trade receivables, this ratio might conceal further liquidity problems since a failure to collect trade receivable balances may also result in a higher ratio

Receivables turnover:

- the ratio has deteriorated over the two years as it now takes, on average, 16 more days to collect debts than last year

- the fact that it takes longer this year to collect debts than last year may be due to liquidity problems of customers, an increase in irrecoverable debts or a failure to chase up overdue debts which might point to failures of management of working capital

Payables turnover:

- the number of days taken to pay trade payables has fallen a little over the two years

- this does not suggest that the company has had difficulty in finding funds to pay trade payables and, therefore, does not appear to have liquidity problems that have forced the business to pay trade payables more slowly

- the decrease may be due to inefficiencies in management and the failure to make full use of credit terms, but it is possible that trade payables have tightened up on the period of credit allowed which might indicate suspicions about the liquidity of the company

Inventory turnover:

- this ratio has deteriorated over the two years as it now takes 17 days longer to sell inventories than it did last year

- this shows that there may be problems with inventory control which may point to overstocking or to increasing amounts of old inventories being included against which provisions may be required to be made.

15 Consolidated accounts: statement of financial position

Workbook Activity 6

Consolidated statement of financial position
Dunsley Ltd and its subsidiary undertaking, Ravenscar Ltd, as at 31 December 20X1

	£000
ASSETS	
Non-current assets	
Goodwill (W1)	447
Property, plant and equipment (5,210 + 1,750)	6,960
Current assets	
Inventories (1,520 + 610)	2,130
Trade receivables (1,120 + 520)	1,640
Cash and cash equivalents (120 + 85)	205
	3,975
Total assets	11,382
EQUITY AND LIABILITIES	
Equity	
Share capital	3,000
Share premium	1,000
Retained earnings(W3)	4,160
Non-controlling interest (W2)	902
Total equity	9,062
Current liabilities (1,610 + 710)	2,320
Total equity and liabilities	11,382

Workings

(W1) **Goodwill**

	£000
Price paid	1,800
Share capital acquired (60% × 600)	(360)
Retained earnings acquired (60% × 1,155)	(693)
Fair value adjustment (60% × (1,750 – 1,250))	(300)
	447

(W2) **Non-controlling interest**

	£000
Share capital attributable to NCIs (40% ×600)	240
Retained earnings attributable to NCIs (40% × 1,155)	462
Fair value adjustment (40% × (1,750 – 1,250))	200
	902

(W3) **Retained earnings**

	£000
100% Dunsley Ltd	4,160
There are no post acquisition reserves of Ravenscar Ltd.	0
	4,160

Workbook Activity 7

Shireoaks Ltd and its subsidiary undertaking, Harkhill Ltd, as at 31 December 20X1

Statement of financial position as at 31 December 20X1

	£000
ASSETS	
Non-current assets	2,160
Goodwill (W1)	
Property, plant and equipment (17,500 + 5,750 + 400)	23,650
Current assets (4,750 + 1,520)	6,270
Total assets	32,080
EQUTY AND LIABILITIES	
Equity	
Share capital	8,000
Share premium	1,500
Retained earnings (W3)	11,998
Non-controlling interest (W2)	2,292
	23,790
Non-current liabilities	
Debentures (4,100 + 1,000)	5,100
Current liabilities (2,250 + 940)	3,190
Total equity and liabilities	32,080

Workings

(W2) Goodwill

	£000
Price paid	5,100
Share capital acquired (60% × 1,500)	(900)
Retained earnings acquired (60% × 3,000)	(1,800)
Fair value adjustment (60% × 400)	(240)
	2,160

(W3) Non-controlling interest

	£000
Share capital attributable to NCIs (40% ×1,500)	600
Retained earnings attributable to NCIs (40% × 3,830)	1,532
Fair value adjustment (40% × 400)	160
	2,292

(W4) Retained earnings

	£000
100% Shireoaks Ltd	11,500
60% Harkhill Ltd (3,830 – 3,000))	498
	11,998

Workbook Activity 8

Tolsta plc
Consolidated statement of financial position as at
31 October 2008

	£000
ASSETS	
Non-current assets	
Goodwill (W1)	7,540
Property, plant and equipment (47,875 + 31,913 + 4,500)	84,288
Current assets	
Inventories	30,509
Trade receivables (14,343 + 3,656 – 2,000)	15,999
Cash	2,003
	48,511
Total assets	140,339
EQUITY AND LIABILITIES	
Equity	
Share capital	45,000
Share premium	12,000
Retained earnings (W3)	25,388
Non-controlling interest (W2)	10,152
Total equity	92,540
Non-current liabilities	
Long-term loan	27,000
Current liabilities	
Trade and other payables (14,454 + 3,685 – 2,000)	16,139
Tax liabilities	4,660
Total equity and liabilities	140,339

Workings

(W1) Goodwill

	£000
Price paid	32,000
Share capital acquired (70% × 18,000)	(12,600)
Retained earnings acquired (70% × 9,750)	(6,825)
Fair value adjustment (70% × 4,500))	(3,150)
	9,425
Goodwill impairment 20%	(1,885)
Goodwill on CSoFP	7,540

(W2) Non-controlling interest

	£000
Share capital attributable to NCIs (30% ×18,000)	5,400
Retained earnings attributable to NCIs (30% × 11,340)	3,402
Fair value adjustment (30% × 4,500)	1,350
	10,152

(W3) Retained earnings

	£000
100% Tolsta Ltd	26,160
70% Balallan Ltd (11,340 – 9,750)	1,113
Goodwill impairment	(1,885)
	25,388

16 Consolidated accounts: statement of comprehensive income

Workbook Activity 4

Consolidated income statement for the year ended 31 December 20X1

	£000
Revenue (W1)	18,400
Cost of sales (W2)	(9,100)
Gross profit	9,300
Distribution costs (1,600 + 450)	(2,050)
Admin costs (1,450 + 375)	(1,825)
Profit from operations	5,425
Finance costs (760 + 125)	(885)
Profit before tax	4,540
Tax (1,200 + 400)	(1,600)
Profit for the year	2,940
Attributable to:	
Equity holders of the parent	2,740
Non-controlling interest (W3)	200
	2,940

Workings

(W1) Revenue:

	£000
Malton Ltd	14,100
Whitby Ltd	5,100
Less inter-company sales	(800)
	18,400

(W2) Cost of sales:

	£000
Malton Ltd	7,150
Whitby Ltd	2,750
Less inter-company purchase	(800)
	9,100

(W3) Non-controlling interest:

20% of £1,000	200

Workbook Activity 5

Consolidated income statement for the year ended 31 March 20X7

	£000
Revenue (W1)	49,406
Cost of sales (W2)	(26,611)
Gross profit	22,795
Distribution costs	(9,254)
Admin costs	(6,453)
Profit from operations	7,088
Finance costs	(742)
Profit before tax	6,346
Tax	(2,134)
Profit for the year	4,212
Attributable to:	
Equity holders of the parent	3,985
Non-controlling interest (W3)	227
	4,212

Workings

(W1) **Revenue:**

	£000
Wraymand plc	38,462
Blonk Ltd	12,544
Less inter-company sales	(1,600)
	49,406

(W2) Cost of sales:

	£000
Wraymand plc	22,693
Blonk Ltd	5,268
Less inter-company purchase	(1,600)
Provision for unrealised profit adjustment	250
	26,611

(W3) Non-controlling interest:

25% of (£1,156 – 250)	227

(W4) PUP adjustment

Selling price	1,600
Cost of goods sold	(1,100)
Profit	500
Provision for unrealised profit (500 × ½)	250

17 Consolidated accounts: parents, subsidiaries and associates

Workbook Activity 3

Task 1

Calculation of goodwill on acquisition of Clive Ltd as at 31 March 20X5:

	£000	£000
Cost of investment		25,160
Less group share of net assets at acquisition:		
Share capital (60% × 20,000)	12,000	
Share premium (60% × 5,000)	3,000	
Retained earnings (60% × 10,600)	6,360	
Fair value adjustment (60% × (33,520 – 30,520))	1,800	(23,160)
Goodwill		2,000
Less impairment of goodwill (10% × 2,000)		(200)
Goodwill as at 31 March 20X5		1,800

Task 2

(a) Investment in associate

Goodwill on acquisition of Grant Ltd	£000
Cost of investment	5,000
Less group share of net assets at acquisition:	
£18,000 × 25%	(4,500)
Goodwill on acquisition	500
Less impairment (500 × 10%)	(50)
	450

Investment in associate	
Group share of net assets at statement of financial position date:	
25% × 19,000	4,750
Add goodwill	450
Investment in associate	5,200

(b) IAS 28 defines an associate as an entity over which the group exerts significant influence but not control. This would usually be a shareholding of between 20% and 50%.

MOCK ASSESSMENT

1 Mock Assessment Questions

SECTION 1

Task 1.1

You have been asked to help prepare the financial statements of NJP Ltd for the year ended 31 March 20X1. The company's trial balance as at 31 March 20X1 is shown below.

NJP Ltd

Trial balance as at 31 March 20X1

	Debit £	Credit £
Share capital		150,000
Share premium		20,000
Revaluation reserve at 1 April 20X0		15,000
Trade payables		17,842
Land & buildings – value/cost	350,000	
accumulated depreciation at 1 April 20X0		90,000
Plant and equipment – cost	176,000	
accumulated depreciation at 1 April 20X0		85,888
Trade receivables	32,184	
Allowance (provision) for receivables		1,200
7% bank loan repayable 20X8		50,000
Cash and cash equivalents	1,800	
Retained earnings		118,004
Interest paid	1,750	
Sales		850,328
Purchases	638,589	
Distribution costs	42,326	
Administrative expenses	33,257	
Interest received		4,200
Inventories at 1 April 20X0	120,556	
Dividends paid	6,000	
	1,402,462	1,402,462

Further information:

(i)   The inventories at the close of business on 31 March 20X1 cost £150,250. Included in the closing inventory is inventory costing £15,000. It has an expected selling price of £15,500 and expected selling costs of £1,800.

(ii)   Depreciation is to be provided for the year to 31 March 20X1 as follows:

    Buildings   2% per annum
    Straight line basis

    Plant and equipment   20% per annum
    Reducing balance basis

    Depreciation is apportioned as follows:

	%
Cost of sales	60
Distribution costs	30
Administrative expenses	10

    Land, which is non-depreciable, is included in the trial balance at a value of £100,000. The total land and buildings have been revalued to £480,000 at 31 March 20X1. This revaluation is to be included in the financial statements for the year ended 31 March 20X1.

(iii) Trade receivables figure includes a debt of £840 which has to be written off at the year end. The allowance for receivables of 5% is to be provided at the year end. Irrecoverable debts and changes in allowances for receivables should be charged to administrative expenses.

(iv)   NJP Ltd has paid interest for half of the bank loan.

(v)   Distribution costs of £3,687 owing at 31 March 20X1 are to be accrued.

(vi)   Administrative expenses of £4,386 relates to the following year.

(vii) The corporation tax charge for the year has been calculated as £28,330.

All of the operations are continuing operations.

(a) Draft the statement of comprehensive income for NJP Ltd for the year ended 31 March 20X1.

(b) Draft the statement of financial position for NJP Ltd as at 31 March 20X1.

Note: Additional notes and disclosures are not required, you should present your answers to the nearest £.

Task 1.2

Data

The directors of Caroline plc have recently undertaken an expansion programme. The directors would like to acquire property, plant and equipment in the next period. The directors are uncertain about the initial recording, subsequent measurement and depreciation of the property, plant and equipment.

Prepare brief notes for the directors of Caroline plc to answer the following questions:

(a) What is the definition of an asset?

(b) What is meant by a property, plant and equipment in accordance with IAS 16?

(c) What should be included when the property, plant and equipment is initially measured (i.e. capitalised) and subsequently remeasured?

(d) What are the key disclosure requirements for property, plant and equipment?

Task 1.3

This task consists of 6 true/false/multiple choice type questions.

(1) An increase in payables from the previous year means that less cash is held by the entity.

Is this statement true or false?

(2) Walker Ltd has provided the following information for the year ended 31 December 20X2:

	£
1/1/20X2 – Plant and machinery at cost	35,000
1/1/20X2 – Plant and machinery accumulated depreciation	15,000

During the year plant was sold for £3,000. It cost £5,000 and had accumulated depreciation of £1,800.

Walker Ltd depreciates all plant at 20% per annum on a reducing balance basis. No depreciation is charged on assets disposed during the year.

What is the depreciation charge for the year ended 31 December 20X2?

A   £6,000

B   £4,000

C   £3,360

D   £3,200

(3) The following information has been provided by E Ltd:

(i)   In the current year the company discovered there was a fraud amounting to £300,000 which was carried out in the previous year.

(ii)   The company changed the depreciation method from 10% per annum on a straight line basis to 15% per annum on a reducing balance basis on all plant and equipment.

Which of the above is would require a prior period adjustment according to IAS 8 Accounting Policies, Changes in estimate?

A   (i) only

B   (ii) only

C   Neither of them

D   Both

(4)   F Ltd has provided the following information for four assets:

Assets	Value in use	Fair value less costs to sell	Carrying amount
	£	£	£
i	15,000	12,000	15,500
ii	10,000	27,000	22,000
iii	3,000	7,000	11,000
iv	17,000	6,500	18,000

What is the total value of the impairment loss (if any) that must be charged to the Income Statement in accordance with IAS 36 Impairment of assets?

A   £3,000

B   £35,000

C   £21,500

D   £5,500

(5)   At 31 July 20X9, K Ltd has provided the following information relating to two projects:

(i)   Project X – This related to development expenditure incurred of £100,000 on improving the efficiency of a product. The criteria for capitalisation have been met.

(ii)   Project Y – The total expenditure of £120,000 was incurred on a product. Unfortunately a competitor has introduced a similar product. The management of K Ltd has decided to abandon this project.

In accordance with IAS 36 Intangible assets, what accounting treatment should be followed for the above two projects?

A   Write off the costs incurred totalling £220,000 of both the projects to the income statement.

B   Capitalise a total of £220,000 as an intangible asset to the statement of financial position.

C   Write off the costs incurred totalling £120,000 of project Y to the income statement and capitalise £100,000 of project X as an intangible asset to the statement of financial position.

D   Write off the costs incurred totalling £100,000 of project X to the income statement and capitalise £120,000 of project Y as an intangible asset to the statement of financial position.

(6) B Ltd signed a contract on 1 Jan 20X9 to lease a piece of machinery from R Ltd. The lease term is 1 year, and the asset is expected to have a useful economic life of 20 years. R Ltd is responsible for all maintenance and insurance.

In B Ltd's financial statements this lease will be classified in accordance with IAS 17 *Leases* as:

A   A finance lease

B   An operating lease

Task 1.4

Data

On 1 April 20X1 P plc acquired 70% of the issued share capital of S Ltd for £2,400,000 and 30% of A Ltd for £300,000. At that date S Ltd and A Ltd had retained earnings of £420,000 and £50,000 respectively.

Extracts of the statements of financial position for the companies later at 31 March 20X3 are as follows:

	P plc £000	S Ltd £000	A Ltd £000
ASSETS			
Investment in S and A Ltd	2,700		
Non-current assets	5,800	2,530	300
Current assets	3,000	1,690	250
Total assets	11,500	4,220	550
EQUITY AND LIABILITIES			
Equity			
Share capital	6,000	1,000	200
Retained earnings	4,000	720	250
Total equity	10,000	1,720	450
Non-current liabilities	1,000	1,980	60
Current liabilities	500	520	40
Total liabilities	1,500	2,500	100
Total equity and liabilities	11,500	4,220	550

Additional data:

(i) Buildings in S Ltd at 1/4/X1 was carried at £600,000 but had a fair value of £850,000. This has not yet been reflected in the books of S Ltd. As a result of the fair value adjustment extra depreciation of £50,000 will need to be provided for consolidation purposes.

(ii) During the P plc sold goods to S Ltd amounting to £40,000 of which a quarter is still in the inventory of S Ltd. Goods are sold at a mark-up of 25%.

(iii) The inter- company receivables and payables were as follows:

	£000
In P plc – Receivable (from S Ltd)	25
In S Ltd – Payable (to P plc)	20

The difference was due to a cheque sent by S Ltd before the year end which has not yet been received by P plc.

(iv) Non-controlling interests are to be valued at their proportionate share of net assets. Goodwill is to be impaired by 10%.

(a) Draft the consolidated statement of financial position for P plc and its subsidiary and associate undertaking as at 31 March 20X1.

Your calculations should work to the nearest £000.

Data

P plc acquired 90% of the issued share capital of S Ltd and 30% of A Ltd on 1 April 20X0.

Extracts from their statements of comprehensive income for the year ended 31 March 20X1 are shown below:

	P plc £000	S Ltd £000	A Ltd £000
Continuing operations			
Revenue	1,200	710	110
Cost of sales	(760)	(460)	(68)
Gross profit	440	250	42
Distribution costs & administrative expenses	(180)	(100)	(12)
Investment income	50		
Profit before tax	310	150	30
Tax	(130)	(60)	(10)
Profit after tax	180	90	20

Additional data:

(i)   S Ltd sold goods to P plc for £250,000 during the year. However at the year end £100,000 remained in the closing inventory of P plc. Goods were sold by S Ltd to P plc at a gross profit margin of 20%.

(ii)   S Ltd paid a total dividend of £40,000 during the year to its shareholders. P plc has accounted for the dividends and has included them in the investment income.

(b)   Prepare a consolidated statement of comprehensive income for P plc (incorporating the results of S Ltd and A Ltd) up to and including the profit before tax line for the year ended 31 March 20X1.

SECTION 2

Task 2.1

Data

You have been asked to calculate ratios for MP Ltd in respect of its financial statements for the year ending 31 March 20X1 to assist your manager in his analysis of the company.

MP Ltd's statement of comprehensive income and statement of financial position are set out below.

MP Ltd – Statement of comprehensive income for the year ended 31 March 20X1

	20X1 £000
Continuing operations	
Revenue	48,000
Cost of sales	(28,000)
Gross profit	20,000
Distribution costs	(8,200)
Administrative expenses	(5,400)
Profit from operations	6,400
Finance costs	(1,250)
Profit before tax	5,150
Tax	(1,545)
Profit for the period from continuing operations	3,605

MP Ltd – Statement of financial position as at 31 March 20X1

	£000
ASSETS	
Non-current assets	
Property, plant and equipment	310,500
Current assets	
Inventories	15,000
Trade receivables	8,500
Cash and cash equivalents	3,725
	27,225
Total assets	337,725
EQUITY AND LIABILITIES	
Equity	
Share capital	150,000
Retained earnings	152,795
Total equity	302,795
Non-current liabilities	
Bank loans	15,000
	15,000
Current liabilities	
Trade payables	17,100
Tax liabilities	2,830
	19,930
Total liabilities	34,930
Total equity and liabilities	337,725

(a) **State the formulas that are used to calculate each of the following ratios:**

    (i)   Gross profit percentage

    (ii)   Operating profit percentage

    (iii) Return on capital employed

    (iv) Net asset turnover

    (v)   Current ratio

    (vi) Acid test ratio

    (vii) Trade payable collection period

    (viii) Inventory holding period (days)

    (ix) Gearing ratio

    (x)   Interest cover

(b) **Calculate the above ratios. (All ratios have to be calculated to the nearest first decimal place except for ratios (vii) and (viii), which have to be calculated to the nearest day.)**

Task 2.2

Data

You are an AAT student and have been given the following information by the management of CAP Ltd, for the years ended 31 December 20X1 and 20X2.

	20X2	20X1
Gross profit	14.9%	11.4%
Inventory days	26 days	22 days
Receivables days	30 days	43 days
Payable days	28 days	30 days
Gearing	47%	52%

Required:

Prepare a report to the management that:

Analyses the performance of CAP Ltd over the two-year period, suggesting possible causes of the changes in each ratio shown above, between 20X1 and 20X2.

Briefly states whether the company's performance has improved or deteriorated.

Task 2.3

The Conceptual Framework for Financial Reporting 2010 gives guidance on a number of items.

(a)   Identify **five** user groups and their information needs.

(b)   What are the basic objectives of financial statements and identify the two key underlying assumptions?

(c)   Explain, briefly, the **four** enhancing qualitative characteristics of useful information.

APPENDIX

Alternative format for Task 1.1

SECTION 1

Task 1.1

Data

The most recent statement of comprehensive income and statement of financial position (with comparatives for the previous year) of Smith Ltd are set out below.

Smith Ltd – Statement of comprehensive income for the year ended 31 March 20X1

Continuing operations	£000
Revenue	7,580
Cost of sales	(6,442)
Gross profit	1,138
Distribution costs	(225)
Administrative expenses	(180)
Profit from operations	733
Investment income	48
Finance costs	(45)
Profit before tax	736
Tax	(460)
Profit for the period from continuing operations	276

Smith Ltd – Statement of financial position as at 31 March 20X1

	20X1	20X0
	£000	£000
ASSETS		
Non-current assets		
Property, plant and equipment	3,800	2,500
Investments	2,100	1,850
	5,900	4,350
Current assets		
Inventories	685	700
Trade and other receivables	715	485
Interest receivable	12	18
Cash in hand	130	125
Cash at bank	0	338
	1,542	1,666
Total assets	7,442	6,016
EQUITY AND LIABILITIES		
Equity		
£1 Share capital	2,400	2,300
£1 Share premium	1,900	1,800
Revaluation reserve	100	0
Retained earnings	1,262	1,046
Total equity	5,662	5,146
Non-current liabilities		
Bank loans	380	225
	380	225

Current liabilities

Trade payables	650	582
Finance costs accrued	15	12
Tax liabilities	550	51
Bank overdraft	185	0
	1,400	645
Total liabilities	1,780	870
Total equity and liabilities	7,442	6,016

Further information:

(i) The total depreciation charge for the year was £510,000.

(ii) During the year, plant with a carrying value of £160,000 was sold for £190,000. The profit on disposal has been included within administrative expenses.

(iii) Investment income comprises dividend received of £10,000 and interest receivable of £38,000.

(iv) Finance costs comprise the interest payable.

(v) All sales and purchases were on credit. Other expenses were paid for in cash.

(vi) A dividend was paid during the year.

(vii) There were no disposals of non-current asset investments.

(viii) The company has accumulated tax losses brought forward from the previous period.

Required:

(a) Draft the statement of changes in equity for Smith Ltd for the year ended 31 March 20X1.

(b) Prepare a reconciliation of profit from operations to net cash from operating activities for Smith Ltd for the year ended 31 March 20X1.

(c) Prepare the statement of cash flows for Smith Ltd for the year ended 31 March 20X1.

2 Mock Assessment Answers

SECTION 1

Task 1.1

(a) **NJP Ltd – Statement of comprehensive income for the year ended 31 March 20X1**

	£
Continuing operations	
Revenue	850,328
Cost of sales (W1)	(624,008)
Gross profit	226,320
Distribution costs (W2)	(52,920)
Administrative expenses (W2)	(32,380)
Profit from operations	141,020
Investment income – (interest received)	4,200
Finance costs (7% × £50,000)	(3,500)
Profit before tax	141,720
Tax	(28,330)
Profit for the period from continuing operations	113,390
Other comprehensive income for the year	
Gain on revaluation (W3)	225,000
Total comprehensive income for the year	338,390

(b)   **NJP Ltd – Statement of financial position as at 31 March 20X1**

	£
ASSETS	
Non-current assets	
Property, plant and equipment (W4)	552,090
Current assets	
Inventories (W1)	148,950
Trade receivables (W5)	29,777
Administrative expenses prepaid	4,386
Cash and cash equivalents	1,800
	184,913
Total assets	737,003
EQUITY AND LIABILITIES	
Equity	
Share capital	150,000
Share premium	20,000
Revaluation reserve (W6)	240,000
Retained earnings (W6)	225,394
Total equity	635,394
Non-current liabilities	
Bank loans	50,000
Current liabilities	
Trade payables	17,842
Distribution costs owing	3,687
Loan interest accrued (£3,500 – £1,750)	1,750
Tax liability	28,330
	51,609
Total liabilities	101,609
Total equity and liabilities	737,003

Workings

(W1) Cost of sales

		£
Inventories at 1 April 20X0		120,556
Purchases		638,589
Inventories at 31 March 20X1	£150,250	
Inventory at cost price	£15,000	
Expected selling price	£15,500	
Less: Expected selling costs	(£1,800)	
	———	
Net selling price	£13,700	
	———	
Reduction in closing inventory	(£1,300)	
	———	
Adjusted closing inventory		(148,950)
Buildings depreciation (W2)		
£5,000 × 60% = £3,000		3,000
Plant and equipment depreciation (W2)		
£18,022 × 60% =		10,813
		———
		624,008
		———

(W2)	Distribution costs £	Administrative expenses £
Per trial balance	42,326	33,257
Depreciation:		
Buildings (2% × £250,000 = **£5,000** × 30%/10%)	1,500	500
Plant and equipment		
(20% × [£176,000 – £85,888] = **£18,022** × 30%/10%)	5,407	1,802
Irrecoverable debt		840
Increase in allowance for receivables		
Closing allowance – 5% × (32,184 – 840) = £1,567		
Opening allowance £1,200		
Therefore increase in allowance		367
Distribution costs owing	3,687	
Administrative expenses prepaid		(4,386)
	———	———
	52,920	32,380

(W3)

	£	£
Land and buildings at valuation at 31/3/20X1		480,000
Land and buildings b/f	350,000	
Less: Buildings accumulated depreciation b/f	(90,000)	
Less: Buildings depreciation charge for the year (W2)	(5,000)	
Carrying value at 31/3/20X1		255,000
Revaluation gain		225,000

(W4)

	£	£
Land and buildings at valuation at 31/3/20X1		480,000
Plant and equipment – cost b/f	176,000	
Less: Accumulated depreciation b/f	(85,888)	
Less: Depreciation charge for the year (W2)	(18,022)	
Carrying value at 31/3/20X1		72,090
Total at 31/3/20X1		552,090

(W5)

	£
Trade receivables per trial balance	32,184
Less: Irrecoverable debt	(840)
Less: Closing allowance for receivables (W2)	(1,567)
	29,777

(W6)

	Revaluation reserve £	Retained earnings £
Opening balance	15,000	118,004
Revaluation gain during the year (W3)	225,000	
Profit for the period from continuing operations		113,390
Less: Dividends paid		(6,000)
Closing balance	240,000	225,394

Task 1.2

(a) **What is the definition of an asset?**

An asset is a **resource controlled** by an entity as a result of **past events** and from which **future economic benefits** are expected to flow to the entity."

(b) **What is meant by a property, plant and equipment in accordance with IAS 16?**

Property, plant and equipment are tangible assets held by an entity for more than one accounting period for use in the production or supply of goods or services, for rental to others, or for administrative purposes.

(c) **What items are to be included when the property, plant and equipment is initially measured (i.e. capitalised) and subsequently remeasured?**

This should represent the initial measurement of the value of property, plant and equipment. Cost should include all costs directly attributable to bringing an asset into working condition for its intended use.

Items to be included would be the purchase price, delivery costs, legal costs, site preparation costs, installation costs, etc.

Subsequent cost should be capitalised only if **additional** economic benefits are expected to flow into the business, over and above those expected at the time of the asset's original acquisition (e.g. an extension built to an existing building, adding a part to a machine which will increase productive capacity and increase useful life).

(d) **What are the key disclosure requirements for property, plant and equipment?**

Disclosure requirement – for each classification of asset must:

- State the cost or revalued amount at the beginning of a period and at the year end date

- Accumulated depreciation at the beginning of a period and at the year end date.

- Must also disclose this year's charge to the income statement

- Must show all movement in a period i.e. acquisitions, disposals, revaluations, transfers, effect of impairment and depreciation

- Carrying amount at the beginning of the period and at the year end date

- State depreciation method used

- State the useful lives or the depreciation rates used

- If considered material, must disclose the effect of revaluations, changes in useful life and residual values.

- If considered material, must disclose the effect of a change in the depreciation method in a period.

Task 1.3

(1) **False.** An increase in payables from the previous year means that more cash is held by the entity. A reduction in receivables would lead to an increase in cash and cash equivalents.

(2) C

Plant and machinery

Carrying value b/f (£35,000 – £15,000)	£20,000
Less: Disposal at carrying value (£5,000 – £1,800)	£(3,200)
Carrying value after disposal	£16,800
	x 20%
Depreciation charge for the year	**£3,360**

(3) A

(i) The discovery of fraud in the current year relating to the previous would require a prior period adjustment (i.e. a retrospective adjustment, therefore the opening figures would need to be adjusted).

(ii) Is a change in an accounting estimate therefore the adjustment should be made prospectively (adjustments must be made in the current and future periods).

(4) D

According to IAS 36 (para 8) an asset is impaired when its carrying amount exceeds its recoverable amount. The recoverable amount of an asset is the **higher** of its fair value less costs to sell and its value in use (para 6). On this basis, assets I, III and IV are impaired.

Assets	Value in use	Fair value less costs to sell	Carrying amount	Impairment loss
	£	£	£	£
(i)	15,000	12,000	15,500	500
(ii)	10,000	27,000	22,000	No impairment loss
(iii)	3,000	7,000	11,000	4,000
(iv)	17,000	6,500	18,000	1,000
Total				5,500

(5) C

Write off the costs incurred totalling £120,000 of project Y to the income statement since the project no longer satisfies the criteria of capitalisation according to IAS 38.

Capitalise £100,000 of project X as an intangible asset to the statement of financial position because the criteria of IAS 38 are met.

(6) B

A finance lease transfers substantially all the risks and rewards of ownership to the lessee (IAS 17 para 4).

An operating lease is a lease that is not a finance lease (IAS 17 para 4).

In this case substantial risks and rewards of the lease are still with R Ltd.

Task 1.4

(a) **P plc – Consolidated statement of financial position as at 31 March 20X1**

	£000
ASSETS	
Goodwill (W3)	1,108
Non-current assets (£5,800 + £2,530 +	8,530
FV adjustment + £250	
– Depreciation adjustment – £50)	
Investment in associate (W6)	360
Current assets (£3,000 + £1,690	4,668
less PUP on inventory adjustment	
[£40 × ¼ × 25/125 = £2]	
less inter-company receivables £25 and	
add cheque in transit £5	
Total assets	14,666
EQUITY AND LIABILITIES	
Equity	
Share capital	6,000
Retained earnings (W5)	4,110
Non-controlling interest (W4)	576
Total equity	10,686
Non-current liabilities (£1,000 + £1,980)	2,980
Current liabilities (£500 + £520	1,000
less inter-company payables £20)	
Total liabilities	3,980
Total equity and liabilities	14,666

Workings

(W1)

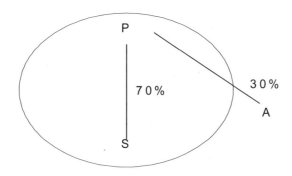

NCI in S Ltd will be 30%.

(W2)

Note (i)

The fair value adjustment of £250,000 (£850,000 – £600,000) will be dealt with as follows:

	£000
Dr Buildings	250
Cr Revaluation reserve	250

This revaluation reserve will then be allocated 70%/30% to P plc (W3) and NCI (W4) respectively.

The depreciation adjustment will be dealt with as follows:

	£000
Dr Retained earnings of S Ltd	50
Cr Buildings (accumulated depreciation)	50

This depreciation adjustment will then be allocated 70%/30% to P plc (W5) and NCI (W4) respectively.

Note (ii)

The unrealised profit adjustment on inventory (PUP) will be £40,000 × ¼ × 25/125 = £2,000.

This will be dealt with as follows:

	£000
Dr Retained earnings of P plc	2
Cr Inventory (in Statement of financial position)	2

Note (iii)

The inter-company receivables and payables will need to be cancelled (i.e. reduced) and the bank balance will need to increase. The adjustment will be dealt with as follows:

	£000
Dr Payables (reducing the inter-company payables)	20
Dr Bank (increasing the bank balance of P plc)	5
Cr Receivables (reducing the inter-company receivables)	25

Note (iv)

The goodwill impairment will be:

Dr Retained earnings of P plc (W5)

Cr Goodwill (W3)

(W3) Calculate Goodwill

Goodwill of S Ltd	£000
Price Paid	2,400
Share capital acquired (70% × £1,000)	(700)
Retained Earnings acquired (70% × £420)	(294)
Revaluation adjustment (70% × £250)	(175)
	———
Goodwill at acquisition	1,231
Impairment (10% × £1,231) (W5)	(123)
	———
Goodwill in SFP	1,108
	———

(W4) Non-controlling interest

	£000
Share Capital attributable to NCI (30% × £1,000)	300
Retained Earnings attributable to NCI (30% × (720 – 50)	201
Revaluation adjustment (30% × 250)	75
	———
Total	576
	———

(W5) Retained Earnings

	£000
Parent	4,000
Subsidiary 70% × ([720 – 50] – 420)	175
Associate 30% × (250 – 50)	60
Goodwill impairment (W3)	(123)
Provision for unrealised profit	
£40 × ¼ × 25/125	(2)
	———
Total	4,110
	———

(W6) Investment in associate (A Ltd)

	£000
Cost of investment in associate	300
Share of post acquisition profits	
30% × (250 – 50)	60
	———
	360
	———

(b) P plc – Consolidated statement of comprehensive income for the year ended 31 March 20X1

Continuing operations	P plc	S Ltd	Adjustments		Total
	£000	£000	£000		£000
Revenue	1,200	710	(250)		1,660
Cost of sales	(760)	(460)	250	}	(990)
PUP on inventory					
(£100 × 20%) (W2)		(20)		}	
		———			———
Gross profit					670
Distribution costs & administrative expenses	(180)	(100)			(280)
Investment income	50		(36) (W3)		14
Income from associate (£20 × 30%)			6		6
Profit before tax					410
Tax	(130)	(60)			(190)
		———			———
Profit after tax		70			220
		———			———

Attributable to:

Equity holders of P plc (balancing figure)	213
Non-controlling interest (10% × £70)	7
Total	220

Workings

(W1)

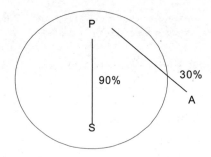

NCI in S Ltd will be 10%.

(W2) The unsold goods at the end of the period are multiplied by the gross profit margin. The figure is shown in S Ltd's column since S Ltd was the selling company.

(W3) The inter-company dividend to be cancelled out will be £36,000 (i.e. Total dividend paid by S Ltd multiplied by P plc's share – £40,000 × 90%).

SECTION 2

Task 2.1

(a) and (b) Formulas and calculation of the ratios

(a)   (b) 20X1

(i)   Gross profit percentage

$$\frac{\text{Gross profit}}{\text{Revenue}} \times 100 \qquad \frac{20{,}000}{48{,}000} \times 100 \qquad = 41.7\%$$

(ii)   Operating profit percentage

$$\frac{\text{Profit from operations}}{\text{Revenue}} \times 100 \qquad \frac{6{,}400}{48{,}000} \times 100 \qquad = 13.3\%$$

(iii)   Return on capital employed

$$\frac{\text{Profit from operations}}{\text{Total equity} + \text{non - current liabilities}} \times 100 \qquad \frac{6{,}400}{302{,}795 + 15{,}000} \times 100 \quad = 2\%$$

(iv)   Net asset turnover

$$\frac{\text{Revenue}}{\text{Total equity} + \text{non - current liabilities}} \qquad \frac{48{,}000}{302{,}795 + 15{,}000} \qquad \begin{array}{l}= 0.2 \\ \text{times}\end{array}$$

(v)   Current ratio

$$\frac{\text{Current assets}}{\text{Current liabilities}} \qquad \frac{27{,}225}{19{,}930} \qquad = 1.4{:}1$$

(vi)   Acid test ratio

$$\frac{\text{Current assets - inventories}}{\text{Current liabilities}} \qquad \frac{27{,}225 - 15{,}000}{19{,}930} \qquad = 0.6{:}1$$

(vii)   Trade payable collection period

$$\frac{\text{Trade payables}}{\text{Cost of sales}} \times 365 \qquad \frac{17{,}100}{28{,}000} \times 365 \qquad \begin{array}{l}= 223 \\ \text{days}\end{array}$$

(viii)   Inventory holding period (days)

$$\frac{\text{Inventories}}{\text{Cost of sales}} \times 365 \qquad \frac{15{,}000}{28{,}000} \times 365 \qquad \begin{array}{l}= 196 \\ \text{days}\end{array}$$

(ix)   **Gearing ratio**

$$\frac{\text{Non - current liabilities}}{\text{Total equity + non - current liabilities}} \times 100 \qquad \frac{15,000}{302,795 + 15,000} \times 100 \qquad = 4.7\%$$

(x)   **Interest cover**

$$\frac{\text{Profit from operations}}{\text{Finance costs}} \qquad \frac{6,400}{1,250} \qquad \begin{array}{l} = 5.1 \\ \text{times} \end{array}$$

Task 2.2

(a)   **Report**

    To: Management of CAP Ltd

    From: AAT student

    Subject: Performance of CAP Ltd

    Date: xxxxxxxxxx

As requested I have looked into the financial situation of CAP Ltd.

(i)   The **gross profit ratio** has improved, which is a positive sign as more gross profit is being generated by sales.

       This improvement may be due to an increase in selling price, a reduction in the cost of goods purchased, or perhaps a change in the product mix with higher margin products being sold in greater quantities.

(ii)   The **inventory days** ratio has worsened as it now takes 26 days to convert inventory into sales revenue, compared with just 22 days in the previous year.

       This could be due to poor inventory management, a large purchase before the year end, (e.g. a special build-up of inventories, for example for a marketing campaign at the start of the next year).

(iii) The **receivables days** ratio has improved as it now takes less time to collect in the cash due from credit customers. This could be due to improvements in credit control and debt collection procedures. The enterprise might also have begun to offer attractive discounts for early payment, which many customers are taking.

(iv)   **The payables days ratio** has gone down since the company is taking fewer days credit from its credit suppliers. This could be due to taking up the discounts offered by the suppliers, buying more goods for cash, credit supplier reducing their credit period.

(v)   The **gearing ratio** has improved, indicating that a lower proportion of long-term finance of the enterprise is now provided by long-term debts, and a greater proportion is financed by equity.

The improvement could be due to the repayment of some debt financing or the increase in financing from equity/ordinary shareholders. In view of the rise in gross profit, it seems likely that the total profits have been quite high, and a proportion of those profits have been retained. This would increase total equity financing and reduce the gearing ratio.

(b)   From the information provided the overall position of the company has improved. The gross profit percentage, receivables days and gearing ratios have improved. The payables days has gone down slightly. The inventory days has worsened and will require further investigation.

Task 2.3

(a)   **Identify five user groups and identify their information needs?**

Shareholders and potential investors – Investors (current/existing) assess risk and return. They are primarily concerned with receiving a return on their investment (e.g. amount of dividends receivable and changes in the share price)

Lenders – Whether to lend to the business and also will the business be able to pay back the loan and the interest on the loan.

Management – This user group is concerned with the overall performance and position of the business e.g. profitability, solvency, liquidity, risk, etc.

Employees/trade unions – They are concerned with job security and will look at the future prospects of the business. They will also be concerned with the going concern of the business.

Suppliers – Whether to supply goods and services to the business on credit. Can the business pay for the goods and services.

Customers – Whether to buy goods and services to the business. Will the business continue to be a going concern, guarantee of warranty on goods, etc.

Competitors – The check on the performance of the business. They will also look at market share, growth, etc.

Government – Whether the company will be able to pay the taxes due.

Analyst advisor group – This user group will be interested in the investment potential and going concern of the business.

Public – What is the business doing regarding the local and general community (e.g. social, investment, ethical policy, etc).

Please note only five user group were required.

(b) What are the basic objectives of financial statements and identify the two key underlying assumptions?

The objective of financial statements is to provide information about the financial position, performance and changes in financial position of an entity that is useful to a wide range of users in making economic decisions.

The two key underlying assumptions are:

(i) **Accrual basis**

The accrual basis of accounting means that the effects of transactions and other events are recognised as they occur (i.e. on a receivable and payable basis) and not as cash or its equivalent is received or paid.

(ii) **Going concern**

The going concern basis assumes that the entity will continue for the foreseeable future. Hence it has neither the need nor the intention to liquidate or curtail materially the scale of its operations

(c) **Explain, briefly, the four enhancing qualitative characteristics of useful information**

Comparability

It should be possible to compare an entity over time and with similar information about other entities.

Verifiability

If information can be verified (e.g. through an audit) this provides assurance to the users that it is both credible and reliable.

Timeliness

Information should be provided to users within a timescale suitable for their decision making purposes.

Understandability

Information should be understandable to those that might want to review and use it. This can be facilitated through appropriate classification, characterisation and presentation of information.

APPENDIX

Answers for alternative Task 1.1

SECTION 1

Task 1.1

(a) **Smith Ltd – Statement of changes in equity for the year ended 31 March 20X1**

	Share Capital £000	Share premium £000	Revaluation reserve £000	Retained Earnings £000	Total Equity £000
Balance at 1 April 20X0	2,300	1,800	0	1,046	5,146
Changes in equity for 20X1					
Profit for the year				276	276
Dividends paid **(balancing figure)**				**(60)**	**(60)**
Revaluation gain			100		100
Issue of share capital	100	100			200
Balance at 31 March 20X1	2,400	1,900	100	1,262	5,662

(b) **Smith Ltd**

Reconciliation of profit from operations to net cash from operating activities

	£000
Profit from operations	733
Adjustments for:	
Depreciation	510
Gain on disposal of property, plant and equipment (£190 – £160)	(30)
Decrease in inventories (£685 – £700)	15
Increase in trade receivables (£715 – £485)	(230)
Increase in trade payables (£650 – £582)	68
Cash generated by operations	1,066
Interest paid (W1)	(42)
Tax refund (W2)	39
Net cash from operating activities	1,063

(c) **Smith Ltd – Statement of cash flows for year ended 31 March 20X1**

	£000	£000
Net cash from operating activities		1,063
Investing activities		
Dividends received	10	
Interest received (W3)	44	
Proceeds on disposal of property, plant and equipment	190	
Payment for non-current asset investments (£2,100 – £1,850)	(250)	
Payment for property, plant and equipment (W4)	(1,870)	
Net cash used in investing activities		(1,876)
Financing activities		
New bank loans received (£380 – £225)	155	
Proceeds of share issue (W5)	200	
Dividends paid **[from task 1.1 (a)]**	(60)	
Net cash from financing activities		295
Net decrease in cash and cash and cash equivalents		(518)
Cash and cash equivalents at beginning of year (£125 + £338)		463
Cash and cash equivalents at end of year (£130 – £185)		(55)

Workings

(W1) **Finance costs**

	£000
Balance b/d	12
Income statement charge	45
Balance c/d	(15)
	——
Paid from bank	42

(W2) Tax

	£000
Balance b/d	51
Income statement charge	460
Balance c/d	(550)
	———
Tax refund	39

(W3) Interest receivable

	£000
Balance b/d	18
Income statement charge note (iii)	38
Balance c/d	(12)
	———
Interest received	44

(W4) Property, plant and equipment (CV)

	£000
Balance b/d	2,500
Revaluation	100
Disposal	(160)
Depreciation	(510)
Balance c/d	(3,800)
	———
Additions	1,870

(W5) Share issue

	£000 20X1	£0 20X0	£000 Increase
Share capital	2,400	2,300	100
Share premium	1,900	1,800	100
Proceeds of shares			200

INDEX